Student's Book

MORE! 2

**Gerngross · Puchta
Holzmann · Lewis-Jones · Stranks**

Zeichenerklärung

 Dazu gibt es eine Tonaufnahme auf CD.
(Obere Zahl: CD Nummer / Untere Zahl: Tracknummer)

 Dazu gibt es ein Video auf DVD.

 Bei dieser Übung stehen dir zwei Varianten zur Verfügung.

 Dazu gibt es eine Hausübung im Internet. (www.helbling-ezone.com)

 Dazu gibt es im Internet einen Progress Check. (www.helbling-ezone.com)

 Dazu gibt es passende Übungen im Workbook (auf Seite 15).

 Diese Übung enthält wichtige Inhalte und sollte nicht ausgelassen werden.

2 Diese Übung kann bei Zeitmangel im Sinne eines "Fast track" durch die Unit ohne Probleme ausgelassen werden.

Mithilfe der kostenlosen **MORE! Media App** kannst du passend zu den Übungen im Schulbuch verschiedene Inhalte über ein Smartphone oder Tablet aufrufen und abspielen. Folgende Symbole zeigen dir an, welche Inhalte über die App verfügbar sind:

 Zu dieser Übung gibt es eine Audioaufnahme, welche über ein Smartphone oder Tablet abgespielt werden kann. Zusätzlich findest du die Audioaufnahme auch im Internet (www.helbling-ezone.com).

 Von diesem Text gibt es eine *graphic story* (Version im Comic-Stil), welche du dir auf einem Smartphone oder Tablet ansehen bzw. auch anhören kannst.

 Zu diesem Inhalt gibt es ein Grammatik-Erklärvideo oder ein Video über Lucy & Leo (*The Twins*), welches du dir auf einem Smartphone oder Tablet ansehen kannst.

Your Portfolio Ein Portfolio ist eine Mappe, in der du von dir verfasste Texte sammeln kannst. Du kannst dein Portfolio auch in digitaler Form anlegen, wenn du die Texte mithilfe eines Computers schreibst und abspeicherst. Dann kannst du eventuell auch Ton- oder Videoaufnahmen (zum Beispiel von Rollenspielen in der Klasse) hinzufügen. Dein Portfolio hilft dir dabei, deine Sprachkenntnisse und deinen Lernfortschritt selbst einzuschätzen und dir auch selbstständig Ziele für dein Sprachenlernen zu setzen.

Contents

Unit 1: Welcome back — 8-13

Get talking	Talking about your day
Vocabulary	School subjects
Grammar	Present simple (revision) / Past simple (revision)
Reading	A school day in Ghana and New Zealand Story time: First day at school A webpage: The blue-ringed octopus
Listening	Oliver's timetable
Writing	My summer holidays
MORE!	A song 4 U: Where did you go? / A poem: The furious octopus

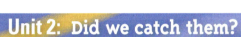

Unit 2: Did we catch them? — 14-21

Get talking	Talking about the past
Vocabulary	*hypnotise, stage, assistant, floor, hypnotist, wallet, pick up, medal*
Grammar	Past simple negation (revision) / Past simple questions / More irregular verbs / Grammar chant (Past simple)
Reading and listening	Time for a sketch: "Pronto!"
Writing	A dialogue
MORE!	The Story of the Stones 1: It's only a dream
Everyday English	*I mean. Oh, come on. I promise.*

Unit 3: How embarrassing! — 22-27

Get talking	Acting out a dialogue / Giving reasons
Grammar	*one/ones / why – because*
Reading	Embarrassing stories / A webpage: Online dos and don'ts
Listening	A story: Modern art
Writing	A picture story
Pronunciation	/w/
Developing speaking competencies	The Twins 1: The bike tour (mistakes / apologising / expressing dismay)

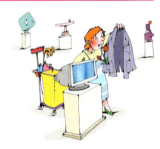

Unit 4: Halloween — 28-33

Get talking	Creating an ending to a story
Vocabulary	Halloween
Grammar	*should – shouldn't*
Reading and listening	A webpage: Halloween traditions Story time: Trick or treat
Writing	Ideas for a Halloween party
Pronunciation	*should – shouldn't*
MORE!	A song 4 U: When they come after you A poem: I'm not so keen on Halloween The Story of the Stones 2: We're all in danger
Everyday English	*Here you are. I don't get it. How can that be?*

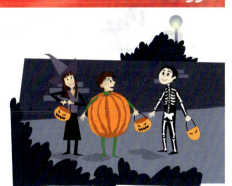

Unit 5: Amazing animals 34-41

Get talking	A guessing game: Animals / Talking about animals
Vocabulary	Adjectives: *small, strong, hairy, clever, heavy, big, dangerous*
Grammar	Comparatives / *as … as* / Superlatives
Reading	A newspaper text: Saved by a pig / Gaming cards / A magazine article: The most amazing animals in the world
Listening	The animal quiz
Writing	A creature from Atlantis
Pronunciation	/dʒ/ /tʃ/
MORE!	A song 4 U: Teatime in Atlantis / A poem: Shark in the park Kids in NYC 1: Homework first
Everyday English	*It depends. Ready? Can you do me a favor? Hang on.*

Unit 6: Where's the post office? 42-49

Get talking	Giving directions / Acting out a dialogue
Vocabulary	Directions / Buildings
Grammar	Directions (Prepositions of place)
Reading	Dialogues: Asking the way / Story time: Missing tourist finally found!
Listening	Dialogues: Asking the way
Writing	A text message: How to get to my house
MORE!	A Song 4 U: This is where you go
Developing speaking competencies	The Twins 2: The way to the station (around town / interrupting politely / checking understanding)

Unit 7: Outdoor adventure 50-55

Get talking	Describing a picture / Making plans
Vocabulary	Places
Grammar	*have to – don't have to*
Reading	Story time: Treasure hunt
Listening	A treasure hunt
Writing	An email home from a youth camp
Pronunciation	*have to*
MORE!	The Story of the Stones 3: The new girl
Everyday English	*I'm off now. Too late! Poor you! Hang on.*

Unit 8: We might go out 56-61

Get talking	Intentions / Acting out a dialogue / Plans for the weekend
Vocabulary	*watch a DVD, do your homework, do the shopping, stay at a friend's house, tidy your room, have a party, play basketball, do nothing*
Grammar	*going to* (negative) / Grammar chant (*not going to*) / *might – might not*
Reading	Messages / Story time: William, the worrier
Listening	Dialogues: Weekend plans
Writing	A party invitation
Pronunciation	*going to*

Unit 9: Strange things from space! 62-69

Vocabulary	Science fiction
Grammar	Past simple (revision) / Past time markers
Reading	Story time: A new home / A magazine article: UFOs – are they really out there?
Listening	An interview: UFOs
Writing	Write an ending to a story
Pronunciation	/ɪd/ /d/ /t/
MORE!	A song 4 U: Song of the Trojans The Story of the Stones 4: You can run, but you can't hide
Everyday English	*In that case. Calm down. One thing at a time. Look.*
Developing speaking competencies	The Twins 3: At the cinema (problems / buying a cinema ticket / expressing disappointment)

Unit 10: Are you ready to order? 70-77

Get talking	Acting out a dialogue: Ordering food at a restaurant
Vocabulary	Food
Grammar	*some – any*
Reading	A dialogue: In a restaurant / Time for a sketch: The best restaurant in town
Listening	People's shopping baskets
Writing	A visit to a restaurant
MORE!	A song 4 U: My dream Kids in NYC 2: The baseball star
Everyday English	*By the way. It's no trouble at all. It isn't fair.*

Unit 11: The curse of the pharaoh 78-84

Get talking	Completing a story
Vocabulary	Ancient Egypt
Grammar	Irregular plurals / Questions with "*Who …?*"
Reading	A magazine text: Life in ancient Egypt / More about the pyramids / The story of Howard Carter / Story time: The curse of the pharaoh
Listening	Ancient Egypt quiz / An interview: The pyramids at Giza
Writing	An ending to a story
Pronunciation	/dʒ/ /tʃ/
MORE!	The Story of the Stones 5: It's you!
Everyday English	*Hopefully. It wasn't your fault. That's for sure. Not exactly.*

Unit 12: Families 85-91

Get talking	Who's who? / Favourite activities / Acting out a dialogue / Rules at home
Vocabulary	Family / Activities
Grammar	*like (doing) / mustn't*
Reading	A webpage: A famous mother / What's in a family? / A magazine article: The coolest things kids learn / An anecdote: Norbert Wiener
Listening	Listen and write names / Children talking about their favourite activities / Dialogue between Fred and his mum
Writing	A leaflet: What people must know about our hotel
Developing speaking competencies	The Twins 4: The pizza (pizza toppings / ordering food / changing your mind)

Unit 13: Magic   92-98

Get talking	Acting out a sketch
Vocabulary	*car boot, nail, put a spell on someone, feather, roast potatoes, fence, cooker, deckchair, sprinkle, prison*
Grammar	Adverbs of manner
Reading	Time for a sketch: The school for young ghosts Story time: Abracadabra, one, two, three
Listening	An interview: Favourite TV series
Writing	A picture story
MORE!	A song 4 U: Welcome The Story of the Stones 6: Farewell!
Everyday English	*I'm afraid so. Believe me. It doesn't matter. I'm afraid not.*

Unit 14: Where we live   99-105

Get talking	A memory game: Things in a room / Remembering / Acting out dialogues
Vocabulary	Inside a room
Grammar	*Whose … ?* / Possessive *'s* / Possessive pronouns
Listening	Finding out where people are / Completing conversations
Reading	A magazine text: Houses and homes
Writing	The best place in my house
Pronunciation	/juː/ /ʊ/
Developing speaking competencies	The Twins 5: Leo's watch (materials and patterns / describing an object / checking what someone says)

Unit 15: Feeling better   106-113

Get talking	Aches and pains / Acting out dialogues
Vocabulary	Aches and pains
Grammar	Present perfect / Past participle / Grammar chant (Present perfect)
Reading	A webpage: Jenny's jokes / A magazine text: The world's new gold
Listening	"Doctor, doctor" jokes / People's aches and pains / Matching short dialogues to pictures
Writing	A text message/An email to a friend who is in hospital
Pronunciation	/p/ /b/ /æ/ /e/
MORE!	Kids in NYC 3: The city quiz
Everyday English	*Let's see. Have fun. Who cares? I have no clue.*

Unit 16: Light rain in the north   114-119

Get talking	Acting out dialogues / Asking about the weather / Acting out a sketch
Vocabulary	Weather
Grammar	*will*-future
Reading	The weather today / Time for a sketch: "And the weather for tomorrow … " / Two magazine texts: The hottest place in the USA, The wettest place in England
Listening	Short weather reports
Writing	An email about the weather on your last holiday
Pronunciation	/l/

Unit 17: Get active! 120-127

Get talking	Sports / Asking questions with *Have you ever …?*
Vocabulary	Sports
Grammar	Present perfect with *already* and *yet* / Present perfect with *ever* and *never*
Reading	Two magazine articles on extreme sports
Listening	Completing profiles about American teenagers
Writing	My favourite sport
Pronunciation	/ɒ/ /ɔː/ /əʊ/
MORE!	A poem: The game
Developing speaking competencies	The Twins 6: The sports party (sports / making requests and offers / responding to requests and offers)

Unit 18: Caring for animals 128-135

Get talking	A memory game: Looking after your pet / Asking about pets
Vocabulary	Looking after your pet
Grammar	*So do/have I. – Neither do/have I.*
Reading	A picture story: A new pet / Story time: The story of Happy Feet
Listening	Interviews about pets
Writing	My pet
MORE!	A song 4 U: Getting a pet Kids in NYC 4: The missing cat
Everyday English	*I don't get it. Got you. What for? Right here.*

Extra unit: Holidays 136-137

Reading	A holiday diary

Life in the USA 138-141

Reading	School life in the USA / Favourite sports / American national parks / Extreme weather
Listening	The highschool prom / Sports quiz / A visit to Redwood national park / The Storm Chasers

GRAMMAR 142-151

CLASSROOM LANGUAGE 152

ENGLISH SOUNDS 153

WORDLIST 154-174

UNIT 1   Welcome back

You learn
- about the present simple (revision)
- about the past simple (revision)
- about school subjects

You can
- talk about daily routines
- talk and write about your holidays
- talk about school subjects

A song 4 U

1 Listen and sing.

Where did you go?

Hey, hey, hey!
Where did you go for
your holiday?

Did you go to Paris?
And did you go to Rome?
Did you go to Lisbon?
Or did you stay at home?

I didn't go away
on a holiday.
I was glad to stay
at home.

Were you on a cruise ship?
Were you at a spa?
Were you in the jungle?
Did you travel far?

I didn't go away
on a holiday.
I was glad to stay
at home.

Did you see the North Pole?
Did you see Madrid?
Did you go Down Under?
Tell me what you did.

I didn't go away
on a holiday.
I was glad to stay
at home.
Yeah, I was glad to stay
at home.

2 CHOICES

A Read about Jacob from New Zealand. Then write the times.

My name's Jacob. I live in Queenstown on the South Island of New Zealand. I usually wake up at 7.30. I wash, get dressed and have breakfast with my mum and dad. At ten past eight, my mum drives me to school. I play with my friends there. School starts at 8.45. I really like school. My teacher takes us on a lot of trips – I like that best. School ends at 4 o'clock. Then I usually go to rugby practice with my friends. I get home at 6 o'clock. Then I go for a quick walk with my dog. At 8 o'clock, we have dinner. After dinner, I watch TV or read a bit. I usually go to bed at 9.30.

1 Jacob wakes up at ......7.30 a.m.......
2 Jacob goes to school at ....
3 Jacob's lessons start at ....
4 Jacob gets home at ....
5 Jacob goes to bed at ....

B Read about Abeeku from Ghana. Then cover up the text and write notes in the boxes. Check with a partner.

My name's Abeeku and I go to school in a village 200 kilometres from Accra in Ghana. I usually wake up early in the morning, around 4 a.m., so I can study a bit and do my household chores*. People here get up early because it is better to do your chores when it is not so hot. First, I say my morning prayers. Then I sweep the house, wash, make breakfast and put on my school uniform. I always get to school around 6.30 a.m. As soon as I get to school, I sweep my classroom – this is what I and my friends do every day. At 7 a.m., we all meet in assembly, where we usually hear some important information. Our first lesson starts at 7.30 a.m., and lasts for 80 minutes. Every day, we have five lessons. We have a break at 10.10 a.m. and we start again at 10.40 a.m. The older kids have more lessons, of course. But when we finish, I don't go home right away. I stay for private classes with one of our teachers. I get home at about 3.30 p.m. I have my lunch, then go for water for the house. After that, I help my mum to prepare food for our supper. I do my homework after supper. I usually go to bed at 10 p.m.

VOCABULARY: *household chores – Aufgaben im Haushalt

4 a.m.	6.30 a.m.	7.30 a.m.	3.30 p.m.	10 p.m.
Abeeku wakes up				

Get talking Talking about your day

  Work in pairs. Talk about your daily routines.

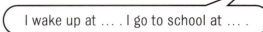

I wake up at … . I go to school at … .

Vocabulary School subjects

  Listen and number the school subjects. Say which subject you like best.

- ☐ Maths
- ☐ English
- ☐ Geography
- ☐ History
- ☐ Science
- ☐ Music
- ☐ Art
- ☐ Information Technology (IT)
- ☐ French
- ☐ Design and Technology
- ☐ Physical Education (PE)

  Oliver is from England. Here is his timetable. Listen and complete.

	Monday	3	6	8	Friday
9 – 9.55 a.m.	English	Maths	Science	French	11 ....
10 – 10.55	1	English	History	Science	IT
			BREAK		
11.15 – 12.10	Design and Technology	4	Maths	9	History
			LUNCH		
1 – 1.55 p.m.	Maths	Science	7	English	12 ....
2 – 2.35	Art	French	....	10	English
2.40 – 3.15	2	5	....	Music	Geography

Story time

6 Read the story.

First day at school

It was the first day of the new school year. All the kids were really excited. There were a lot of holiday stories to tell. Everyone wanted to talk. The new teacher, Miss Cross, asked everyone to sit down and listen.

"OK," she said. "Who wants to tell me about their holidays?"

Twenty arms went up in the air.

"Let's start with Sara," said Miss Cross.

We didn't hear any other stories in that lesson. Sara's family always go somewhere exciting for their holidays. This year was the same.

"My family – that's me, my mum, my dad and my five-year-old brother Michael – went to Australia," she said. "We went to North Queensland. It was really beautiful and we had a great time swimming in the sea and playing on the beach."

"Boring!" said Andrew Wilson.

"Sh!" said Miss Cross. Sara went on.

"One day, my brother was near the sea on his own. When he came back, he had a beautiful shell in his hand. He showed it to us."

"So what?" said Andrew Wilson.

"Well, I saved my brother's life."

"I don't believe you," said one boy.

"How?" shouted another.

"My brother looked in the shell. He told us there was a strange blue and yellow thing inside. He started to put his fingers inside. He wanted to pull it out. Then I remembered about the blue-ringed octopus."

"The what?" Andrew Wilson asked.

"The blue-ringed octopus – I read about it before we went. It lives in the sea, near Australia and Japan. It's small, but it's really poisonous. It can kill you with one bite. I hit my brother's hand and the shell fell onto the sand. Then we saw a small blue and yellow octopus come out of the shell. Of course, we didn't touch it."

"We don't believe you," said lots of the students.

"There's no octopus that's so dangerous," said Andrew Wilson.

"There's one way to find out," said Miss Cross. "Let's check on the internet!"

7 How many of these tasks can you do?

Circle T (True) or F (False).

1. It's the last day of the school year.   T / F
2. The children were excited.   T / F
3. Not many children wanted to tell their holiday stories.   T / F

Choose the correct answer.

4. How many people are there in Sara's family?   ☐ 3   ☐ 4   ☐ 5
5. Where did Sara's brother find the shell? ☐ in the sea   ☐ on the beach   ☐ behind some rocks
6. What did Sara remember about the octopus?
   ☐ it's only from Australia   ☐ it's not very big   ☐ it lives in shells

Answer the questions.

7. How can a blue-ringed octopus kill a person? ....
8. How did Sara save her brother's life? ....
9. Why does Miss Cross tell them to go onto the internet? ....

8 Check your answers with a partner. Then listen to the story.

9 Read the webpage for the blue-ringed octopus.

The blue-ringed octopus is very dangerous. It lives in the sea from Japan down to Australia. It lives for about two and a half years. The blue-ringed octopus has blue rings on its body and on its eight arms. It's about the size of a golf ball. It's dark yellow, but when you attack it, it turns bright yellow. The rings turn bright blue. The blue-ringed octopus hunts during the day. It eats fish. It bites the fish and kills them with its poison. The blue-ringed octopus also uses the poison to kill attackers. The poison is so strong and dangerous that it can kill a person. There is no medicine against the poison.

10 Complete the questions with the question words in the box. Then write the answers to the questions.

| How |
| What |
| Where |
| When |
| How |
| What |

1 .... does the blue-ringed octopus live?
....

2 .... long does it live?
....

3 .... many arms has it got?
....

4 .... colour is it?
....

5 .... does it hunt?
....

6 .... does it eat?
....

11 Listen to the poem. Then read it.

The furious octopus

The octopus, the octopus
is sometimes very furious.
You shake his first arm and you see
some octo-ink right on your knee.
You shake the others – two to eight –
and suddenly it's much too late
to get away.

The octopus, the octopus
is getting really furious.
He covers you in ink so black.
It's on your head and legs and back.
And then he hugs you really tight.
Believe me, this is quite a sight:
you and the eight-armed octopus.
It's furious, so furious.

⑫ CHOICES

Writing for your Portfolio

Tricia is from Brighton in the UK. Read her email to you.

From: tricia_p05@mailconnect.com
Subject: My summer holidays

Hi,
This year my family stayed at home. I got up late every day. In the mornings, I usually watched TV. After lunch, I played volleyball or went swimming. In the evenings, I played on my computer. I sometimes went to the cinema. It was the perfect holiday.
Bye,
Tricia

A Write an email answer to Tricia (30–35 words). Tell her about your holidays. Write about:

- the place (*I was in … / We went to …*)
- who was with you (*My parents, my …*)
- what the weather was like (*It was sunny / …*)
- how good it was (*The holidays were good / …*)

B Write your answer to Tricia (70–80 words). Tell her:

- where you went
- who you went with
- how long you stayed
- what you did all day
- who you met
- what interesting things you did
- why you enjoyed / did not enjoy your holidays

GRAMMAR

Present simple (revision)

Du verwendest das Present simple, um über Tatsachen zu sprechen.

The blue-ringed octopus **eats** fish.
When you **attack** it, it **turns** bright yellow.
The octopus **doesn't hunt** at night.

I **do** my homework after supper.
Our first lesson **starts** at 7.30 a.m.
I **don't believe** you.

Past simple (revision)

Mithilfe des Past simple berichtest du über Ereignisse und Situationen in der Vergangenheit.

Bei regelmäßigen Verben (regular verbs) hängst du ein *-ed* an das Verb:

play – We **played** on the beach.
show – He **showed** it to us.

Einige Verben haben unregelmäßige Formen im Past simple:

go – We **went** to Australia.
read – I **read** about it before the holiday.

UNIT 2 Did we catch them?

You learn
- about past simple questions
- about past simple negation (revision)
- more irregular verbs

You can
- ask questions about the past
- use negation (*Verneinung*)
- understand a sketch
- write a dialogue

Vocabulary

  Listen and look at the picture. Then write the numbers next to the words. How many can you remember?

- [ ] hypnotise
- [ ] stage
- [ ] assistant
- [ ] floor
- [ ] hypnotist
- [ ] wallet
- [ ] pick up
- [ ] medal

Time for a sketch

  Read the sketch.

"Pronto!"

The characters

Charles Granger, a hypnotist
Vivien Tate, his assistant
Roger Allen, a man at the show
Claire Grimes, his girlfriend
Inspector Lime
Sergeant Lewis
a doctor at the hospital

SCENE 1

A show with Charles, a hypnotist, on stage. With him is his assistant Vivien. In front of them there are tables with people sitting at them.

Charles And now, ladies and gentlemen, we need a man for a little experiment. What about you, sir?

Roger No, thank you.

Claire Oh, come on, Roger. Maybe it's fun. Please do it.

Roger Oh, alright.

Charles   Come up here, sir.

(Roger walks on stage. Applause.)

   What's your name?

Roger   I'm Roger.

Charles   Please have a seat, Roger. I'm going to hypnotise you. Look at this medal. I'm going to swing it. You follow it with your eyes – that's all.

Roger   And then?

Charles   And then I'm going to give you some commands. And you are going to do what I say.

Claire   Tell him to do the washing-up every day!

(Laughter.)

Charles   Right, here we go. You only hear what I say. You only follow my commands.

(He hypnotises Roger.)

   Good! Stand up! Stand on one leg. Hop around. Very good. Jump down to your friend. Kiss her hand. Very good. Come back here again. Give me your watch. Thank you, very good. When I say "Pronto" – you wake up again. You don't remember anything, of course! One, two, three – "Pronto".

Roger   What happened? What did you do? Did you hypnotise me? What did I do?

Charles   It's alright. You gave me your watch.

Roger   I didn't. *(He checks.)* I did. Give it back to me.

Vivien   Here you are, sir. Thank you, sir.

Charles   Applause for the gentleman.

(Applause.)

SCENE 2

After the show, Charles and Vivien are alone.

Vivien   Did it work?

Charles   Of course it did. I gave Roger the secret commands.

Vivien   So, we're going to be rich?

Charles   Very rich, baby, very rich.

Vivien   Do you think he can break into the museum?

Charles   Yes, he can. He's very strong.

Vivien   Did you tell him to throw the jewels in the bushes?

Charles   I did. We pick up the jewels. The police pick up Roger.

(They both laugh.)

SCENE 3

In a room of the museum. In the background there is a broken window. There is broken glass everywhere.

Inspector Lime	Come on, Lewis. Tell me the facts.
Sergeant Lewis	Somebody broke into the museum, took the Deng Jewels and jumped out of the window.
Inspector Lime	Jumped out of the window? Why didn't he use the door?
Sergeant Lewis	The alarm went off when he broke in and the security guards came.
Inspector Lime	I see. Any clues?
Sergeant Lewis	Yes, we found blood under the window, but no thief.
Inspector Lime	Ah, what have we got here? A wallet!
Sergeant Lewis	Don't touch it, sir.
Inspector Lime	But my hands are clean!
Sergeant Lewis	I know, sir. But we need the fingerprints. The thief's fingerprints. Not yours!
Inspector Lime	Ah, yes. Hm, hm. Sorry, errm. And just look at all the mess around here.
Sergeant Lewis	Don't walk around in it, sir.
Inspector Lime	You're right. My shoes are getting dirty.
Sergeant Lewis	No, the footprints, sir.
Inspector Lime	Am I making footprints? Well, the museum people can clean them up.
Sergeant Lewis	Not your footprints, sir. The thief's footprints. I have to go now, sir. See you at the station.
Inspector Lime	Yes, yes. Good man. Off you go.

SCENE 4

Sergeant Lewis is at the door of Claire's house.

Sergeant Lewis I'm trying to find Mr Allen. I've got his wallet. This address was in it.

Claire Oh yes, he's my boyfriend.

Sergeant Lewis I see. Can I talk to him?

Claire Is it about the accident? He's still in hospital. And he can't remember what happened.

Sergeant Lewis An accident? Tell me more about it.

SCENE 5

In a room at the hospital.

Sergeant Lewis Sir, can you hear me?

Claire He can't hear you.

Sergeant Lewis Sir, please, talk to me. It's very important.

(The door opens, and a doctor comes in.)

Doctor What are you doing here? This man is in shock.

Sergeant Lewis I'm from the police, sir.

Doctor I don't care. I want you out now. Pronto!

(Suddenly Roger sits up and starts walking stiffly towards the door.)

Doctor Hey, what's going on? Don't get out of bed!

Claire Goodness me, you said "Pronto". That's what the hypnotist said.

Sergeant Lewis The hypnotist? Tell me more.

SCENE 6

In Inspector Lime's office at the police station.

Inspector Lime Look at the paper, Lewis!
Sergeant Lewis Why, sir?
Inspector Lime It says "Inspector Lime solves another case! Jewels back at the museum." Let me read it to you.
Sergeant Lewis No, sir. Thank you, sir.
Inspector Lime Alright. I like that. "Inspector Lime solves another case!" Where did you catch them, Lewis? The paper doesn't say.
Sergeant Lewis The hypnotist and his friend were already on a plane to Singapore. I phoned the police in Singapore this morning and they arrested them an hour ago.
Inspector Lime Fantastic! We did an excellent job!
(He takes the newspaper.)
"Inspector Lime solves another case!" I like that!

THE END

3 How many of these tasks can you do?

Choose the correct answer.
1 Charles hypnotises ☐ Roger. ☐ Claire. ☐ Inspector Lime.
2 What does Roger give to Charles? ☐ his wallet ☐ a kiss ☐ his watch
3 Who gives Roger the secret commands? ☐ Charles ☐ Vivien ☐ Charles and Vivien

Complete the sentences.
4 Roger steals the jewels from the ....
5 Sergeant Lewis finds Roger's address in ....
6 When the doctor says "Pronto" Roger ....

Answer the questions.
7 Why is Inspector Lime happy with the newspaper story? ....
8 Why do you think that Sergeant Lewis doesn't want to hear the newspaper story?
....
9 Where are the criminals at the end of the story? ....

4 Check your answers with a partner. Then listen to the sketch.

Get talking Talking about the past

5 Ask your partner about yesterday. Use the verbs in the box to form questions.

| play | do | read | go | go | help | have | watch |

… your homework?   … your brother/sister with the dishes?
… to the cinema?   … a video game?
… TV?   … for a run?
… a book?   … a good time?

Did you go to the cinema?

Grammar chant Past simple

6 A chant. Listen and repeat.

What did you do?
Did you steal anything?
Did you take my ring?
Did you hypnotise me?
Did you take my key?

No, I didn't.
You're wrong.
It was really
Harry Strong.

7 CHOICES

Writing for your Portfolio

A Use the phrases in the box to complete the dialogue. There is one phrase you can't use. Write the dialogue in your exercise book (I = Inspector, W = Witness).

he didn't
did I
did he
did he
did you see
did you

I What ¹……………………………… ?
W I saw a man with a large bag in his hands.
I What ²……………………………… do?
W He threw the bag into the bush over there.
I And then?
W Then he walked away.
I ³……………………………… look nervous?
W No, ⁴……………………………… . He looked very calm.
I Why ⁵……………………………… call the police then?

B Somebody broke into a shop and stole an expensive watch. An inspector (I) is asking a witness (W). Write the dialogue (60–70 words).

GRAMMAR

Past simple negation (revision)

The thief **didn't take** everything.
The inspector **didn't catch** the thief.
I **didn't do** it.

Wichtig: Kein *did* oder *didn't* mit *was, were* und *could*!
Roger **wasn't** at home.
Vivien and Charles **weren't** on a plane to Paris.
Sergeant Lewis **could not** talk to Roger.

Past simple questions

Did you **hypnotise** me?
Did you **read** the newspaper?

Wichtig: Kein *did* oder *didn't* mit *was* und *were*!
Was Roger a thief?
Were Charles and Claire on their way to Singapore?

Complete. Write *did* or *didn't*.

So bildest du die Verneinung im Past simple: person + [1].......................... + *base form* of the verb.
So bildest du Fragen im Past simple: [2].......................... + person + *base form* of the verb.

More irregular verbs

| break – **broke** | find – **found** | take – **took** | catch – **caught** |
| give – **gave** | get – **got** | have – **had** | say – **said** |

The Story of the Stones 1

It's only a dream

1 Match the names to the characters.

Darkman
Sarah
Sunborn
Daniel
Emma

2 Watch Episode 1 and complete the sentences with the names from **1**.

1 .... makes a promise.
2 .... has three dreams about Darkman.
3 .... dreams she is on a rope.
4 .... says they have to speak to Sunborn.
5 .... thinks Darkman is dead.

3 Write a message to Sunborn from the children.

....
....
....
....

Everyday English

4 Watch Episode 1 again. Complete the sentences with the words in the box.

> I mean   Oh, come on   I promise

Daniel Yeah, let's get in touch with her.

Sarah ¹.. . They're only dreams.

Darkman I'll get them. ².. .

Daniel It's the third time this week.

Sarah Me too. ³.. , I have almost the same dream.

UNIT 3 How embarrassing!

You learn
- how to use *one / ones*
- how to use *why – because*
- about online behaviour

You can
- ask why something happened
- give reasons
- use the internet responsibly
- write a picture story

1 CHOICES

THE PARTY THAT WASN'T A SURPRISE (by Alan S., 12)

At the end of the last school year my friends and I wanted to organise a surprise party for Mr Harris, our English teacher. He had a job at a new school. So we wanted to say thank you and goodbye. We made a big cake and we bought a big box of chocolates, too.

Two days before the party I wrote an email to the kids from my class. I said, "Don't forget! The party for Mr Harris is a SURPRISE! So don't tell him!" Then I pressed SEND. The next day at school my friends told me about my mistake. I had sent* the email to them and I had sent it to Mr Harris, too!

VOCABULARY: *had sent – hatte geschickt

A Read Alan's story. Then match the questions and answers. There is one extra answer.

1 What did Alan's class plan for their teacher?
2 What did they want to give him?
3 What did Alan write in his email?
4 What mistake did he make?

☐ He sent the email to Mr Harris, too.
☐ A big box of chocolates, and a cake.
☐ He made a mistake.
☐ He wrote, "Don't tell Mr Harris about the party!"
☐ They planned a surprise party.

MUM'S MISTAKE (by Sophie K., 13)

A few months ago my best friend Karen's dad needed to go to hospital for an operation. She was really worried. When I told my mum about the operation, she asked me for Karen's email address. She wanted to send her a message to wish the family luck. The next time I saw Karen, she wasn't very happy. "I'm a bit upset with your mum's message," she said. I was really confused, but then she showed me the message. "Dear Karen. I hope the operation is a success. We are all thinking of you. LOL Mrs Beeton." When I got home, I asked Mum, "Why did you write LOL in your message to Karen?" "Because I wanted to send her lots of love." "Mum," I explained, "LOL doesn't mean 'lots of love', it means 'laugh out loud'." My mum was so embarrassed and phoned Karen immediately to say sorry. Luckily the operation was a success. Now we can all laugh at my mum's embarrassing mistake.

B Read Sophie's story. Then answer the questions.

1 Who is Karen?
....
2 Why did Sophie's mum want to write to Karen?
....
3 Why was Sophie confused?
....
4 What three words did Sophie's mum want to write?
....

2 Listen to the story *Modern art* and circle T (*True*) or F (*False*).

1. Mrs Smith had a new job in a shop. T / F
2. The director went to check on Mrs Smith's work. T / F
3. The floor was still dirty. T / F
4. Part of the modern sculpture was missing. T / F
5. The jacket with five roses was missing. T / F
6. The jacket with the roses was part of a sculpture. T / F

3 Think of the stories in and . Who do you think said these sentences?

1. What an old jacket!
2. Oh no! I didn't take his address out.
3. I can't believe that she wrote that.
4. What's the matter, you look upset?
5. There's something missing here.
6. Oh no! I must phone her immediately.

I think Alan / Karen / Sophie / Sophie's mum / the cleaning lady / the director of the museum said, "…"

4 Listen to the dialogue. Then act it out.

Richard	Dad?
Dad	What is it?
Richard	Can I have another T-shirt?
Dad	Why? What's wrong with the blue one?
Richard	Nothing, but I want my extra large one. The one that has got an alien on it.
Dad	Sorry, I can't give you that one.
Richard	Why not?
Dad	I put it in the washing machine. And now it's extra small.
Richard	Oh, Dad!

Sounds right /w/

5 Listen and repeat.

Why and **wh**y and **wh**y!
Why is it always **wh**y?
Why not ask me **wh**en,
or **wh**ere or **wh**at or who?
It's something you could do.

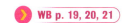

6 Read the webpage.

Online dos and don'ts

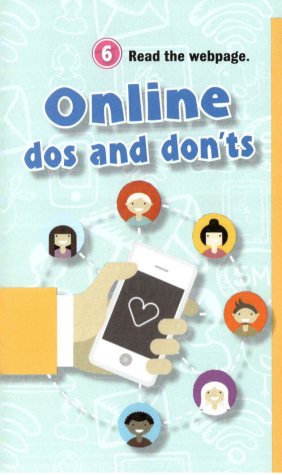

Home | Advice | Contact us | Blog

Why was 14-year-old Jacob so upset when he opened the door of his house? Because there were about a hundred young people in the garden for his birthday party. Some of them he knew. Most of them he didn't know.

Why were they there? Because Jacob posted his invitation on Facebook. But why did so many people turn up? Because Jacob didn't check who could see his postings. So not only his real friends turned up, but also friends of his friends.

Jacob was lucky because one of his neighbours called the police and the people went away. The garden was a mess, but the house was fine.

Jacob made a terrible mistake. Jacob is not the only one to make such a mistake. There are lots of stories about something going wrong because of wrong behaviour on the web. So here are some important tips for when you go online:

- Think before you post something and check who can see it.
- Think about what you write or what sort of pictures you send. You never know how many people can read your text or look at the picture. Your best friend could send it on to his or her best friend and so on. Do you really want that?
- Don't give your passwords to anyone. And don't post your real name and home address online.
- When you hear something bad about someone, don't pass it on to other people. Maybe it's not true.
- When someone bullies you online, talk to an adult.

7 Match the answers to the questions.

1 Why were there lots of people in Jacob's garden?
2 Why was Jacob upset?
3 Why was Jacob lucky?
4 Why is it a good idea to check who can see your postings?
5 Why is it not a good idea to give your password to other people?
6 Why is it a good idea to talk to an adult?

☐ Because a neighbour called the police.
☐ Because you don't want everyone to know your plans.
☐ Because they can help when someone bullies you.
☐ Because he posted his invitation on Facebook.
☐ Because you don't want other people to use it.
☐ Because lots of people turned up for his birthday.

Get talking Giving reasons

8 Work in pairs. Talk to your partner about the following: a TV series, a school subject, a book, a CD. Make short dialogues. Use words from the box.

| exciting | fun | cool | interesting | funny | great | boring |
| bad | too long | confusing | scary | difficult | silly | awesome |

A Do you like Science?
B Yes, I do.
A Why do you like it?
B Because it's exciting.

A Do you like Science?
B No, I don't.
A Why not?
B Because it isn't interesting.

9 CHOICES

Writing for your Portfolio

A Look at the pictures. Write a story (30–40 words). You can use the words below to help you.

This morning Tom was …
He looked … and saw …
He ran …
His friends … because … slippers*.

VOCABULARY
*slippers – Hausschuhe

B Look at the pictures. Write a story (70–80 words). Add a good title.

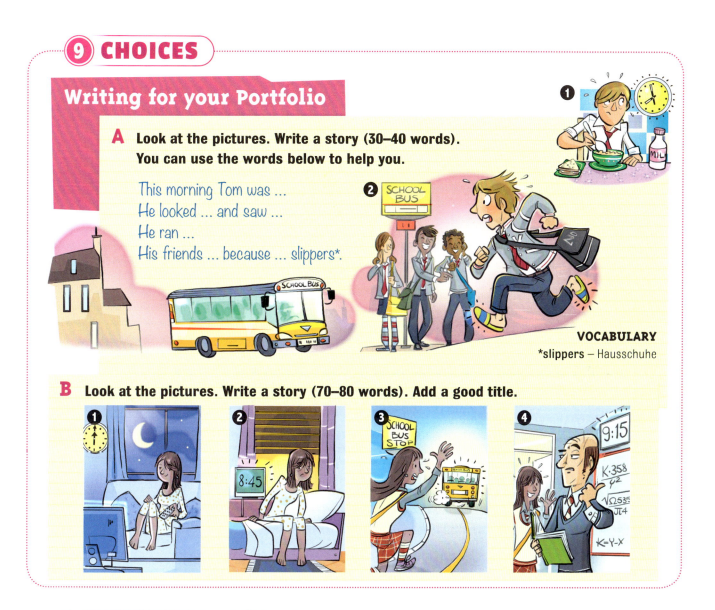

GRAMMAR

one / ones

Wenn du über gleiche Dinge sprichst, aber das Nomen nicht immer wiederholen möchtest, dann kannst du das Nomen durch **one** oder **ones** ersetzen.
I needed an email with everyone's address in it so I used the **one** Mr Harris sent.

Complete with *one* or *ones*.

Du verwendest [1]………………… , wenn du ein Nomen im Singular nicht wiederholen willst.
Du verwendest [2]………………… , wenn du ein Nomen im Plural nicht wiederholen willst.

why – because

Why were the people there? – **Because** Jacob posted his invitation on Facebook.
But **why** did so many people turn up? – **Because** Jacob didn't check who could see his postings.

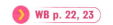 

The Twins 1
DEVELOPING SPEAKING COMPETENCIES

Language function
- apologising (*sich entschuldigen*)

Speaking strategy
- expressing dismay (*Missfallen ausdrücken*)

The bike tour

Vocabulary Mistakes

1 Look at the photos. Match them with the mistakes. Listen and check.

- [ ] send a text message to the wrong person
- [ ] break someone's camera
- [ ] eat someone's chocolate
- [ ] lose someone's pen

2 Watch or listen to the dialogue. Then read it. Why does Leo say sorry?

Leo Lucy, I'm really sorry. I made a terrible mistake.
Lucy What did you do?
Leo Well, you told me to invite Emily Clarke … for the bike tour.
Lucy And?
Leo I wanted to text her, but I sent the message to Emily White.
Lucy What? You know I don't really like her. She's a bit boring.
Leo I know. I feel really bad about it.
Lucy You fool. She's so boring.
Leo I'm sorry. It was a mistake. I know.

Lucy But how could you do that?
Leo Hang on a minute. Here's her answer: *Great idea. Thanks. See you both near the old castle at two. Say hi to Lucy.*
Lucy Oh, no!

3 Complete the sentences with *Lucy*, *Leo* or *Emily*.

1 …………………… invited the wrong person for a bike tour.
2 …………………… got an invitation to go on a bike tour with Lucy and Leo.
3 …………………… knows what …………………… thinks about Emily White.
4 …………………… thinks that Emily White is boring.
5 …………………… tells …………………… that she will join them.
6 When …………………… hears that she is not happy at all.

Useful phrases Apologising

4 Write the sentences that Leo uses to apologise to Lucy. Then check with ②.

1 sorry / really / I'm ....
2 about / I / really / bad / it / feel ....

? What do you think? Answer the questions.

- Do they meet Emily White?
- What happens on the bike tour?

Mobile homework

Watch part 2 of the video. Use a verb from the box and your own ideas to complete the sentences.

| meet | stop | apologise | have | ride |

1 Lucy and Leo .... near ....
2 The three kids .... their bikes ....
3 They .... next to ....
4 Emily .... a surprise ....
5 In the end, Lucy ....

Speaking strategy Expressing dismay

5 Try to complete the phrases. Check with the dialogue in ②.

1 **Leo** I sent the message to Emily White.
   Lucy W.............................. ?

2 **Leo** I know. I feel really bad about it.
   Lucy You f.............. . She's so boring.

3 **Leo** I'm sorry. It was a mistake. I know.
   Lucy But h.............. c.............. y.............. d.............. that?

6 CHOICES

A Work in pairs. A apologises to B for a mistake. B shows dismay.

send / text message
break / mobile phone
lose / pen
eat / ice cream

A I sent the text message to Pam, not to Paula. I'm so sorry.

B How could you do that?

B ROLE PLAY: Look at the situations from A. Choose one. Work in pairs and extend it into a longer dialogue. Take 2 or 3 minutes to practise it. Don't write it down. Act it out in class.

UNIT 4 Halloween

You learn
- Halloween words
- how to use *should / shouldn't*

You can
- talk about Halloween
- create an ending to a story
- make suggestions (*Vorschläge*)
- write an email based on a mind map

Vocabulary Halloween

   1 Listen and look at the picture. Then write the numbers next to the words.

- ☐ apple bobbing
- 1 a ghost
- ☐ a pumpkin
- ☐ a haunted house
- ☐ a vampire
- ☐ a witch

A Song 4 U

  2 Listen and sing.

When they come after you

We are brave, we are strong.
Here's our Halloween song:

We aren't scared of witches.
We smile at every ghost.
We do not fear the zombies.
In fact, we like them most.

*But what will you do
when they come after you?*

We are brave, we are strong.
Here's our Halloween song:

We say hello to pirates
and wizards are our friends.
We do not fear the vampires
that fly until night ends.

*But what will you do
when they come after you?*

We are brave, we are strong.
Here's our Halloween song:

We love the Halloween monsters.
We think they are alright.
It's all a great big party.
A party for a night.

3 Read the webpage about Halloween. Who do you think has the most fun and why?

The question was: Do you have any Halloween traditions or fun things to do? Your answers were:

George, USA, aged 11
My mum gets a scary film from the DVD shop. We change the house into a haunted castle and then we invite friends for a Halloween party. My brother and I have got a CD of scary noises, and when our friends walk up the stairs in the dark, we play it. After a tour of the house we eat popcorn and watch the film.

Megan, Ireland, aged 14
We always have a party. Everyone wears a mask. We're vampires, witches and ghosts. And we also play apple bobbing. There are lots of apples in a bowl of water and you try to take them out with your mouth. You can't use your hands. It's difficult, but fun. I often win the game because I'm a vampire. And with my vampire teeth it's easy to get the apple.

Steve, UK, aged 12
Me and my brothers usually go out on Halloween. We knock on people's doors and say "Trick or treat". People sometimes give us a treat; sweets, etc. But if they don't, we play a trick on them. Last year our neighbour Mr Eliot didn't give us a treat, so we put some vampire stickers on his front window.

Henry, Canada, aged 11
Every year we take a pumpkin to school. We cut off the top and take out everything inside. Then we cut a scary face in it. Finally, we put a candle inside the pumpkin. This year my pumpkin face was the best. It was so scary that the teacher said: "Let's keep it for our Halloween party at school." I was very proud. Henry – Master of Horror!

4 Read the sentences below. Which of the four texts on the webpage in **3** do they go with? Write the names: *George*, *Megan*, *Steve* or *Henry*.

1 That's really scary, well done! All we need now is a candle. ....
2 My clothes are really wet. I must get another T-shirt! ....
3 Wait for me before you start the film! ....
4 Can I borrow your knife, please? ....
5 Those pictures look really scary! ....
6 This is unfair. Your teeth are so long. ....
7 Wow, that's a lot of sweets. ....
8 What was that? Did you hear that? What an awful sound! ....

Story time

5 Read the story.

Trick or treat

Last Halloween, I went trick-or-treating with my twin sister Kerry. "Larry and Kerry, don't go too far away," our mum said. But we didn't listen and soon we were on the other side of town. There we met a boy about the same age as us. He told us his name was Jim. He said he wanted to go trick-or-treating with us. "There are some really good houses in this street," he told us. So we went with him.

At the end of the street was a really big old house with a big gate and a long drive up to the front door. We stopped and looked at it. It was the kind of house you see in horror films. "Let's try this house," said Jim.

"We shouldn't go in there," I said. "And you shouldn't be a baby," said Jim. "Come on." Jim walked up the long drive. We followed. An old man opened the door. He wasn't very happy to see us. "Trick or treat?" Jim asked. The old man looked at us. "Go away," he said. "Go away – now!" He closed the door. "Come on," I said. And we walked to the gate. At the gate Jim stopped. "That man was mean," he said. "We should play a mean trick on him." "OK," I said. "Let's make ghost noises." "No," said Jim. "We should play a really mean trick on him." "Let's throw a stone at his window," said Kerry. "No," said Jim. "Let's put superglue in his door lock." "I think we should go home," I said. But it was too late.

6 How many of these tasks can you do?

1 Larry *tells* / *doesn't tell* his mum where they are going.
2 The kids *know* / *don't know* Jim.
3 The big house is *old* / *new*.

4 Larry thought the house was like one from ....
5 Jim calls Larry .... because he doesn't want to go into the house.
6 The old man tells the children .... and then shuts the door.

7 Why does Jim want to play a trick on the old man? ....
8 What trick does Kerry want to play on the old man? ....
9 What trick does Jim want to play on the old man? ....

7 Check your answers with a partner. Then listen to the story.

Get talking Creating an ending to a story

8 Work in pairs. Think of an ending to the story.

9 Now listen to the end of the story.

10 Complete Sarah's list of suggestions for going trick-or-treating. Write *should* or *shouldn't*.

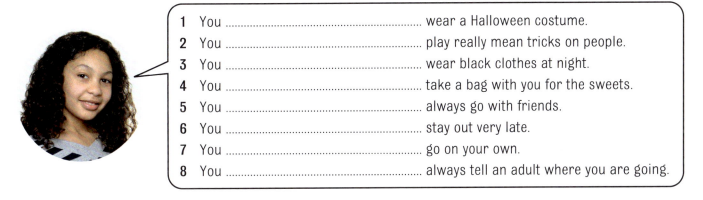

1 You .... wear a Halloween costume.
2 You .... play really mean tricks on people.
3 You .... wear black clothes at night.
4 You .... take a bag with you for the sweets.
5 You .... always go with friends.
6 You .... stay out very late.
7 You .... go on your own.
8 You .... always tell an adult where you are going.

Sounds right *should – shouldn't*

11 Listen and check. Then say the sentences in **10** yourself.

Writing for your Portfolio

12 Read Sarah's email to you. Then answer her in an email.

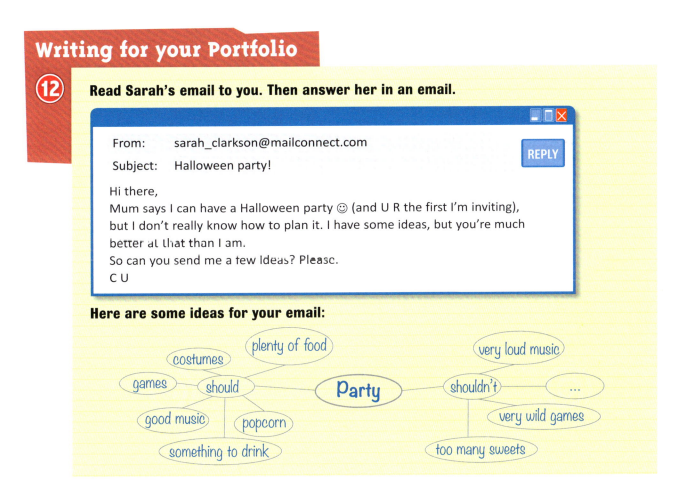

From: sarah_clarkson@mailconnect.com
Subject: Halloween party!

Hi there,
Mum says I can have a Halloween party ☺ (and U R the first I'm inviting), but I don't really know how to plan it. I have some ideas, but you're much better at that than I am.
So can you send me a few ideas? Please.
C U

Here are some ideas for your email:

should: costumes, plenty of food, games, good music, popcorn, something to drink
Party
shouldn't: very loud music, ..., very wild games, too many sweets

Listen to the poem. Then read it.

I'm not so keen on Halloween

I'm not so keen
on Halloween.
When my friends meet
for trick or treat,
I'm not the one
who thinks it's fun
to run around
as witch or ghost.

What scares me most
is other kids
who hunt for treats,
who look for sweets.
They don't play tricks
but just give kicks
to get their treats,
to get your sweets.

GRAMMAR

should – shouldn't

Lies die Beispielsätze.

We **should go** home – it's late.
We **shouldn't go** in there – it's dangerous.
What **should** I **do**?

We should take our umbrellas.

Complete the sentences with should or shouldn't.

Wenn du sagen willst, was jemand tun sollte,
dann verwendest du ¹.................................. .
Wenn du sagen willst, was jemand nicht tun sollte,
dann verwendest du ².................................. .
Wenn du um Rat fragst, dann verwendest du
ebenfalls ³.................................. .

Bildung: *should / shouldn't* + *base form* of the verb.

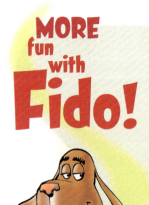

MORE fun with Fido!

Trick or treat!

A bone?

Why didn't they like my treat?

The Story of the Stones 2

We're all in danger

1 Look at the pictures from Episode 1 and put them in the correct order.

2 Can you remember who morphs into each of these animals? Write the names.

❶ .... ❷ .... ❸ ....

3 Watch Episode 2 and answer the questions. Circle a, b or c.

1 Who is Darkman's master?
   a) The Black Knight   b) Demon Eyes   c) The Lord of the Fire
2 What does Darkman's master want?
   a) the belt and stones b) a spaceship   c) the three stones
3 Which Lord wanted all the stones?
   a) The Lord of the Earth b) The Lord of the Fire c) The Lord of the Water
4 Who is trying to find the stones?
   a) Sunborn   b) Darkman   c) The Lords

Everyday English

4 Watch Episode 2 again. Complete the sentences and match them with the person who said them.

| Here you are | get it | How can that be |

1 .... ? He's dead, isn't he?   ☐ Emma
2 Only your stones can protect you now. ....   ☐ Sarah
3 But I still don't .... Why didn't Darkman die? ☐ Sunborn

UNIT 5 Amazing animals

You learn
- about comparatives and superlatives
- about amazing animals
- words to describe animals

You can
- compare things
- talk about animals
- write about an imaginary animal

 Read the text.

Saved by a pig

August 5th, 2004 was a hot day in Worcester. Judith Crowe, her 5-year-old son Jeff and their little pig Bacon went swimming in the river near their home. Bacon was a very good swimmer. In fact, he was better than Jeff.

Judith and her son played and swam in the water for an hour. All the time Bacon was with them. Then Jeff's mother got out of the water to get a towel. "Stay here for a minute," she said. When she turned round, she saw Jeff in the middle of the river. The water was deeper and more dangerous there. He was in trouble.

Jeff's mother jumped into the water and started to swim. But Bacon was faster than Judith and got to the boy first.

The little boy put his arms around the pig. But he was bigger than the pig and he was heavier. The boy and the pig both disappeared under the water.

Jeff's mother didn't know what to do. Then suddenly she saw the little pig again. Jeff was on the pig's back. Her son was safe.

2 How many of these tasks can you do?

1 Judith is Jeff's mother. T / F
2 Bacon is Jeff's friend. T / F
3 They went swimming in a river. T / F
4 .... was near their house.
5 Bacon was a .... than Jeff.
6 Judith left Jeff in the water to ....
7 Where was Jeff when he got into trouble? ....
8 Who got to Jeff first? ....
9 Why did Jeff pull Bacon under the water? ....

3 Check your answers with a partner.

Vocabulary Adjectives

4 Match the pictures with the adjectives. Write the numbers.

☐ small ☐ strong ☐ hairy ☐ clever ☐ heavy ☐ big ☐ dangerous

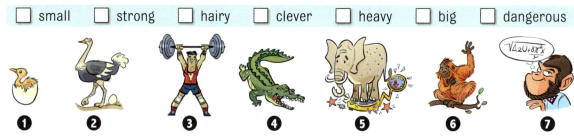

① ② ③ ④ ⑤ ⑥ ⑦

Get talking A guessing game

5 Choose one of the animals. Make sentences using comparatives. Your partner guesses what animal it is. Use the words in the box in **4** to help you.

A It's bigger than a mouse.
B Is it a guinea pig?
A No, it's heavier than a guinea pig.
B Is it a rabbit?
A That's right.

6 Read the gaming cards for these animals from Atlantis.

ANIMALS OF ATLANTIS — THE RUCKLE
The Ruckle was very exotic. It was half land animal and half bird, but it didn't fly. It was as big as a rabbit. It was very friendly and many Atlantians had them for pets.

ANIMALS OF ATLANTIS — THE BUGBOY
The Bugboy was a small reptile. It was as small as a mouse, but it was as dangerous as a snake. In fact, it was as poisonous as a blue-ringed octopus. Every year, hundreds of people died from its bite.

ANIMALS OF ATLANTIS — THE SNAPKLE
The Snapkle was a kind of dragon. It lived in the mountains outside of Atlantis. It was as big as an elephant. But it wasn't as beautiful as an elephant. In fact, it was very ugly.

ANIMALS OF ATLANTIS — THE HIPCOP
The Hipcop wasn't as friendly as the Ruckle, but it was also a popular pet. It was as clever as a chimpanzee.

7 Read the cards again and circle T (*True*) or F (*False*).

1 Atlantians had Ruckles in their homes. T / F
2 The Ruckle was bigger than a rabbit. T / F
3 The Bugboy was very dangerous. T / F
4 The Bugboy was a kind of octopus. T / F
5 The Snapkle was bigger than an elephant. T / F
6 The Snapkle wasn't a beautiful animal. T / F
7 The Hipcop was friendlier than the Ruckle. T / F
8 The Hipcop wasn't as clever as a chimpanzee. T / F

WB p. 33, 35, 36

8 Look at the pictures and write four sentences using *as ... as* and *not as ... as*.

The yellow car is not as expensive as ...

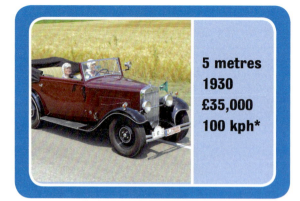

5 metres
1930
£35,000
100 kph*

4 metres
1930
£30,000
100 kph

VOCABULARY: *kph – short for "kilometres per hour"

Sounds right /dʒ/ /tʃ/

9 Listen and repeat.

His name's **J**im,
I'm more beautiful than him.
He's a **ch**impanzee,
and he's as big as me.

10 Read the magazine article. Complete it with the missing numbers from the box. Then listen and check.

| 150 | 2 | 8 | 3 | 110 | 1 | 3 |

a The Estuarine crocodiles of South East Asia are the longest crocodiles in the world. They can be .... metres long – as long as two cars together!

b The world's most poisonous snake is the taipan. It lives in the deserts of Australia. It can be more than .... metres long.

c The biggest animal on land or in the sea is the blue whale. It's also the heaviest. It weighs .... tons.

d The bumblebee bat from Thailand is the smallest mammal in the world. It is .... centimetres long and weighs .... grams.

e The most dangerous animal in the world is the mosquito. It can carry malaria. Every year more than .... million people worldwide die from malaria.

f The fastest land animal in the world is the cheetah. It can run very fast – more than .... kph.

The most Amazing Animals in the world

11 Whose eye is it? Match the eyes and the animals.

- [ ] antelope
- [ ] giraffe
- [ ] rhino
- [ ] ostrich
- [ ] chimpanzee
- [ ] dolphin

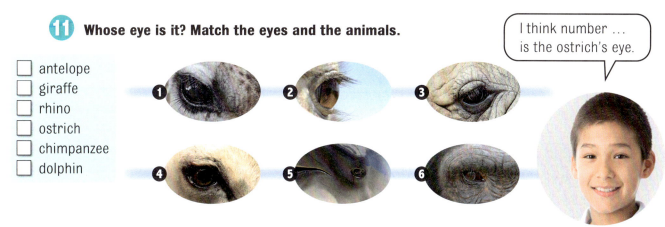

I think number … is the ostrich's eye.

12 Listen and check.

13 Put the animals in order. Write 1, 2 and 3 in the boxes.

The animal quiz

❶ Which is the tallest?
- a ☐ a giraffe
- b ☐ an ostrich
- c ☐ an elephant

❷ Which is the longest?
- a ☐ an anaconda
- b ☐ a whale shark
- c ☐ a crocodile

❸ Which is the fastest?
- a ☐ a lion
- b ☐ a rabbit
- c ☐ an antelope

❹ Which is the most intelligent?
- a ☐ a dolphin
- b ☐ a pig
- c ☐ a chimpanzee

❺ Which is the heaviest?
- a ☐ a rhino
- b ☐ a blue whale
- c ☐ an elephant

Get talking Talking about animals

14 Discuss your answers with a partner. Then listen and check.

A I think the elephant is the tallest.

B I don't think so. I think the …

A song 4 U

15 Listen and sing.

Teatime in Atlantis

It's teatime in Atlantis
and everyone is there.
They drink and sing
and you can hear
them really everywhere.

The Hipcop and the Ruckle
went for a cup of tea.
They sat down on a sofa.
Guess what!
Who did they see?

It's teatime in Atlantis …

The Bugboy and the Snapkle,
the Huffump and his son,
they had ten cups of orange tea
and had a lot of fun.

It's teatime in Atlantis …

16 Listen and say the poem.

Shark in the park by Roger McGough

Ever see*
a shark
picnic
in the park?

If he offers
you a bun,

run.

VOCABULARY: *ever see – short for "Have you ever seen … ?"

Writing for your Portfolio

17 **Read about the Huffump.**

The Huffump was a kind of shark. It lived in the sea around Atlantis. It was as big as a whale and it was very dangerous. It had a really big mouth and more than 4,000 teeth. Every year it killed and ate more than 200 Atlantians. The Atlantians were very scared of swimming in the sea.

18 **Design your own animal from Atlantis. Make up a name for the creature and write a text of 50–70 words about it.**

GRAMMAR

Comparatives

Wenn du zwei Dinge vergleichst, die verschieden sind, dann verwendest du das Wort *than*. An die englischen Eigenschaftswörter mit einer Silbe (*fast, slow, deep, old, ...*) hängst du *-er* an.
He's old**er than** me.   She's fast**er than** me.

An die englischen Eigenschaftswörter mit zwei Silben, die auf *-y*, *-le* und *-ow* enden (*happy, simple, slow, ...*) hängst du ebenfalls *-er* an.

Bei manchen Eigenschaftwörtern verändert sich jedoch die Rechtschreibung:
hot, big, fat, etc. – It's hot**ter** today than yesterday.
heavy, angry, hungry, etc. – Joe's heav**ier than** me.

Wenn das Eigenschaftswort mehr als zwei Silben hat (*dangerous, difficult, interesting, ...*), dann verwendest du *more + adjective*.
The book is **more interesting than** the film.

Ausnahmen:
good – **better**   He was **better than** Jeff.
bad – **worse**   I'm bad at football, but he's **worse than** me!

as ... as

Wenn du sagen willst, dass zwei Dinge / Tiere / Personen gleich groß, klein usw. sind, dann verwendest du *as ... as*:
It was **as** small **as** a mouse.
It was **as** dangerous **as** a snake.

Wenn du sagen willst, dass ein/e Ding / Tier / Person nicht so groß, klein usw. ist wie ein/e andere/s Ding / Tier / Person, dann verwendest du *not as ... as*:
It was **not as** friendly **as** the Ruckle.

Superlatives

Wenn du ausdrücken willst, dass etwas am größten, schwersten, schnellsten usw. ist, hängst du *-est* an das Adjektiv an:
fast, slow, deep, old, etc. – The cheetah is **the** fast**est** mammal in the world.

Bei einigen Adjektiven ändert sich die Schreibung:
hot, big, fat, etc. – The blue whale is **the** big**gest** animal in the world.
heavy, angry, hungry, etc. – The blue whale is **the** heav**iest** animal in the world.

Bei Adjektiven, die aus drei oder mehr Silben bestehen, verwendest du *the most + adjective*:
dangerous, interesting, etc. – The mosquito is **the most dangerous** animal in the world.

Ausnahmen:
good – **the best**   She's **the best** player in the team.
bad – **the worst**   It's **the worst** restaurant in town.

Kids in NYC 1

Homework first

Before you watch

1 Write the words under the pictures.

bedroom
living room
hall
kitchen

1 .... 2 .... 3 .... 4 ....

2 What order do you think these pictures come in the DVD? Write 1–4.

Watch the story

3 Check your answers to **2**.

4 Complete the sentences.

1 Steve is in the ....
2 Steve and Jenny want ....
3 Steve's .... isn't done.
4 Jenny did the Geography ....
5 Jenny wants to ring her sister to ....

40 KIDS IN NYC 1

5 Complete the dialogue.

need
see
listen
want
remember
get
do
think

Jenny Clare? Hi, it's me. ¹.................................... , can you ².................................... me a favor?
Clare It depends. What do you ³.................................... ?
Jenny I ⁴.................................... my Geography homework – it's in my school bag.
Can you ⁵.................................... it?
Clare Where is it?
Jenny In my room, I ⁶.................................... .
Clare Hang on then. Jenny? I'm in your room, but I don't ⁷.................................... your bag.
Jenny I'm really sorry, Clare, but I ⁸.................................... now – I left it in the kitchen.

6 Answer the questions.

1 Where's Jenny's Geography homework? ....
2 Does Clare find the bag in the bedroom? ....
3 Where does Clare find the bag? ....
4 Why does Steve say "This isn't right"? ....

Everyday English

7 Complete the dialogues.

Note:
favor = American English
favour = British English

It depends.   Ready?   Can you do me a favor?   Hang on

UNIT 6 Where's the post office?

You learn
- to understand directions
- how to use prepositions of place
- words for buildings

You can
- ask the way
- give directions
- write a text message with directions to your place

Vocabulary Directions

  Gretta the witch is explaining to Sir Florestan, a knight, how to get to the dragon's place. Listen and follow the way. Write *D* where the dragon lives.

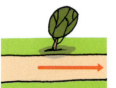 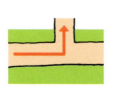 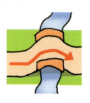 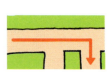

go past the tree   go straight ahead   turn left   cross the bridge   take the second right

Vocabulary Buildings

 2 Listen and look at the pictures. Then write the numbers next to the words.

☐ bank ☐ police station ☐ chemist's ☐ post office ☐ tourist office ☐ railway station
☐ church ☐ supermarket ☐ cinema ☐ restaurant ☐ music shop ☐ hospital

❶ ❷ ❸ ❹ ❺ ❻
❼ ❽ ❾ ❿ ⓫ ⓬

③ CHOICES

A Read the dialogue and draw the sign for the post office in the map.

DIALOGUE 1

Woman	Excuse me, where's the post office?
Man	The post office? Go straight ahead. Go past the supermarket.
Woman	Alright. And then?
Man	Then take the first left.
Woman	OK.
Man	Go past the bank. The post office is next to it.

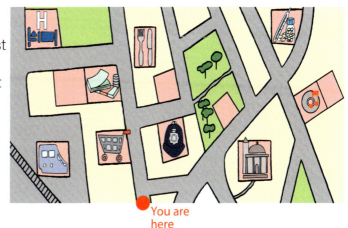

You are here

B Read the dialogue and draw the sign for the cinema in the map above.

DIALOGUE 2

Boy	Excuse me.		Boy	OK, past the police station …
Woman	Yes, dear?		Woman	Then there's a little park in front of you. Go through the park. Turn right, then left, and then right again. The cinema is behind the large music shop.
Boy	Can you tell me where the Odeon cinema is?			
Woman	The Odeon? Well, let me think. It's in Hill Road.			
Boy	How do I get there?		Boy	Thank you.
Woman	Go straight on, take the second right and go past the police station.		Woman	Not at all.

  Listen to two more dialogues and draw the other two signs on the map in ③.

Get talking Giving directions

5 Work in pairs. Student A works with the map here, student B works with the map in the Workbook (page 43).

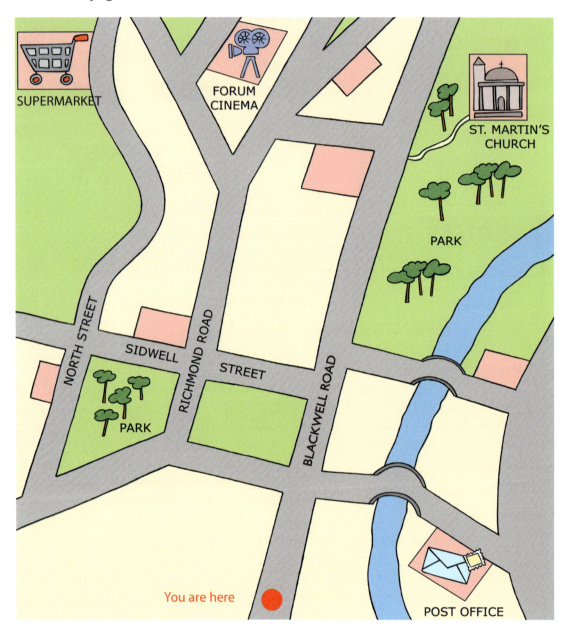

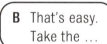

You ask your partner the way to the tourist office, the restaurant, the police station and the bank.

A Excuse me, how do I get to the tourist office? (Excuse me, I'm trying to find … / Excuse me, I'm looking for …)

B That's easy. Take the …

Story time

6 Read the story.

Missing tourist finally found!

Romanian tourist found safe and well after three days.

Mr Vasile Belea (63) from Romania came to London three days ago. He wanted to have a holiday with his son's family. His son picked him up from the airport and they went into London by underground. When they changed trains at Stockwell Station, Mr Belea's son, Radu, jumped on the next train and the doors closed. Mr Belea was too slow and the doors closed in front of him.

"I came back right away," Radu Belea said, "but Dad wasn't there. So I looked around the station, and then I went to the next stop again, but I really couldn't find him."

We know now that Mr Belea went back into the street and tried to ask a policeman for help. When he finally found one, the policeman was very friendly, but he didn't understand a word Mr Belea said to him. And Mr Belea didn't know a word of English! So he walked around and hoped to see his son somewhere, but, of course, he didn't. He asked another policeman and another – they were all very friendly, but they didn't understand him and he didn't understand them. Mr Belea had only £17 in his pockets, he didn't know where his son lived, and he couldn't talk to people. When it got dark, he sat in a bus stop and spent the night there. In the morning, he started walking again. When he was cold, he went into a shopping centre. He stayed there most of the time, and in the evening he went to a bus stop again.

After two days and nights like this he saw a man reading a newspaper. On the cover of this newspaper he saw a picture: It was him!

Mr Belea had one pound left. So he bought a newspaper and with the newspaper he went to a police station. He showed the paper to a policeman there, and after half an hour, Mr Belea was back with his son's family.

"We're so glad to have him back," his son said. "And I think it's great that the paper helped so much. They put an extra large photo of my dad on the cover. I really want to thank everybody for their help."

7 How many of these tasks can you do?

1. Mr Vasile Belea is ☐ English. ☐ British. ☐ Romanian.
2. Vasile Belea was in London
   ☐ on business. ☐ for a conference. ☐ for a holiday with his son's family.
3. Mr Belea got lost
   ☐ on the underground. ☐ on a bus. ☐ in a shopping centre.
4. The policeman didn't speak ....
5. Vasile Belea only had a little .... on him.
6. Vasile Belea did not know his son's ....
7. Where did Vasile Belea spend the nights? ....
8. Why did Vasile Belea buy the newspaper? ....
9. Why was the paper a big help? ....

8 Check your answers with a partner. Then listen to the story.

A Song 4 U

9 Listen and sing.

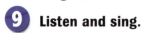

You want to go to Newtown?
Then simply go ahead.
Just cross the bridge
and don't forget
to stop when lights are red.

*Right and left and straight ahead,
this is where you go.
Right and left and straight ahead,
that's what you need to know.*

You want to go to Market Square?
Then take the second right.
Then turn left
and left again.
That's Market Square alright.

Right and left and straight ahead …

You want to find the cinema?
Go past the music shop,
and opposite
the restaurant
take a few steps more and stop.

Right and left and straight ahead …

10 Put the dialogue in the correct order. Compare with your partner. Then act it out.

	Jasmine	The Carlton? The film's at the Odeon. Hurry up!
	Jasmine	I'm in front of the cinema, too. The Odeon cinema.
1	Jasmine	Hey, Ron, where are you?
	Jasmine	Go up Broad Street and turn left after the bank.
	Ron	What's the quickest way?
	Ron	I'm in front of the cinema.
	Ron	Right. See you in five minutes.
	Ron	Oh dear. Wrong cinema. I'm in front of the Carlton cinema.

Writing for your Portfolio

 Your friend is coming to visit you. She sent you a text message. Send her a text message with directions to your house.
(Write 40–60 words.)

GRAMMAR

Directions (Prepositions of place)

So sagst du jemandem, wie er/sie an ein bestimmtes Ziel gelangen kann:

Go straight ahead.
Take the first left / **second right.**
Go past the post office.
Turn left / **right.**
Cross the bridge / street.
Walk up the hill **as far as** the church.

opposite

So sagst du jemandem, wo ein bestimmtes Ziel zu finden ist:

The cinema is **behind** the shopping centre.
Next to the bank, there's the post office.
The restaurant is **opposite** the church.
There's a little park **in front of** you.
On the corner of the next street, there's a large bank.
It's just **round the corner**, beside the bank.

round the corner — in front of

MORE fun with Fido!

The Twins 2

DEVELOPING SPEAKING COMPETENCIES

Language function
- interrupting politely (*jemanden höflich unterbrechen*)

Speaking strategy
- checking understanding (*nachfragen, ob man etwas richtig verstanden hat*)

The way to the station

Vocabulary Around town

 Match the places and the pictures. Then listen and check.

bridge bus stop fountain traffic lights statue clock tower

1 .... 2 .... 3 ....

4 .... 5 .... 6 ....

 Watch or listen to the dialogue. Then read it. What items from ❶ do Lucy and Leo mention?

Tourist	Excuse me.
Leo	Yes?
Tourist	I'm sorry to bother you, but can you tell me the way to the railway station?
Leo	Sure, no problem.
Lucy	Can you see that bus stop over there?
Tourist	Yes.
Lucy	Go past it and take the second left.
Tourist	Second left.
Lucy	Yes, the second left. Then go straight ahead and turn left at the traffic lights.
Tourist	Sorry?
Lucy	Straight ahead and then left at the traffic lights. The railway station is at the end of the road.
Tourist	So that's second left after the bus stop, then left at the traffic lights.
Lucy	That's right. You can't go wrong.
Tourist	Thank you.

48 DEVELOPING SPEAKING COMPETENCIES ▶ WB p. 45

3 Cover up the dialogue in 2. Try to complete the directions. Then check.

Walk past the ¹.................... and then take the ².................... left. Go straight ahead until you get to some ³.................... lights. Turn ⁴.................... . The ⁵.................... is at the end of the road.

Useful phrases Interrupting politely

4 Write the words in the correct order to make sentences. Then check with the dialogue in 2 to find a good answer to the phrases.

1 me / excuse ....
2 sorry / bother / I'm / to / you ....

? What do you think? Answer the questions.

- The tourist asks Leo for directions. Why does Lucy tell him the way?
- What happens next?

Mobile homework

Watch part 2 of the video and complete the sentences with *Lucy* and/or *Leo*.

1 .... is angry with ....
2 .... gives the directions to the next tourist.
3 .... tells the tourist to follow the man.
4 .... laugh at the end.

Speaking strategy Checking understanding

5 Complete. Check with the dialogue in 2.

Lucy	Then go straight ahead and turn left at the traffic lights.
Tourist	¹.. ?
Lucy	Straight ahead and then left at the traffic lights. The railway station is at the end of the road.
Tourist	².. second left after the bus stop, then left at the traffic lights.
Lucy	That's right. You can't go wrong.

6 CHOICES

A Work in pairs. Use the prompts.

first / second / third right
first / second / third left

A Take the third right. Then take the second left and then the first right.

B Sorry?

A Give directions. → B Check understanding.

B ROLE PLAY: Work in pairs. Then swap roles.

Student A: You are a tourist. Where do you want to go? Ask student B the way. Interrupt politely and check his/her directions.

Student B: Give student A directions. Make sure he/she understands.

UNIT 7 Outdoor adventure

You learn
- words for places
- how to use *have to* / *don't have to*

You can
- make/suggest a plan
- write an email home from a youth camp
- describe a picture

Vocabulary Places

 Listen and look. Then write the numbers next to the words.

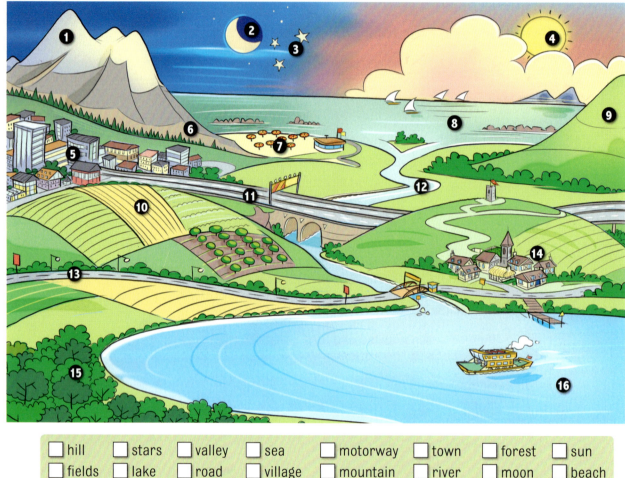

☐ hill ☐ stars ☐ valley ☐ sea ☐ motorway ☐ town ☐ forest ☐ sun
☐ fields ☐ lake ☐ road ☐ village ☐ mountain ☐ river ☐ moon ☐ beach

2 Work in pairs. Look at the picture above for half a minute. One of you closes the book. Ask and answer questions.

Student A

Where | 's / are | the | village? / sea? / lake? / … / fields? / …

Student B

On the right-hand side.
On the left-hand side.
In the middle.
In the top right-hand corner.
In the bottom left-hand corner.
Next to the …

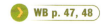

Get talking Making plans

  3 **Listen and complete the dialogue.**

A Let's ¹.................................. on Monday.
B Canoeing? I'm not sure.
A Well, you don't have to come along. I'll go alone, then.
B Wait a minute. I think I'll join you.
A Great. But bring ².................................. ! And you have to ³.................................. a life jacket in the boat all the time.
B Of course. I know that.

Build a tree house!
When: Thursday 3 p.m.
Don't be late!
Bring a hard hat!

Go for a picnic!
When: Sunday 12 a.m.
Bring your own food and drink!
Clean up the picnic area after the picnic!

Go rock climbing!
When: Friday 11 a.m.
Bring warm clothes and good shoes.
Read the camp guide carefully.

Visit the waterfalls!
When: Saturday 2 p.m.
Don't be late!
Wear an anorak near the waterfalls.

4 **Work in pairs. Look at the notices above and act out dialogues.**

A Let's visit/go/build ... .
B ... I'm not ... .
A Well, you don't ... .

B Wait ... .
A Great. But ... . And you ... .

Sounds right have to

  5 **Listen and repeat.**

A I can't stay here, I **have to** go.
B You **have to** go? But why?
A I **have to** move to London!
B I **have to** say goodbye.

  6 **Listen to Emma and Harry talking about a treasure hunt. Take notes.**

	When?	What did you find?	Where did you find it?
Emma			
Harry			

WB p. 47, 49, 51

UNIT **7** 51

Story time

 7 Read the story.

Treasure hunt

When Dad said that Gillie and I could go to an adventure holiday camp, I wasn't too excited. I didn't want to go on a holiday camp with my nine-year-old sister! But Gillie really loved the idea. So I couldn't say no. But the camp was great! Lots of new friends and Gillie was OK, too (most of the time ☺). What I liked most about the camp were the surprise activities: wild water canoeing, rock climbing, a visit to the waterfall – these things were never boring! No wonder – Rick, Pamela, Laura, Jack and Ron (our guides) were fantastic. Especially Ron! He was really cool.
One Friday, Gillie was very excited: "Chris, come quickly, there's a geo-caching treasure hunt with Ron tomorrow. Quick, only 20 kids can go!" "Geo-caching???" I thought. I had no idea what it was – but I didn't want to ask. I was fourteen. And she was nine, you know! "Geo-caching? Not a bad idea," I said. When we wrote our names on the list, I saw this note:

I went to speak to Ron later to find out more about geo-caching and this was what I learnt: for geo-caching you need a GPS unit. The camp guides tell you where you can find the 'treasure'. But they don't say things like "go through the forest until you come to a little pond" etc. They only tell you the coordinates of the place (for example 1.27 mi S: GCG8V5), and you put them in your GPS and off you go! Oh, there's something else: The treasure is usually several small things in a box (the so-called 'cache'!). You can take out as many as you want. But for every treasure you take out, you have to put in something new.
The next day we started our geo-caching hunt. We looked for three hours, and we looked everywhere, behind every tree, under every stone, in every hole in the ground. Nothing! "Let's go back!" I said. Then suddenly Gillie shouted "Here it is!" She had her hand in a hole in the ground and when she took her hand out, I knew that it wasn't a cache! In her hand, my nine-year-old sister Gillie had a handful of old coins!

GEO-CACHING TREASURE HUNT!
WHEN: WEDNESDAY 1 P.M.
BRING: GOOD SHOES, A SNACK AND A BOTTLE OF WATER.
DON'T FORGET: ONE OR TWO SMALL THINGS FOR THE CACHE!
WRITE YOUR NAME ON THE LIST – ONLY 20 KIDS CAN GO!
SEE YOU!
RON

Back at the camp, we showed the coins to Ron. He laughed. "Old coins? Ha, ha, ha! Good joke! They're not old. But give them to me!" Ron was very nice. He gave me a DVD and my sister a bar of chocolate for the coins! Later in the evening, Gillie showed me a coin. "I didn't give him this one," she said. "I wanted to keep it." "Silly idea," I thought. But I didn't say much. After all, she was only nine.

Two days later, there was a visit to a museum in a town near our camp. Ron went, so of course Gillie and I went along, too. We saw lots of interesting things. Gillie suddenly shouted. "Look! The coins! The coins! They look like my coins!" Gillie was very excited. She looked at the coin in her hand. It looked exactly like the old Roman coins behind the glass window.

There was a man in uniform at the other end of the room. When Ron saw him, he got very nervous. "Be quiet, you silly girl!" he shouted. But the man in the uniform saw the coin. "Where did you find this coin?" he asked. "In the forest," Gillie said. "But not only this one. We found lots of them. And Ron has got them all. Ron has got them!"

Gillie pointed at Ron. Suddenly he did not look very cool any more. He turned around and ran away! Then things happened very quickly. The man in the uniform phoned the police. Two very friendly police officers came and took us to the police station in a car. "These coins are Roman coins. They're very old," one of them said.

"And when you find old coins, you have to give them to the museum. Nobody can keep them! We're going to find this young man, Ron. He has to give the coins to the museum!" Two days later the police found Ron. They took the coins away from him. They are now behind glass in the museum. And next to them is a little sign:

Gillie is very proud of this. Well, after all, she is only nine ...

8 How many of these tasks can you do?

1. Chris was excited by the idea of a holiday camp.   T / F
2. Chris changed his ideas when he got to the camp.   T / F
3. Ron was a guide at the camp.   T / F

4. For geo-caching you do not need ☐ a map. ☐ a GPS unit. ☐ small objects.
5. Gillie found the treasure ☐ under the ground. ☐ behind a tree. ☐ under a stone.
6. Gillie gave Ron ☐ all the coins. ☐ the coins and a DVD. ☐ nearly all the coins.

7. How did Gillie find out that her coins were really old coins? ....
8. Why was the man at the museum upset? ....
9. What happened to the coins? ....

9 Check your answers with a partner. Then listen to the story.

WB p. 48, 50

Writing for your Portfolio

10 Samantha is at a youth camp. Read her email to her mum. Which paragraph (1, 2 or 3) talks about

a) what she did yesterday? ☐ b) the rules of the camp? ☐
c) all the different things you can do at the camp? ☐

From: sam06@hello.uk
Subject: Youth camp

Hi Mum,
[1] The camp is really great! There are lots of things to do here like football and volleyball, for example. We can go horse riding too. We can go swimming in the river – it's fantastic! We never get bored.
[2] Yesterday I went on a great canoeing trip! We went down the river for two hours and then we had a picnic. Jack, our guide, made a fire and we sang songs and played games.
[3] Everything is great, but of course there are rules. We have to go to bed at ten.
We have to help in the kitchen. We have to make our beds. But we don't have to wash up – that's good. I hope you and Dad are well. See you soon.
Love,
Sam

11 CHOICES

A Imagine you are at the same youth camp as Samantha. Write an email of 30–40 words to a friend. Write about:

- what sports you can do
- what sport you played yesterday

B Imagine you are at a different youth camp. Write an email to your parents (100–120 words). Write about:

- what the camp is like
- how you like it there
- what you can do there
- the rules in the camp
- what you did yesterday
- what you are going to do tomorrow
- what you like best
- what you don't like

GRAMMAR   have to – don't have to

You have to wear a helmet!

You **have to** wear a life jacket. You **don't have to** come along.

Complete the rule with *have to* or *don't have to*.

Mit [1] .... sagst du, dass etwas **notwendig** ist.
Mit [2] .... sagst du, dass etwas **nicht notwendig** ist.

54   UNIT 7   WB p. 51, 52, 53   CYBER Homework 20

The Story of the Stones 3

The new girl

1 Match the sentence halves to complete the summary of Episode 2.

1 The children tell Sunborn   ☐ Darkman is alive.
2 The children learn that   ☐ to the children.
3 Sunborn tells the children   ☐ about their dreams.
4 Sunborn gives the stones   ☐ into animals.
5 The children morph   ☐ the story of the stones.

2 Look at the picture from Episode 3 and say what you can see. What do you think happens in this episode?

3 Watch Episode 3 and put the sentences in order to tell the story.

☐ The children hear a cry for help.
☐ The children learn the new girl's name is Gillian.
☐ The tiger rescues the girl.
☐ The children talk about their dreams.
☐ Emma morphs and jumps in the river.
☐ Daniel thinks it's a trap.

Everyday English

4 Watch Episode 3 again. Match the pictures with the expressions.

I'm off now.
Too late … !
Poor you!
Hang on.

1 Maybe it's a trap.

UNIT 8 We might go out

You learn
- how to use *might / might not*
- how to use *not going to*
- how to talk about freetime activities

You can
- talk about things that might happen
- talk about what you are (not) planning to do
- write an invitation

Get talking Intentions

 What are these people's plans? Talk about them with your partner. Use the words in the box to help you.

| watch a DVD | do the shopping | tidy (your) room | play basketball |
| do (your) homework | stay at a friend's house | have a party | do nothing |

A What's she going to do?

B She's going to do her homework.

  Listen to the dialogues and tick (✓) the correct box.

	Sharon	Nick	Chloe	Bill
have a party				
do nothing				
do homework				
stay at a friend's place				

③ CHOICES

A Read the dialogue and complete it with the phrases from the box. There is one phrase you don't need. Then listen and check. Act out the dialogue.

> I'm going to watch TV.   I'm going to do nothing.   And your school project?

Steve What are your plans for the weekend?
Luke 1 ....
Steve What about TV?
Luke I'm not going to watch TV. There's nothing good on.
Steve 2 ....
Luke I'm not going to do any work this weekend.

B Work with a partner and complete the dialogue with your own ideas. Then act out the scene.

Kevin Have you got any special plans for the weekend?
Dawn Well, I'm going to watch DVDs tomorrow night. Do you want to watch them with me?
Kevin I'd love to*, ...
Dawn Oh, why not?
Kevin I'm going to Jenny's party.
Dawn .... !

VOCABULARY: *I'd love to … – Ich würde gerne …

Grammar chant *not going to*

4 A chant. Listen and repeat.

Hey, Dad, listen. I'm sorry.
I'm not going to tidy my room.
I'm not going to make my bed.
I'm not going to work for school.
I'm going to take it easy instead.

Listen, Sam. That's fine, but …
I'm not going to cook for you.
I'm not going to drive you around.
I'm not going to buy you sweets.
I'm not going to give you a pound.

Hey, listen Dad. That was only a joke. Honestly …
I am going to tidy my room.
I am going to make my bed.
I am going to do my work,
I am now going to go ahead.
Really! Believe me, Dad!

Sounds right *going to*

5 When we say *going to*, it often sounds like *gonna*. Listen and repeat.

I'm **going to** write a letter,
I'm **going to** put it in the post.

And the letter's **going to** tell you
that I love you the most.

Get talking Plans for the weekend

6 Find out about your partner's plans for this weekend.

> **A** Are you going to watch TV?

> **B** No, I'm not. I'm going to watch DVDs. What about you?

7 Look at the mixed-up messages. Match them with the types of communication in the box. Write letters A–I.

☐ ☐ text messages   ☐ ☐ ☐ emails   ☐ ☐ notes
☐ invitation   ☐ Facebook post

A I've just come home. We had a great Sunday out. We, that's Mum, Dad, me and my sister Mia. We went to Brighton to see Grandma. Mia and I climbed a tree – see the photo! She's cool. I really like my sister.
Like Comment

B Mia, I saw your note about Sunday this morning. No way! We're all going to visit Grandma, and you're coming with us. You've got another 5 days to do your work for school. No excuse, please.

C Hi, Zoe. There was a phone call from Mia. She's not feeling well. She's not going to come over today. Dad

D Hey, Mum. I'm really sorry. I've got a lot of work for school this week. So I'm not going to come along to see Grandma on Sunday.

E From: zoe_f@likeit.com
Subject: photos on FB
Hi Mia, I saw the photos your brother posted on FB. I can see you had a lot of fun. But why did you tell me you're ill? Zoe

F From: mia_hd@hello.uk
Subject: party
Hello Zoe, thanks for your invitation for Sunday. Great! My parents and my little brother Lucas are going to visit Grandma. I'm not going with them. I'll tell them I've got a lot of work for school. LOL! Mia

G OK, I understand. I'm going to join you all, of course. Mia

H From: mia_hd@hello.uk
Subject: Sorry!!!
Hi there, I really, really, really wanted to see you today, Zoe. Then my mum said no. I felt ashamed and didn't want to tell you I had to go with them. It was a big mistake! Sorry for telling you a lie. Can we meet up tomorrow after school? Mia

I Dear Mia,
Come to my birthday party next Sunday.
Time: 10 a.m. – 6 p.m.
Place: 7, Station Road
Love, Zoe

8 Read the messages in 7 again. Tick the correct answer.

1 What does Mia say in her email to Zoe about Sunday?
- [ ] She's going to visit her grandma with her family.
- [ ] She's going to climb a tree with her brother.
- [ ] She's not going to visit her grandma with her family.

2 What message does Mia give Zoe's dad?
- [ ] She's going to come over to Zoe's place two hours later.
- [ ] She's not feeling well and isn't going to come over to Zoe's place.
- [ ] She's not feeling well, but she's going to come over anyway.

3 What does Zoe see on Mia's brother's Facebook page?
- [ ] A photo of Mia's family and their grandma.
- [ ] A photo of Lucas and his grandma.
- [ ] A photo of Lucas and Mia.

4 How does Mia feel when Zoe finds out what she did?
- [ ] She feels sorry she didn't tell Zoe the truth.
- [ ] She's very angry with herself.
- [ ] She's angry with Lucas because he posted the photo.

9 Read the messages again. In what order do they come? Write the letters A–I in the correct order.

1 [I] 2 [ ] 3 [ ] 4 [ ] 5 [ ] 6 [ ] 7 [ ] 8 [ ] 9 [ ]

Story time

10 Read the story.

William, the worrier

William has got a driving test in the morning, and he's worried. William is always worried!

"We're going to the cinema. Do you want to come?"

"No, thanks. We might miss the last bus home and I have to get to bed early tonight."

"Do you want to go for a practice drive?"

"No, thanks. I might crash the car. I need the car for my test tomorrow."

The next morning.

"I'm sorry, William. Your test was yesterday!"

11 Here are some more of William's worries. Match the sentence halves.

1. I don't want to go to the beach –
2. I don't want to go skiing –
3. I'm going to study tonight –
4. I don't want to go near that dog –
5. I don't want to answer the teacher's question –
6. I don't want to ride your bike –
7. I'm not going to eat that –
8. I'm not going to go trick-or-treating –

☐ I might break my leg.
☐ I might not get it right.
☐ I might fall off.
☐ it might be poisonous.
☐ the sun might be too hot.
☐ I might get into trouble.
☐ we might have a test tomorrow.
☐ it might bite.

12 Work in pairs. Take turns to test your partner.

A: Why doesn't William want to go to the beach?
B: Because the sun might be too hot.
A: That's right.

13 CHOICES

Writing for your Portfolio

A Read Jill's invitation to her birthday party. Imagine it's your birthday next week. Invite a friend (30–40 words). Write about:
- why there is a party
- when and where it is
- what there is going to be at the party

B Imagine there is going to be a fancy dress party at your school. Draw a mind map first – see the example below. Then use your ideas to write an invitation to a friend (60–70 words).

Party invitation

It's my birthday on Friday and I'm going to have a party on Saturday at my place. There's going to be lots of food and drink and there's going to be a DJ, too. It's going to be great. The party starts at 6 p.m. Don't be late.
See you on Saturday,
Jill

Mind map: fancy dress party
- lots of food
- DJ
- what?
- midnight surprise
- costume: me: pirate, you: catwoman?
- 18:00 – 21:00
- Friday evening
- at school

GRAMMAR

going to (negative)

Du verwendest *going to*, wenn du etwas planst oder beabsichtigst, etwas zu tun.
Beim Verb *go* verwendest du normalerweise kein *going to*. Also: *I'm going to a party.*

So bildest du die Verneinung mit *going to*:
negative of *be* + *going to* + *base form* of the verb.

I**'m not going to play** tennis tomorrow.
You **aren't going to like** the film.
He/She **isn't going to do** the shopping.
It **isn't going to rain** this afternoon.
We **aren't going to do** our homework.
They **aren't going to play** volleyball on Sunday.

might – might not

Wenn du sagen willst, dass etwas möglicherweise (nicht) eintreten wird, verwendest du:
might (not) + *base form* of the verb.

I **might go** to the party. I'm not sure.
It **might rain**, so take a coat.
I **might not sleep** well.

UNIT 9 Strange things from space!

You learn
- space vocabulary
- about the past simple (revision)
- how to use past time markers

You can
- talk about science fiction / UFOs / space
- write an ending to a story

Story time

1 Read the story.

A new home

The president of the planet Trojan spoke to all the people.

"People of Trojan!" she said. "I'm sorry, but I have bad news for you. Two months ago, we found out that a planet is coming towards us. A hundred years from now, the other planet is going to hit us, and the planet Trojan is going to explode. We can't stop this – it's going to happen."

The Trojan people were very scared. The president said more. "People of Trojan, we have only got one hundred years. But we've got a plan. We're going to build spaceships – huge spaceships, the biggest spaceships in the history of the universe. Each spaceship is going to be big enough to carry 10,000 people – and we are going to build 20,000 spaceships! In this way, we can take every Trojan man, woman and child to another place – a safe place – before the other planet hits us."

The people asked: "Where? Where is this place that we can all go to?"

The president said: "There is another planet, very far from here. It is a planet where Trojan people can live. The air is like our air; the water is like our water; and there is room for us. The name of this planet is: Earth! Earth is going to be our new home. Now, we have to get ready!"

The next day, the people of Trojan started to build the spaceships. It took them a very long time – more than fifteen years – to build the first 1,000 spaceships. And after fifty years, 5,000 spaceships were ready. And finally, all the 20,000 spaceships were ready. The spaceships were round, like huge yellow footballs – so big that 10,000 Trojans could go inside.

Then, one day, the people of Trojan said goodbye to their home. They went into the spaceships. And, one by one, the spaceships took off. And the Trojans began the journey to their new home. Twenty years later, the spaceships arrived at the planet Earth.

One day, Jenny was in her garden. It was a nice, sunny morning. Her dog, Josh, was with her – and suddenly he started to bark very loudly. "What's the matter, Josh?" she said, and she walked over to him. In the air, there were lots of strange, round, yellow seeds. The seeds fell from the sky, and one by one they landed on the grass. Jenny looked around – there were thousands of the seeds on the ground. Just then, her father came out of the house.
"What are you looking at, Jenny?" he asked. "Come here, Dad," she said. "Look at this!" Her

father came over and looked at the yellow seeds. "How strange!" he said. "But I haven't got time to look at them now. I've got to go to work. Jenny, tidy up here, please!" And her father walked to his car. He walked on some of the seeds and they went "Crack!!" Jenny's father got into his car and went to work. Jenny went into the house. She got a broom and came back to the garden. Then she started to sweep up the little yellow seeds. She put them into the dustbin.

2 How many of these tasks can you do?

1. The planet Trojan is going to explode in 10 years.   T / F
2. Each spaceship can take 10,000 Trojans.   T / F
3. Trojan is very similar to Earth.   T / F
4. The spaceships were like ....
5. The journey to Earth took ....
6. Jenny was .... with her dog.
7. Why was Josh barking? ....
8. Why was Jenny's dad in a hurry? ....
9. Jenny's dad asked her to ....

 3 Check your answers with a partner. Then listen to the story.

Vocabulary Science fiction

4 Match the words and the pictures.

☐ spaceship   ☐ galaxy   ☐ alien   ☐ time machine   ☐ astronaut   ☐ space station

Sounds right /ɪd/ /d/ /t/

5 Which is the odd one out? Listen and check.

1 arriv**ed** / land**ed** / plann**ed**   2 look**ed** / start**ed** / bark**ed**   3 ask**ed** / walk**ed** / visit**ed**

6 Complete the sentences. Use the verbs in the box in the past simple.

| see | pick | go | ~~be~~ | hear | put | see | turn |

They never saw him again!

James ..was.. alone in a town.   He .... a strange noise.   He .... round.   He .... a gold key on the ground.

He .... it up.   He .... a green light in a window.   He .... the key in the door of the house.   He .... into the house.

7 Look at the pictures again. Then write the story.

Sentence 1: *One day …*
Sentence 2: *Suddenly …*
Sentences 3–5: *He …*
Sentence 6: *At that moment …*
Sentence 7: *Then …*
Sentence 8: *Finally, …*

A Song 4 U

8 Listen and sing.

Song of the Trojans

*Trojans, Trojans,
let's leave this place.
Trojans, Trojans,
off into space.*

*Goodbye sweet, sweet Trojan.
Goodbye sweet, sweet home.
Let's board all our spaceships.
Into space we will roam.*

*Goodbye sweet, sweet Trojan.
The ships they all wait.
We're leaving our Trojan.
We hope it's not too late.*

Trojans, Trojans, …

*Goodbye sweet, sweet Trojan.
Sleep well, all my friends.
And dream of our planet.
Our Trojan time ends.*

*Goodbye sweet, sweet Trojan.
To Earth we now go.
And a new planet Trojan
out there we will grow.*

Trojans, Trojans, …

9 Read the text and match the sentence halves.

UFOs – are they really out there?

There are people who believe in UFOs, ufologists, and there are people who don't. There are thousands of photos of unidentified flying objects (UFOs). Many of them are nothing but clouds or balloons and airplanes. And some of them are fakes. Here is one of the most famous UFO photographs and the story behind it:

On May 11th, 1950 Evelyn Trent was in the garden of her farm in McMinnville, Oregon. On her way back to the house, she saw a metallic disk flying in her direction. She called out to her husband. He quickly got a camera and took pictures of the disk.

Even today ufologists believe that this photo shows a UFO; other people say it is a hoax, a trick to fool people. The Trents died many years ago, so we will never know the truth from them. In 2013, there was a big investigation into the photograph. Scientists used the most modern technology to study the photo, but the experts still couldn't decide if it was real or not.

1 A ufologist   ☐ thought she saw a UFO in the back garden.
2 Evelyn Trent   ☐ are no longer alive.
3 Mr Trent   ☐ studied the photo in 2013.
4 The Trents   ☐ believes in UFOs.
5 Scientists   ☐ took a photo of the "UFO".

10 Listen to an interview with ufologist Paul Brady and George Brendel, who does not believe in UFOs. Take notes to answer the questions below.

1 What does Paul believe aliens are doing?
   ....

2 Why are they doing this?
   ....

3 What does George think about his ideas?
   ....

Writing for your Portfolio

 Here are two endings for the story in . Choose the one you like best and say why.

Ending 1

James went into the house. He saw a chair and he sat down. It was very comfortable! Then he found a button on the floor, near the chair. "What's this?" he said, and he pushed the button. The chair started to go round and round very quickly, but after a minute, it stopped. James went out of the house. He was in the year 2090!

Ending 2

James went into the house. He saw a chair and he sat down. It was very comfortable! He went to sleep. Five hours later, James woke up. In front of him were two strange people with pink eyes. "Why are you here?" said one of the strange people. "You shouldn't be here! Now we have to take you to our planet!"

 Write another ending.

GRAMMAR

Past simple (revision)

Bei regelmäßigen Verben bildest du das Past simple, indem du *-ed* anhängst:

open – open**ed**   laugh – laugh**ed**
look – look**ed**

Es gibt auch viele unregelmäßige Verben:

be – **was/were**   go – **went**
take – **took**   run – **ran**
come – **came**   see – **saw**

Die Verneinung bildest du mit *didn't* + Verb:

They **didn't believe** her.
She **didn't take** another photograph.

***Was/were* verneinst du mit *wasn't/weren't*.**

Mr Brown didn't look before he opened the door.

Past time markers

So kannst du ausdrücken, wann sich etwas in der Vergangenheit ereignet hat:

Two months ago, we found out that a planet is coming towards us.
One day, Jenny was in her garden.
Then she started to sweep up the seeds.
The next day, they started building the spaceships.
After fifty years, five thousand spaceships were ready.
Twenty years later, the spaceships arrived at the planet Earth.
Finally, all the spaceships were ready.

The Story of the Stones 4

You can run, but you can't hide

1 Answer the questions about Episode 3. Tick the right answers.

1 Where were the children?	☐ on the beach	☐ by a river	☐ by a lake
2 Who jumped in the water?	☐ the eagle	☐ the rat	☐ the tiger
3 What is the new girl's name?	☐ Lillian	☐ Gillian	☐ Debbie
4 Why was she in the water?	☐ to save a dog	☐ to save a cat	☐ to save a rabbit

2 Complete the summary of Episode 3 with *Gillian*, *Emma*, *Sarah* or *Darkman*.

¹.................................. goes to Emma's house and gives the children a box of chocolates. Gillian tells them that she met a strange man. The children are worried it was probably ².................................. . He wanted to know about the kids.
Before she leaves, Gillian gives them a box that ³.................................. gave to her. ⁴.................................. opens the box. A gas escapes. She and ⁵.................................. are unconscious*.
⁶.................................. returns and saves them. ⁷.................................. tells her about the morphing.

VOCABULARY: *unconscious – bewusstlos

3 Watch Episode 4 and match the questions with the answers.

1 Why did Emma tell Gillian about the morphing?   ☐ Because he wants the stones.
2 Why does Sunborn want to give Gillian   ☐ Because she can help them make a
  morphing powers?   stronger team.
3 Why does Gillian want them to close the door   ☐ Because she doesn't like fighting.
  quickly?   ☐ Because Darkman is after her.
4 Why doesn't Gillian want to join the team?   ☐ Because she saw the eagle on the floor.
5 Why does Darkman break into the house?

Everyday English

4 Watch Episode 4 again. Complete the sentences.

| In that case | Calm down | One thing at a time | Look |

Gillian He was behind me. I know it.

Emma ¹.................................. , Gillian. You're safe here with us.

Sarah ².................................. – we know who this man is. His name's Darkman and he's after us.

Sunborn Sometimes I feel that Darkman is very close indeed.

Daniel ³.................................. , I think we should give Gillian morphing powers.

Sunborn ⁴.................................. , Daniel. First I have to meet her.

The Twins 3
DEVELOPING SPEAKING COMPETENCIES

Language function
- buying a cinema ticket (*Kinokarten kaufen*)

Speaking strategy
- expressing disappointment (*Enttäuschung ausdrücken*)

At the cinema

Vocabulary Problems

1 Read what these signs say. How would you say them in German?

2 Watch or listen to the dialogue. Then read it. What's the problem for Lucy and Leo?

Leo	Two tickets for the 5 o'clock showing of *They Came From Mars*, please.
Assistant	I'm sorry. It's sold out.
Leo	What a shame.
Lucy	What time is the next showing, please?
Assistant	It's not until 7.30. However, there's a showing at 5.30, but it's in 3D.
Lucy	What film is that?
Assistant	It's the same film: *They Came From Mars*.
Leo	That's great.
Assistant	But it's in 3D, so it's more expensive.
Lucy	That's a pity.
Leo	Lucy? Are you crazy? It's in 3D! Let's go.
Lucy	Oh, OK. Two tickets, please.
Assistant	Where would you like to sit?
Lucy	Just a moment. Er … row 12, please.

3 Read the sentences and correct them.

1 There is only one ticket for the 5 o'clock showing of *They Came From Mars*.
2 The showing at 7.30 is more expensive than the showing at 5 o'clock.
3 Leo does not like 3D films very much.
4 Lucy doesn't think it's a problem that the 3D showing is more expensive.
5 The twins don't buy tickets for the 3D showing.

Useful phrases Buying a cinema ticket

4 Who says what? Write C (*Customer*) or A (*Assistant*).

1 I'm sorry. It's sold out. ☐
2 Two tickets for the … o'clock showing of …, please. ☐
3 What time is the next showing, please? ☐
4 It's not until 7.30. ☐
5 There's a showing at 5.30, but it's in 3D, so it's more expensive. ☐
6 Where would you like to sit? ☐
7 Row 12, please. ☐

? What do you think? Answer the questions.

- What do they do until the film begins?
- Does the film begin on time?

Mobile homework

Watch part 2 of the video. Use the verbs from the box in the correct form and information from part 2 to complete the sentences.

| have got | buy | begin | win | notice | want |

1 Lucy and Leo ………………………… until the film ………………………… .
2 First they ………………………… a hot dog.
3 Leo ………………………… play ………………………… on the mobile.
4 Leo ………………………… the game and he is very ………………………… .
5 Lucy suddenly ………………………… started 15 minutes before.

Speaking strategy Expressing disappointment

5 Complete. Then check with the dialogue in **2**.

1 **Assistant** I'm sorry. It's sold out.
   Leo ………………………… shame.

2 **Assistant** It's in 3D, so it's more expensive.
   Lucy ………………………… pity.

6 CHOICES

A Work in pairs. A mentions a problem (from **1**). B reacts and shows disappointment.

> A The shop's closed.
>
> B What a pity.

B ROLE PLAY: Look at the situations from **1**. Choose one. Work in pairs and extend it into a longer dialogue. Take 2 or 3 minutes to practise it. Don't write it down. Act it out in class.

UNIT 10 Are you ready to order?

You learn
- how to use *some* and *any*
- some food words
- about ordering food in a restaurant

You can
- talk about food
- order food in a restaurant
- write a story

Vocabulary Food

 1 Listen and look at the pictures. Then write the numbers next to the words.

- ☐ pears
- ☐ pork
- ☐ beef
- ☐ chicken
- ☐ plums
- ☐ lamb
- ☐ rice pudding
- ☐ pumpkin pie
- ☐ peppers
- ☐ onions
- ☐ tomatoes
- ☐ chocolate ice cream
- ☐ cabbage
- ☐ cheesecake
- ☐ strawberries
- ☐ turkey
- ☐ pancakes
- ☐ peaches
- ☐ grapes
- ☐ potatoes

 2 Write the food words from **1** in the table below.

fruit	vegetables	meat	desserts

3 Listen and write the names of the people under the shopping baskets.

Henry   Ella   Jacob   Laura

....

4 Write the words under the pictures.

sausages
cheese
ham
mushrooms
olives

  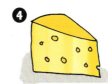 

....

5 Read the dialogue. Then write the names under the pizzas.

Waiter	Are you ready to order?
Mr Hutton	Yes, we are.
Mrs Hutton	I'd like a pizza with ham, cheese and tomatoes.
Waiter	And to drink?
Mrs Hutton	Mineral water, please.
Mr Hutton	I'd like a pizza too – with ham, mushrooms and green peppers. And an orange juice, please.
Ben	For me a pizza with ham, sausage and cheese.
Waiter	And to drink?
Ben	A cola, please.
Vicky	And for me a pizza with mushrooms, tomatoes and sausages.
Waiter	And to drink?
Vicky	An apple juice, please.

....

 6 Listen to the dialogue and act it out.

Time for a sketch

 7 Read the sketch.

The best restaurant in town

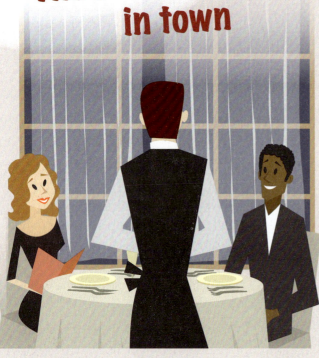

 Menu

Starters:
Onion soup • Tomato soup

Main courses:
Lamb chops with potatoes and cabbage
Chicken with rice and peas
Beef with chips and carrots
Turkey with potatoes and cabbage
Pork chops with chips and peas
Vegetable curry
Fish of the day

Desserts:
Chocolate ice cream
Cheesecake
Rice pudding
Pancakes
Pumpkin pie

SCENE 1
In the restaurant.

Man	A table for two, please.
Waiter	Next to the window, sir?
Man	That's fine.
Woman	Can we have the menu, please?
Waiter	Certainly, madam. Straightaway. Can I get you something to drink?
Woman	Mineral water, please.
Man	The same for me.

(Two minutes later.)

Waiter	Here you are. Are you ready to order?
Woman	Onion soup.
Man	And the onion soup for me, too.
Waiter	Thank you.

SCENE 2
In the kitchen.

Waiter	Two onion soups and …
Chef	Onion soup? We haven't got any onions.
Waitress	I can run over to the supermarket and buy some.
Chef	Too late. Let me think. Run over to Johnny's Restaurant and get two bowls of onion soup.
Waitress	OK.

(Five minutes later.)

Chef	But that's tomato soup.
Waitress	They didn't have any onion soup.

SCENE 3
In the restaurant.

Waiter	I'm sorry. There isn't any onion soup. But we've got some tomato soup. It's a special recipe of the chef's grandma.
Woman	OK. Bring us the tomato soup.

SCENE 4
In the restaurant.

Waiter	How did you like our chef's tomato soup?
Man	It was fine. Now I'd like the beef with chips and carrots.
Woman	And for me, the lamb with potatoes and cabbage.
Waiter	Certainly.

 WB p. 69, 71, 72

SCENE 7

In the kitchen.

Waiter Run over to Johnny's again and get some rice pudding and chocolate ice cream.

Waitress OK.

SCENE 8

In the restaurant.

Waiter For dessert we have rice pudding and chocolate ice cream.
Woman That's fine.
Waiter Here you are.
Man Look. There's a flag on my ice cream. It says: "Johnny's Restaurant".
Woman I don't think we're in the best restaurant in town. Next time we're going to Johnny's.

SCENE 5

In the kitchen.

Waiter One beef and one lamb.
Chef Is there any lamb in the fridge?
Waitress No, there isn't.
Chef What about beef? Have we got any beef?
Waitress No, sorry, there isn't any beef.
Chef What can we do?
Waitress Johnny's Restaurant does a good chicken.
Chef Run over and get two chickens.

SCENE 6

In the restaurant.

Waiter Here you are.
Woman But we ordered lamb and beef.
Waiter Madam, the chicken is the best in town. It's the chef's special recipe. Chicken Volcano.
Woman OK. The chicken then.

8 How many of these tasks can you do?

1 The man and woman sit next to the window.   T / F
2 For a starter they order tomato soup.   T / F
3 The waiter brings them nothing for a starter.   T / F
4 The man orders .... for his main course.
5 The woman wants .... with her lamb.
6 .... is missing from the fridge.
7 How many times does the waitress go over to Johnny's? ....
8 What does the waiter offer the couple for dessert? ....
9 What do the couple decide to do after dessert? ....

9 Check your answers with a partner. Then listen to the sketch.

WB p. 69, 71, 72

A Song 4 U

10 Listen and sing.

My dream

Last night I dreamed of chicken,
of rice and cabbage stew.
Last night I dreamed of pancakes,
and then I dreamed of you.

You served me cakes.
You served me grapes.
You served me pumpkin pie.
You said to me,
you said to me,
you said to me: Please try.

Last night I dreamed of strawberries,
of grapes both green and blue.
Last night I dreamed of ice cream,
and then I dreamed of you.

You served me cakes ...

I tried and tried. I tried and tried.
I felt like a balloon.
Then I woke up. You said to me:
Come on, it's breakfast soon!

11 CHOICES

Writing for your Portfolio

Read these two stories about a visit to a pizza place. Underline the differences in the second text. Which text is more interesting to read, and why is it better?

Last Sunday my dad and I went to a restaurant. We had tomato soup and a pizza. Suddenly Dad stopped eating. There was something under the cheese. It was a coin. Dad called the waiter. The waiter was very sorry and Dad got another pizza.

Last Sunday my dad and I went to a restaurant. We had tomato soup and a pizza. Suddenly Dad stopped eating. "What's the matter?" I asked. "I don't know," Dad said. "There's something under the cheese." "Yes," I said, "your pizza." "Very funny," Dad said. Then he lifted the cheese. There was a coin under it! Dad called the waiter. "I'm so sorry," the waiter said. Dad got another pizza.

A Look at the picture. Write a story about it (50–60 words). Use these words and phrases to help you.

On Saturday Mrs Green went to a ... with her ....
Mrs Green had ..., Sue had ... and James had ....
Suddenly Sue said, "Don't eat your ..., Mum! There's a ...."
Mum called the .... She ....

B Look at the picture. Write a story about it (80–100 words). Use dialogue to make it more interesting.

Complete the sentences with *some* or *any*. Then listen and check.

Dad Sue, are there [1].................... plums and peaches in the fridge?

Sue There are [2].................... plums, but there aren't [3].................... peaches. Are you making fruit salad?

Dad Yes. What have we got?

Sue There are [4].................... grapes and [5].................... pears.

Dad OK. Are there [6].................... strawberries?

Sue No, sorry, Dad. There aren't [7].................... .

 # GRAMMAR   *some – any*

*Run over to the supermarket and buy **some** tomatoes.* (= einige Tomaten)
Du verwendest in diesem Satz *some*, weil nicht angegeben wird, wie viele Tomaten es sind.

*Get **some** rice pudding and chocolate ice cream.* (= etwas Reispudding)
In diesem Satz sagst du *some*, weil du von etwas sprichst, das man nicht zählen kann.

*We haven't got **any** onions.* (= keine Zwiebeln)
Hier verwendest du *any*, weil du ausdrücken willst, dass etwas *nicht vorhanden* ist.

*There isn't **any** onion soup. But we've got **some** tomato soup.*
Hier sagst du, dass etwas *nicht vorhanden* ist (die Zwiebelsuppe), aber etwas anderes *vorhanden* ist (die Tomatensuppe).

 Read the questions. Write *some* or *any*.
*Have we got **any** beef?*
*Can I have **some** ice cream?*
Mit [1].................... fragst du nach etwas, von dem du weißt, dass es vorhanden ist.
Mit [2].................... fragst du, ob etwas vorhanden ist.

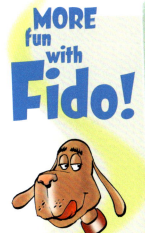   

Kids in NYC 2

The baseball star

Before you watch

1 Write the words under the pictures.

team
pitch
bat
hit

1 .... 2 .... 3 .... 4 ....

2 In what order do you think the pictures come in the DVD? Write 1–4.

Watch the story

3 Check your answers to **2**.

4 Circle the correct answer.

1 Emma *likes* / *doesn't like* baseball.
2 Gerry is *tall* / *short* with blue eyes.
3 The boys have got a big game on *Thursday* / *Friday*.
4 Emma wants to *pitch* / *hit* a few balls.

5 Circle T (*True*) or F (*False*).

1 Emma is a new student at East Central High.   T / F
2 Gerry Wood has blonde hair and blue eyes.   T / F
3 Steve doesn't want Emma to play baseball.   T / F
4 Emma plays baseball on the school team.   T / F
5 The ball hits Gerry on the arm.   T / F

6 Complete the dialogue.

reddish
new
interesting
tall
great
fair

Emma I love watching baseball.
Jenny You love watching baseball or you love watching Gerry Wood play baseball?
Emma Which one's Gerry Wood? Remember, I'm ¹............................ at the school.
Jenny He's pitching now. He's ²............................ with ³............................ hair and blue eyes.
Emma He seems ⁴............................ . But I'm more interested in the baseball.
Jenny Really?
Emma Yeah, what a ⁵............................ game. Why can't girls play? It isn't ⁶............................ .
Jenny Do girls want to play baseball?
Emma Well, I do.

Everyday English

7 Complete the dialogues.

By the way,
it's no trouble at all.
It isn't fair.

Why can't girls play?
....

Do girls want to play baseball?

Hi, Emma, I'm Gerry.

.... I'm Emma. I'm new at the school.

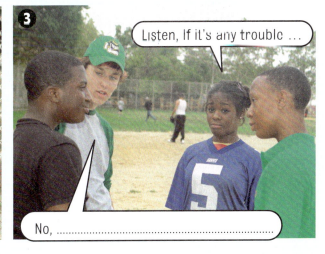

Listen, if it's any trouble ...

No, ...

UNIT 11 The curse of the pharaoh

You learn
- about irregular plurals
- how to form questions with *who*
- about ancient Egypt

You can
- talk about ancient Egypt
- complete a story
- write about the best place in your home

Vocabulary Ancient Egypt

1 Listen and look at the picture. Then number the words.

- 4 a pyramid
- 4 hieroglyphics
- 3 a sphinx
- 7 a mummy
- 2 a temple
- 6 a tomb
- 5 a papyrus

2 Are you good at history? Do the quiz about ancient Egypt and find out. Then listen and check.

— ANCIENT EGYPT QUIZ —

1. What was the name of the Egyptian kings?
   a) presidents   b) lords   **c) pharaohs**   d) emperors

2. What was the most sacred animal of the Egyptians?
   a) the cow   b) the goose   c) the crocodile   **d) the cat**

3. A sphinx has a human head and the body of …
   a) a snake.   **b) a lion.**   c) a hippo.   d) an elephant.

4. A river was very important for the ancient Egyptians. What is its name?
   a) the Amazon   b) the Thames   **c) the Nile**   d) the Seine

5. Religion was very important for the Egyptians. This is why they built lots of …
   a) cathedrals.   b) altars.   c) crosses.   **d) pyramids and temples.**

6. Which of these did the ancient Egyptians invent? (There is more than one right answer.)
   a) bathrooms   b) eye glasses   c) knives   **d) paper**

3 Read the text. Then listen to it.

LIFE IN ANCIENT EGYPT

Q How do we know what life in ancient Egypt was like?

A From documents written on papyrus, from hieroglyphics on stones, and from wall paintings and objects found in tombs.

Q What did people wear?

A People only wore light clothes because it was very hot. They wore sandals on their feet or they went barefoot. The sandals were made of palm leaves. Slaves, workers and children were often naked. People cared a lot about their looks. Men and women wore eye make-up and jewellery. They also used perfumes.

Q What work did the Egyptians do?

A Many Egyptians worked as farmers. They worked on the fields, but they also helped to build the pyramids and temples. There were also other jobs. Weavers, for example, made beautiful clothes. They sold the clothes to other people. People paid for the clothes with food, salt and other things.

Q What did people eat?

A The Egyptians had lots of different food. They hunted fish, ducks and geese. Many people were farmers and had sheep, cattle, goats, pigs, and later also horses. These animals gave them milk, wool, meat and eggs. But they also used the leather, the horns and the fat. The Egyptians even had farms where they kept oxen. They also had lots of vegetables and fruit.

Q What did people do in their free time?

A Hunting and fishing were the most popular sports for the men. Children played with balls and animals made from wood. Rich Egyptians often gave big parties with lots of food and drink. There were musicians, singers, dancers, jugglers and acrobats. Servants put big pieces of perfumed fat on people's heads. When the fat melted, it ran down their faces. This made them smell nice.

4 Circle T (*True*) or F (*False*).

1 Some people in Egypt did not wear clothes.   T / F
2 Men wore make-up and used perfumes too.   T / F
3 Only slaves built the pyramids.   T / F
4 Weavers got a lot of money for their work.   T / F
5 The Egyptians ate meat, vegetables and fruit.   T / F
6 Children went hunting and fishing.   T / F

5 Go through **2** and **3** and underline the plural forms of the following words:

man   child   woman   person   foot   goose   fish   knife   leaf   ox

6 Read about the pyramids at Giza. Put the numbers where you think they go.

100,000   230   20   143   2 million   2,000

The pyramids in Egypt are the tombs of the pharaohs. The biggest pyramid is the one for the Pharaoh Khufu. Did you know?

1 It is ……143…… metres high, and each side is more than ……230…… metres long.
2 There are more than ……100,000 2 million…… stone blocks in the pyramid.
3 Each stone is about ……2,000 100,000…… kilograms.
4 More than ……2 million 100,000…… men worked to build it.
5 It took more than ……100,000 230 20…… years to build it.

7 Listen to the interview and check your answers.

8 CHOICES

A Read more about the pyramids and answer the questions below.

When a pharaoh died, the priests put the mummy inside a pyramid. The Egyptian people believed that after a long time, the pharaoh's spirit woke up. Then it climbed up the steps of the pyramid to meet Ra, the sun god. They also believed that when the pharaoh woke up, he needed many things – for example food, clothes and jewellery. The people put these things in the pyramid with the mummy.

Of course, everyone knew there were wonderful things inside the pyramid. Soldiers guarded the tombs day and night to stop thieves.

But hundreds of years later, robbers found many of the tombs and stole everything inside.

One of the most famous pharaohs was Tutankhamun. He became pharaoh when he was nine, but he died when he was only nineteen. He is famous because the robbers did not find his tomb. When an Englishman called Howard Carter found the tomb of Tutankhamun in 1922, it was still full of wonderful clothes and jewellery.

1 Who put the mummy in the pyramids? the priests
2 Who met the pharaoh's spirit at the top of the pyramid? Ra
3 Who was Ra? the sun god
4 Who guarded the tombs? soldiers
5 Who died when he was only 19? Tutankhamun
6 Who found Tutankhamun's tomb? an Englishman called Howard Carter

MORE! 2 — INFORMATION FÜR ELTERN

Liebe Eltern, liebe Erziehungsberechtigte!

Auch fürs Englischlernen gilt: Übung macht den Meister/die Meisterin! Daher gibt es zu diesem *MORE! Student's Book* eine Vielzahl motivierender Zusatzmaterialien für das Üben zu Hause.
Das **MORE! E-BOOK+** macht das Schulbuch interaktiv und unterstützt gezielt beim Lernen. Auf der **HELBLING e-zone** gibt es zusätzliche kostenlose **Online-Materialien zu MORE!** und mit der **MORE! Media App** kann man auf die audiovisuellen Inhalte des Buches auch unterwegs zugreifen. Für intensives Training zu Hause sind die **MORE! Grammar Practice**, das **MORE! Skills Training – Listening** und das **MORE! Test-Training** perfekt geeignet.

Sie bekommen diese Zusatzmaterialien im Buchhandel oder können sie im Webshop oder per E-Mail ganz bequem bei uns bestellen. Für weitere Informationen finden Sie auf **www.helbling.com** die umfangreichen Produktbeschreibungen.

Ihrem Kind viel Spaß und Erfolg beim Lernen mit MORE!
wünscht das MORE!-Team

MORE! ② E-BOOK+

Das **MORE! E-BOOK+** enthält das gesamte gedruckte Schulbuch und noch viel mehr.
Es bietet alle interaktiven Übungen, Videos und Audios aus dem *MORE! Student's Book*. Eine interaktive *Wordlist* unterstützt Ihr Kind beim Vokabellernen und Aussprachetraining. Der integrierte Lernplaner und regelmäßige Selbstkontrollen führen effizient zum Lernerfolg.

MORE! ② Media App

Die Symbole im *Student's Book* führen zur **MORE! Media App**. Mit dieser App können die Audios, Videos und *Graphic stories* aus dem Buch direkt gestartet und zu Hause oder unterwegs wiederholt werden. Die App kann kostenlos im Apple App Store oder Google Play Store heruntergeladen werden.

Einfach zu bestellen!
- im Webshop: **www.helbling.com**
- per E-Mail: **office@helbling.com**

MORE! 2 — INFORMATION FÜR ELTERN

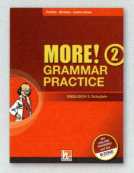

MORE! ② Grammar Practice mit Online Training

Dieses Übungsheft enthält zusätzliche Übungen zu allen wesentlichen Grammatikinhalten. Es orientiert sich an den Inhalten und Themen von MORE!, sodass keine neuen Inhalte erarbeitet werden müssen und die Konzentration voll und ganz auf den grammatikalischen Aufgabenstellungen liegt. Ergänzt wird das Angebot durch die innovativen Online-Übungen auf der HELBLING e-zone.

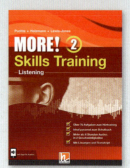

MORE! ② Skills Training – Listening

Hörübungen bei Tests und Schularbeiten müssen keine Hürde mehr sein. Das **MORE! Skills Training – Listening** bietet unterschiedliche Aufgabenformate um spezifische *Listening Strategies* anzuwenden und zu trainieren. Die Hörtexte können über die MORE! Media App abgespielt werden, das Buch enthält alle Hörtexte in abgedruckter Form sowie Lösungen zur Selbstkontrolle.

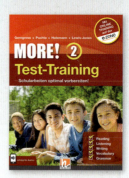

MORE! ② Test-Training

Optimale **Vorbereitung für Tests und Schularbeiten**: Mit den zahlreichen Übungen zu Grammatik, Wortschatz, Lese- und Hörverständnis und Schreibtraining wird der Lernstoff zu Hause effizient geübt und gefestigt. Durch die automatische Auswertung der abwechslungsreichen Übungen kann gezielt weiter trainiert werden.

MORE! ② Holiday Book

Einfache Wiederholung des Jahresstoffs in den Sommerferien! In zehn übersichtlichen Tagesportionen werden die 18 Units aus dem *MORE! Student's Book* aufgegriffen und die Grammatik- und Sprachschwerpunkte wiederholt. Am Ende des Buches gibt es Lösungen zur Selbstkontrolle.

 **Bestellinformation**

Einfach zu bestellen!
- im Webshop: www.helbling.com
- per E-Mail: office@helbling.com

helbling.com

HELBLING Verlagsgesellschaft m.b.H.
6063 Rum · Kaplanstr. 9
Tel.: +43 512 262333-0
Fax: +43 512 262333-111
E-Mail: office@helbling.com

B Read the text. Then put the sentences in the correct order. Write numbers.

THE STORY OF HOWARD CARTER

Howard Carter was born in England in 1874. He was very interested in history. When he was 17, he went to Egypt. He had one wish – he wanted to find the tomb of Tutankhamun. Another Englishman, Lord Carnarvon, had the same dream. He gave Howard some money to find the tomb. For five years Carter tried to find it, but he didn't find anything.

Then he went back to England. When he returned to Egypt, he brought a yellow canary with him. "A golden bird!" shouted one of the Egyptian workers. "The bird will show us the tomb!"

On November 4th, 1922, Carter's workmen discovered the tomb of a pharaoh. Carter wanted to open it the next day. When he came back to his house that night, his servant came up to him and said: "A snake killed your yellow bird. I'm sure it was the pharaoh's snake. Don't open the tomb! There is a curse on the tomb – the curse of the pharaoh! It can kill hundreds of people and animals." But Carter didn't listen to him.

He sent a telegram to Lord Carnarvon in England. Carnarvon arrived in Egypt on November 26th. Carter made a hole in the door of the tomb. He took a candle and looked inside. Behind him, Lord Carnarvon asked: "Can you see anything?" Carter answered: "Yes, wonderful things!" In the tomb there were lots of treasures. There was also the mummy of the boy-king, Pharaoh Tutankhamun!

A few days later, an insect bit Lord Carnarvon on the left cheek. He became ill and died. Back in England, his dog died on the same day.

When workmen took off the bandages from the mummy of Tutankhamun, they saw that there was also a wound on the pharaoh's left cheek. Was there really a curse of the pharaoh?

- ☐ But Howard Carter didn't listen. He sent a telegram to Lord Carnarvon.
- ☐ But when Lord Carnarvon was back in England, he and his dog died on the same day.
- ☐ 1 When Howard Carter was seventeen, he went to Egypt.
- ☐ His servant was scared and said: "Don't open it! There's a curse!"
- ☐ One day, his workmen discovered a tomb.
- ☐ He wanted to find the tomb of Tutankhamun.
- ☐ They found lots of treasures inside, and the mummy of Tutankhamun.
- ☐ When Lord Carnarvon arrived, they opened the tomb.

Sounds right /dʒ/ /tʃ/

9 Listen and repeat the tongue-twister. How quickly can you say it?

Jim juggles jam
and Chuck chooses chickens.

Story time

10 Read the story. Then listen to it.

The curse of the pharaoh

First Hannah, Luke and their parents looked at the pictures on the walls in the tourist centre. They showed scenes from ancient Egypt. There were hundreds of farmers and slaves building a pyramid. Then they took a tour to one of the pyramids. Inside the pyramid it was so much cooler than in the hot sun.

"Stay with me all the time!" the guide said. "It's dangerous in here. There's a curse of the pharaoh!"

"The curse of the pharaoh?" asked another tourist in the group. "What's that?"

"There's one more tomb in this pyramid. But nobody knows where it is," said the guide. "A few years ago, some scientists wanted to find it. They went into the pyramid, but they never came back. People say the curse of the pharaoh killed them!"

"The curse of the pharaoh!" Hannah laughed out loud. "But I'd love to find that tomb!" she whispered to Luke.

Luke didn't say anything. He was in front of a hole in the wall. "That's funny. The guide didn't say anything about this hole!" he said. "Let's go through here! I've got a torch so we can find our way back."

"Shh!!" said Hannah. "Mum and Dad mustn't see us!"

The two children climbed through the hole. Suddenly, there was a loud noise and a second later a big stone filled the hole! Hannah and Luke tried to move the big stone. But they couldn't get out. "The curse of the pharaoh!" whispered Luke.

Get talking Completing a story

11 Work in pairs. Say what you think happened next. Then listen and find out.

12 How many of these tasks can you do?

1 First the family go to the visitor centre.   T / F
2 Inside the pyramid it is not as hot as outside.   T / F
3 The guide tells everyone to stay close.   T / F

4 The guide says there is one .... in the pyramid.
5 The scientists who looked for the tomb ....
6 Hannah really wants to ....

7 What do the children decide to explore? ....
8 What happened when the children climbed through the hole? ....
9 What does Luke try to understand at the end? ....

13 Check your answers with a partner.

14 CHOICES

Writing for your Portfolio

A Write an ending to the story about Luke and Hannah (50–60 words). Use these words and phrases to help you.

| heard voices | walked on | came to a door | some men |
| gold and diamonds | pharaoh | invited them | dream |

B Read the questions below. Think of an ending to the story about Luke and Hannah. Then write the story (100–120 words). Write about:

- what they did
- the people they met
- what the people told them
- how they got out of the pyramid

GRAMMAR

Irregular plurals

Complete. Write *people / children / leaves / women / feet / teeth.*

Einige Nomen (*nouns*) sind unregelmäßig. Sie bekommen im Plural kein *-s*.

man	**men**	woman	³ ~~weman~~
goose	**geese**	person	⁴ ~~persons~~ people
child	¹ children	tooth	⁵ teeth
foot	² feet		

Einige Nomen (*nouns*) haben im Singular und im Plural die gleiche Form:

one fish – two **fish**   one sheep – two **sheep**

Nomen, die auf *-f* oder *-fe* enden, bekommen im Plural meist ein *-ves*.

knife – **knives**   thief – **thieves**   leaf – ⁶ ~~leef leafes~~

Who took the mummy?

Questions with "Who ...?"

Wenn du mit *Who ...?* nach dem Subjekt fragst, verwendest du kein *do/does* oder *did*:

Who put the mummy in the pyramids? (**Not:** Who ~~did~~ put ... ?)
Who found Tutankhamun's tomb? (**Not:** Who ~~did~~ find ... ?)

The Story of the Stones 5

It's you!

1 How well do you remember Episode 4? Circle T (*True*) or F (*False*).

1 Daniel thinks Darkman is trying to kill them.   T / F
2 Darkman attacked Gillian on the beach.   T / F
3 Gillian hit Darkman with her bag.   T / F
4 Gillian doesn't want to join the team.   T / F
5 Gillian is going to meet Sunborn.   T / F

2 Look at the picture. Who do you think says:

1 Hello, Gillian. And welcome to the team.
2 Do you know where he is?
3 How about a wolf?
4 Isn't there a stone for me?
5 Darkman is very close.

3 Watch Episode 5. Complete the sentences with the words in the box. There are some words you don't need.

| wolf | snake | Darkman | kill | Gillian |
| Sunborn | an alien | Emma | Daniel | Darkman |

1 Darkman is trying to .... the children.
2 Gillian wants to be a ....
3 Gillian is really ....
4 .... kills ....

Everyday English

4 Watch Episode 5 again. Complete the sentences.

Sunborn Yes. Hello, Gillian. And welcome to the team. We're happy to have you, ¹........................ .

Daniel Do you know where he is?
Sunborn ²........................ , but he's close.

Emma ... but you didn't know that we had brought him here.
Sunborn No, I didn't. But ³........................ — and you've helped me again.
Sarah And ⁴........................ for the last time!

| hopefully | it wasn't your fault | that's for sure | Not exactly |

UNIT 12 Families

You learn
- family words
- about activities
- how to use *like (doing)*
- how to use *must / mustn't*

You can
- talk about people in a family
- talk about things you like doing
- say and write what people must(n't) do

Vocabulary Family

  1 Listen and write the first names.

William   Natasha   Anthony
Susan   Fred   Jo   Lisa

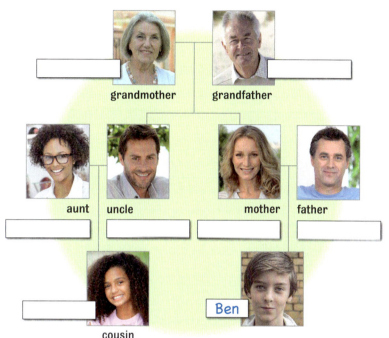

grandmother   grandfather
aunt   uncle   mother   father
cousin   Ben

Get talking Who's who?

2 Work in pairs. Write down the first names of people in your family (uncles, cousins, parents, etc.). Give the list to your partner. Your partner asks you who is who.

A Who's Vera? – B She's my aunt.
A Who are Charlotte and Tina?
B They're my cousins.

3 Read the text about Angelina Jolie and her family.

A FAMOUS MOTHER

Angelina Jolie is an American superstar. In 2001, when she was 26, she became famous all over the world with the film *Lara Croft: Tomb Raider*. But Angelina Jolie is not only a superstar. She also visits refugee* camps in Asia and Africa and in 2001 she gave a million dollars to help refugees. She also built schools in Cambodia and gives money to hospitals for children. In 2002, Jolie adopted her first child, the seven-month-old Maddox Chivan. The boy was born in a small village in Cambodia and had no Mum or Dad. In 2005, Jolie and her third husband Brad Pitt adopted Zahara, a baby from Ethiopia. And a year later their first child, a daughter, was born. Her name is Shiloh Nouvel. In 2007, Jolie adopted a three-year-old boy from Vietnam. His name is Pax Thien. Like Maddox, the boy didn't have a Mum or Dad. In 2008, Jolie had twins, a boy, Knox Léon and a girl, Vivienne Marcheline. American magazines bought the first pictures of the babies for 14 million dollars. The money went to the Jolie-Pitt foundation* that helps children all over the world.

VOCABULARY: *refugee* – Flüchtling; *foundation* – Stiftung

4 Circle T (*True*) or F (*False*).

1 Angelina Jolie gives a lot of money to poor people. **T**/ F
2 Angelina Jolie adopted her first child before she became famous. T /**F**
3 Angelina Jolie has six children. **T**/ F
4 Angelina Jolie sold the picture of her baby twins for a lot of money. **T**/ F

5 Read the magazine article. How did each of these kids learn the things they talk about?

The COOLEST THINGS kids learn

For most parents, what is important is that their child is good at school. Maths, reading, writing, foreign languages … well, yes, of course! But what other things are there that kids have learnt and are proud of? Read our interviews and find out.

Joanna, 12

Make a fire

Two years ago during a summer holiday my mum taught me how to make a fire without burning myself. I loved that. Now, we live in the city, so I can't often make fires. But sometimes we go to the countryside for short holidays, and that's my big chance. There is nothing better than cooking some sausages on a fire you have made yourself. And it's great to sit around a fire with friends in the evening and have a chat.

Jonathan, 13

Drive a tractor

Last summer, my family and I spent two weeks on a farm. First I was a bit bored – I missed my friends. One day, the farmer saw me hanging around, doing nothing. So he asked me if I wanted to help him. I wanted to say no, but said yes of course. We got on the tractor and drove out to the fields. There, he asked me if I could drive the tractor for him. Of course I couldn't. So he showed me and it wasn't that difficult. I so loved it. The coolest holiday ever!

Vicky, 12

Stay calm*

When things went wrong, I often panicked and started to shout or to cry. In my last holiday, my best friend Elisabeth invited me to go on a course with her, *What teens should learn for life*. The first thing I learnt was not to panic. I learnt that when we are in panic, we make big mistakes, we get confused, or get scared and then make bad decisions*. So you know what I learnt? When something goes wrong, breathe, and count to ten. Keep calm.

VOCABULARY: *stay/keep calm – ruhig bleiben; **decision** – Entscheidung

6 Read the article again. Then answer the questions.

1. What does Joanna like about making a fire? ....
2. What did Jonathan think of their farm holidays first? ....
3. Why do you think he said yes when the farmer asked him to help him?
   ....
4. Why does Vicky think it's important to keep cool? ....
5. How does Vicky keep calm? ....
6. What is the coolest thing you can do? ....

Vocabulary Activities

7 Listen and find out what things Natalie and Dylan like doing. Write N or D.

- ☐ making fires
- ☐ building things
- ☐ reading
- ☐ playing football
- ☐ using tools
- ☐ climbing trees
- ☐ going shopping
- ☐ dancing

Get talking Favourite activities

8 Work in pairs. Tell your partner what you like doing. Look at **5** and **7** for words.

9 Read the texts about the families.

What's in a family?

I'm **Lisa,** and I'm from Galway in Ireland. My mum, my mum's boyfriend Mike, my sister Hannah and I live in a large flat. Mike moved in with us three years ago. My real dad also lives in Galway, but he and Mum aren't married any more. He moved out five years ago, and now he lives in a little house with his new wife, Dorothy. Hannah and I go to see them every weekend. Mum says we are a single parent family, but I don't think so. We still see our father, and there are Mike and Dorothy. They're both very nice, and we have a lot of fun with them.

I'm **Les**. I'm from Sydney in Australia. My mum's a single parent and I live with her. My dad lives in Darwin and I don't see him very often. I haven't got any brothers or sisters. My mum works in a restaurant, and I often stay with my grandparents. They live down the road. Sometimes I go and see my mum at the restaurant.

I'm **Amar** and I'm from Birmingham in England. I live with my mum and dad and my brother Vikas and my sister Karisma in a nice house in Selly Oak. My grandmother Jaya also lives with us, and for two years my cousin Kunal also lived in our house. He was here from Allahabad in India. He studied at the university in Birmingham. I like him, and next summer I'm going to visit him in Allahabad.

I'm **Denise**, and I'm from Angola, but I live in the Dukwi refugee camp in Botswana. We had to leave Angola eight years ago because of the war. Now my mum, my dad, my three brothers and my uncle João live in Dukwi camp. I go to school here. My brothers have to help my dad with farming. It's very hard work and we don't have much food. My uncle João works for the Red Cross and translates from Portuguese into English. He likes his job.

10 How many of these tasks can you do?

1 Lisa lives with her *mum* / *dad* in Galway in Ireland.
2 Her dad *doesn't live* / *lives* with his new wife, Dorothy.
3 Lisa *likes* / *doesn't like* her mum's new partner, Mike.
4 Les sees his ...Mum... more often than his ...Dad....
5 When Les' ...Mother... is working, he ...stays... with his grandparents.
6 Amar lives in ...~~England~~ Birmingham..., but his cousin is from ...Allahabad....
7 Who lives with both of their parents? ...Amar and Denise...
8 Who of the four children do you think has the most difficult life? Why?
...Denise, because he is a refugee....
9 Compare Lisa and Les. What is the same about them?
...There parent's are divorsed....

11 Check your answers with a partner.

12 Put the dialogue into the correct order. Then check with a partner. Act it out.

- ☐ Dad — Yes, but you must be home by eight. You mustn't be late, Rory!
- ☐ Dad — No, you mustn't stay out so late. Let's say you must be home by 9.30.
- ☐ Dad — I don't care about the others.
- ☐ Rory — Dad, please. I just want to stay till ten.
- [3] Rory — But Dad. That's not fair. All the others stay till ten.
- ☐ Rory — Great. Thanks, Dad.
- [1] Rory — Dad, can I go?

CD3 19

13 Listen to the dialogue between Fred and his mum. Tick the things he mustn't do.

☐ go into private files ☐ delete a file ☐ print out everything ☐ chat ☐ surf around

Get talking Rules at home

14 Work in pairs. Tell your partner three things you must (mustn't) do at home.

15 Read the anecdote.

> Today's anecdote is about Norbert Wiener (1894–1964). He was a famous mathematician who lived in America. Professor Wiener was a real genius, but he was also a bit absent-minded*. This is why there are a few funny anecdotes about him. Here is our favourite: One day the Wieners moved to another house. His wife gave him a little piece of paper and said: "Norbert, we're moving today. I wrote the new address on this piece of paper." "Thank you," said Wiener and put the piece of paper into his jacket. At the university, he needed a piece of paper to make some notes. He took the paper out of his jacket. He wrote something on it. Later, he left it in his office. Then he walked home – but to the old address. Suddenly he remembered. "Ah yes, a new house, a new address. Damn, where's that piece of paper?" But of course he couldn't find it. Then he looked around and saw a little girl. "Little girl," he said, "do you know where the Wieners live?" "Yes, Dad. Mum sent me to find you. I'll take you home now," the girl answered.
>
> **VOCABULARY:** *absent-minded – zerstreut

16 How many of these tasks can you do?

1. Norbert Wiener was good at maths. — (T)/ F
2. He often forgot things. — (T)/ F
3. Mrs Wiener wrote the new address on some paper. — (T)/ F
4. Mr Wiener worked at _the university_.
5. Mr Wiener wrote _notes_ on the piece of paper.
6. Mr Wiener left his address _in his office_.
7. Where did Mr Wiener go after work? _To his old address._
8. Who was the little girl? _His daughter._
9. Why was she at the house? _Because she knew her father wouldn't remember the new address._

17 Check your answers with a partner.

Writing for your Portfolio

18 The owner of the Horrible Hotel doesn't want young people in his hotel. Think of more rules: *Young people must / mustn't …* . Then write a leaflet "What people must know about our hotel" (70–90 words).

young people must	young people mustn't
• be in bed before 7 p.m.	• eat any sweets between 6 a.m. and 11 p.m.

GRAMMAR

like (doing)

So sagst du, dass jemand etwas gerne macht:
I **like** juggl**ing**. She **likes** roller-skat**ing**.
She **doesn't like** work**ing** out.

Complete. Write in the right order -ing / like / person.
Bildung: ¹……………………… + ²……………………… + ³………………………

must – mustn't

Du verwendest *must*, um zu sagen, dass jemand etwas tun muss.
I **must** get a birthday present for Joanne.
So sagst du, dass jemand etwas nicht tun darf oder etwas nicht geschehen darf:
Bildung: person + *mustn't (must not)* + *base form* of the verb
You mustn't be home later than 8 o'clock. **We mustn't forget** Mum's birthday.

The Twins 4
DEVELOPING SPEAKING COMPETENCIES

Language function
- ordering food (*Essen bestellen*)

Speaking strategy
- changing your mind (*seine Meinung ändern*)

The pizza

Vocabulary Pizza toppings

1 Match the food and the pictures. Listen and check.

pepperoni   mushroom
tomato   cheese
pineapple   ham

1 ....

2 ....   3 ....

4 ....   5 ....   6 ....

2 Watch or listen to the dialogue. Then read it. What toppings from ① do the family choose on their pizzas?

Assistant	Hello, can I take your order?
Dad	Pizzas for everyone?
Leo	Yes, I'd like the ham and pineapple pizza.
Lucy	Can I have a cheese and tomato one?
Mum	And I'll have a pepperoni one.
Dad	So that's one ham and pineapple, one cheese and tomato … two pepperoni. Hang on. Er … Make that one pepperoni and two cheese and tomato.
Assistant	What would you like to drink?
Dad	Four cokes, please. No, wait a second. Make that three cokes and a bottle of water.
Assistant	Eat in or take away?
Dad	Eat in.
Assistant	OK, that's £24, please. If you'd like to take a seat, your food will be ready in ten minutes. Your order is 21.
Dad	Thanks.

90 DEVELOPING SPEAKING COMPETENCIES   WB p. 90

3 Complete the waiter's order.

Order number ¹...........
Pizzas: 1 x ²........................... and ³..........................., 1 x ⁴...........................
            2 x ⁵........................... and ⁶...........................
Drinks: 3 x ⁷..........................., 1 x ⁸........................... Total £ ⁹...........................

Useful phrases Ordering food

4 Read the sentences. Write C (*Customer*) or A (*Assistant*).

1 Can I take your order? ☐
2 I'd like a ham and pineapple pizza. ☐
3 Can I have a cheese and tomato one? ☐
4 Eat in or take away? ☐

? What do you think? Answer the question.

- Does everyone get what they ordered?

Mobile homework

Watch part 2 of the video and circle T (*True*) or F (*False*).

1 Mum falls in the pond.   T / F
2 Dad misses the bus.   T / F
3 Leo is scared on the London Eye. T / F
4 Dad wants his pizza in six slices. T / F

Speaking strategy Changing your mind

5 Complete. Then check with the dialogue in **2**.

Dad   So that's one ham and pineapple, one cheese and tomato … two pepperoni. ¹H................ o................ . Erm … Make that one pepperoni and two cheese and tomato.
Assistant What would you like to drink?
Dad   Four cokes, please. No, ²w................ a s................ . Make that three cokes and a bottle of water.

6 CHOICES

A Work in pairs. Use the prompts.

A Order a pizza. → B Repeat the order. → A Change your mind.

A Can I have a pepperoni pizza, please?
B A pepperoni pizza.
A Hang on. I'd like a ham one.

B ROLE PLAY: Work in fours.

Student A, B and C
You are customers in a pizza restaurant. Order pizzas and drinks.

Student D
- Take the other students' order.
- Ask if it's eat in or take away.

UNIT 13 Magic

You learn
- how to use adverbs of manner

You can
- say how something is done
- write a picture story

A song 4 U

1 Listen and sing. Then put the pictures in the correct order.

Welcome

Welcome, welcome
to our school.
A place for ghosts
and that's so cool.

Here you learn to
pass through doors.
Here you learn to
float above floors.
Here you learn to
rattle chains.
Here you learn to
make big stains.

Welcome, welcome ...

Here you learn to
take off heads.
Here you learn to
float above beds.
Here you learn to
scream at night
and how you can
win a fight.

Welcome, welcome ...

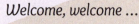
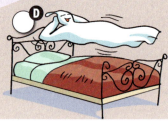

Time for a sketch

 2 Read the sketch.

The school for young ghosts

It's the first night at school for the young ghosts.

Teacher	Good evening.
Ghosts	Oooooooooooooooooooooh.
Teacher	Welcome to our school. On your first night I'm going to teach you ...
Ghost 1	About castles in Britain?
Teacher	No, that's next week. Tonight you're going to learn how to pass through walls.
Ghost 2	And doors?
Teacher	Yes, of course.

Ghost 3	But we can open doors easily.
Teacher	Be quiet, you silly ghost! Passing through locked doors, of course.
Ghost 3	Sorry, sir.
Ghost 4	Do we learn how to scream loudly too?
Teacher	Not this year. That's in year three.
Ghost 5	What about scaring people?
Teacher	That's next month.
Ghost 6	I want to learn how to take my head off.
Teacher	That's in year two. Tonight you're going to learn how to pass through walls. OK?
Ghost 6	Is it difficult to learn?
Teacher	Passing through a wall can be difficult. Sometimes ghosts get stuck.
Ghost 7	I know, sir. My aunt got stuck in a wall when I was a baby. She's still there.
Teacher	The poor woman!
Ghosts	Ooooooooooooooooh!
Teacher	Be quiet! Now, you have to walk quietly. You mustn't say a word.
Ghost 8	Can I rattle my chains?
Teacher	Aren't you listening? You have to walk quietly. No rattling.
Ghost 7	Fast or slowly?
Teacher	Don't walk too fast and don't walk too slowly. I'll show you.
Ghosts	Yes, please.
Teacher	OK, watch me …
Ghost 6	Where's the teacher now?
Ghost 5	In the wall. He got stuck.
Ghosts	Hurray! What a great first lesson!

3 How many of these tasks can you do?

1 It's the first *day / night* at the school for the young ghosts.
2 They are going to learn about castles in Britain *this / next* week.
3 The ghosts are going to learn how to pass through *locked doors / walls*.

4 When do they learn how to scream loudly? ....
5 What do the young ghosts want to know about passing through walls? ....
6 Where is the aunt of ghost 7? ....

7 The teacher says to the ghosts that they mustn't walk too fast or ....
8 The teacher gets .... at the end of the lesson.
9 The ghosts think that the first lesson ....

4 Check your answers with a partner. Then listen to the sketch.

5 Listen to the sketch again and act it out.

WB p. 92, 93, 94

Vocabulary

6 Listen and look at the pictures. Then number the words.

- 10 car boot
- 5 nail
- 9 put a spell on someone
- 8 feather
- 6 roast potatoes
- 1 fence
- 4 cooker
- 2 deckchair
- 3 sprinkle
- 7 prison

Story time

7 Read the story.

Abracadabra, one, two, three

Debbie and her brother Robert were playing ball behind the house. Suddenly the ball landed in their neighbour's garden. "I'll get it," said Robert.

"Be careful," Debbie said, "Mr Blogg loves to eat children for lunch." Robert didn't laugh. Mr Blogg was very unfriendly and Robert was scared of him.

Slowly and quietly, Robert climbed over the fence. He looked through the bushes. The ball was right behind Mr Blogg's deckchair. Then everything happened very fast. Mr Blogg got up and shouted: "This time I'll get you!" Robert quickly climbed back over the fence. After a minute, something came flying through the air. Robert and Debbie looked at it. "That was our ball," Robert said quietly. There was a big nail in the ball.

The following Saturday was Debbie's thirteenth birthday. They had a party in the garden with lots of friends. The young people were having a lot of fun. Suddenly Robert and Debbie's dad came into the garden. "Mr Blogg was here," he said. "You're making too much noise. Come into the house." The young people walked angrily into the house.

"Can we go out later and roast some potatoes over a fire?" Debbie asked.

"Of course," said her dad, "but don't make any noise."

An hour later they went out to roast the potatoes. They were very quiet, but after ten minutes they heard the doorbell. It was Mr Blogg. Then Dad came into the garden and told them to put out the fire. "Mr Blogg says there is too much smoke," he said. "I really don't like Mr Blogg," said Debbie.

Three days later Debbie and Robert were looking for Snowy, their cat. They found her under the bushes near the fence.

Snowy was very ill. Robert also found a rotten fish. "We didn't have fish this week," said Debbie. "I'm sure Mr Blogg threw the fish over the fence." They carried the cat into the house. "Poor Snowy," said Debbie, "I really don't like Mr Blogg."

The next day Debbie was in the garden with a book. "What are you reading?" Robert asked. "It's a book on magic," said Debbie. "Sally gave it to me."

"Why are you reading that?" asked Robert.

"I want to put a spell on Mr Blogg."

"Spells don't work," said Robert.

"Do you want to help me or not?" asked Debbie.

"OK," said Robert. "What do I have to do?"

"The book says that we have to get five things from Mr Blogg," answered Debbie.

"We can do that easily," said Robert.

At ten o'clock that night, Debbie and Robert climbed the fence into Mr Blogg's garden. They found a feather, the rest of a cigar, a piece of bread, half a hot dog and a bottle of beer that was half full. They climbed back into their garden, put all the things in a pot and hid it in the garden shed. The next day they put the pot on the cooker and filled it with water. They cut up the feather, the rest of the cigar, the piece of bread, the rest of the hot dog and threw it in the water together with the beer. Then they filled an empty bottle of orange juice with the brown stuff.

"What do you want to do now?" Robert asked. "We have to go into Mr Blogg's garden and sprinkle this stuff round his house."

They went over to the fence and listened carefully. Nothing. They climbed over and started to sprinkle the brown stuff. When Robert and Debbie got to the garage they stopped. The door of the garage was open and they could see Mr Blogg by his car. He was putting boxes into the boot. When he saw Debbie and Robert, he shouted: "Now I've got you." Debbie and Robert ran as fast as they could.

When they climbed the fence Robert lost one of his trainers. Mr Blogg picked it up.

"I'll show it to your dad when he comes home," he shouted. Then he got into his car and went away. "What can we do now?" asked Robert. "Dad's going to be very angry." "Let's go into town and see Grandma," said Debbie. "We can have dinner with her. And when we get back, everything will be over." When they arrived at Grandma's place they phoned their mum. "We'll be back after dinner," Debbie said. After dinner Grandma brought them back in her car. There was a police car in front of Mr Blogg's house. Debbie and Robert went over and talked to a policeman. "Mr Blogg had an accident in town," the police officer said. "Is he in hospital?" asked Debbie. "No, he's in prison because we found lots of stolen computers in the boot of his car. And the house is also full of stolen things." "So your spell worked," said Robert. "Yes, it did," said Debbie. "But I'm glad he isn't in hospital."

8 How many of these tasks can you do?

1 The children live next door to Mr Blogg. (T) F
2 Robert is afraid of Mr Blogg. (T) F
3 Mr Blogg complains about Robert's party. (T) F
4 What did Mr Blogg give to Snowy? A rotten fish
5 What do the children decide to do? cast a spell on Mr Blogg
6 What do they need for the spell? They need five mr Blogg's things
7 One of ~~children~~ his trainers falls off when he climbs over the fence.
8 The children go their Grandma's haus to help them stop worrying.
9 The police find lots of stolen things in Mr Blogg's house.

9 Check your answers with a partner. Then listen to the story.

10 Listen to the interview with Julia and write the information in your exercise book.

1 two reasons why Julia likes *Wizards of Waverly Place*
2 who is her favourite character, and why
3 how she watches the show

11 Read the text and finish the sentences.

"What can we do?" said a ghost. "We must help our teacher," said the smallest ghost. He gave his chains to another ghost. He walked to the wall. "Don't walk too slowly and don't walk too fast," the others shouted. So the smallest ghost began to walk slowly and quietly through the wall. In the wall, he took the teacher's hand and they both went through the wall. "Hurray!" all the young ghosts shouted and they rattled their chains loudly. "Thank you very much," the teacher said to the smallest ghost. "That's alright," said the smallest ghost.

1 The smallest ghost wanted …
2 He gave his chains …
3 Then he started to …
4 In the wall, he took …
5 They both went …
6 The teacher thanked …

12 CHOICES

Writing for your Portfolio

A Look at the pictures. Use the phrases from the box to help you write a story of about 60 words.

Archibald was a young …
One night he wanted to …
He was very …
Suddenly he heard …
He got scared and …
The dog …
Then Archibald …
In the end, the dog …

B Look at the pictures and write a story of about 120 words. Find a title for your story. Before you write anything, look at each picture carefully. For each picture write down five words you could use. Use at least three adverbs from the box.

quickly
slowly
carefully
angrily
loudly
easily

Start like this: It was the last lesson of the night …

GRAMMAR Adverbs of manner

Mit dem Adverb der Art und Weise drückst du aus, *wie* jemand etwas macht oder *wie* etwas geschieht.

*Young ghosts learn how to scream **loudly**.*
*You have to walk **quietly**.*
*You mustn't walk too **slowly**.*
*Robert climbed back **quickly** over the fence.*
*The young people walked **angrily** into the house.*
*They climbed over the fence and listened **carefully**.*
*We can do that **easily**.*

Bildung: Adjektiv + *ly*

quiet – quiet**ly**
quick – quick**ly**
slow – slow**ly**
careful – careful**ly**

Bei den Adjektiven, die auf *y* enden, wird das *y* zu einem *i*:

easy – eas**ily**
happy – happ**ily**
angry – angr**ily**

Ausnahmen:

fast – **fast**   *Don't walk too **fast**.*
good – **well**   *I'm glad that it worked so **well**.*

Annabel jumped quickly over the fence.

Complete with *adverb* or *adjective*.

Mit einem ¹………………………………… kannst du ein Nomen beschreiben.
Mit einem ²………………………………… kannst du ein Verb beschreiben.

The Story of the Stones 6

Farewell!

1 Use the pictures to tell the story of Episode 5.

2 What do you think happens to these in the final episode?

3 Watch Episode 6 and answer the questions.

1 Why does Sunborn destroy the belt and stones?
2 What happens when she destroys the belt and stones?
3 What can the children no longer do?

4 Complete the sentences about you.

1 My favourite character in *The Story of the Stones* is ....
   because ....
2 My least favourite character in *The Story of the Stones* is ....
   because ....
3 My favourite scene was ....

Everyday English

5 Watch Episode 6 again. Complete the sentences (1–4) with the words in the box. Then match them to the questions (a–d).

| I'm afraid so | believe me | it doesn't matter | I'm afraid not |

☐ 1 That's right, Daniel. But ....
☐ 2 .... There's no place for me here on Earth.
☐ 3 The Lord of the Fire still lives. He won't give up, ...
☐ 4 .... , Sarah. But I'll never forget you.

a Will it all start again?
b So we can't morph any longer?
c Does this mean we won't see you again?
d Can't you stay here?

UNIT 14 Where we live

You learn
- about possessive pronouns
- how to use the possessive 's
- about houses and words for furniture
- how to form questions with *whose*

You can
- talk about your flat or house
- ask to whom things/animals belong

1 Read the text.

Houses and Homes

We all know what a house is. It has a roof, walls, rooms, windows and doors. There might be a staircase. There might be a cellar underneath it or a garden around it. But not all houses are like this. Take a look around the world and see how different houses can be.

Around twenty million Americans live in trailer homes. They usually keep them in special parks. They are like little villages. In the park the owners connect their trailers to electricity and water. Trailers are a cheap way of living in your own home and, if you get tired of one place, you can always move your home to another park.

The Americans aren't the only people who have moveable houses. The Mongolian people in Central Asia move their houses a lot. Their houses are "yurts". When there isn't enough grass for their sheep any more, they take down their houses. They put the parts on the backs of their camels and horses. They then carry the parts to other places where there is enough food for the animals.

In some parts of the world people live in houses that are not on the ground. For example, some people in South East Asia build their houses on stilts*. They do this because their houses are near water. The stilts keep their homes high above the water and out of danger.

Other people actually live on the water. The Uros people live on Lake Titicaca in Peru. There are about two thousand of them on fifty floating islands of reeds. Reeds are long, strong grasses. They use the reeds to build their houses. When the Uros want to visit a neighbour they move from island to island by boat.

Finally, in the jungle of Costa Rica some people live in tree houses. There is even a tree house hotel. There are wooden bridges between the houses so that people can visit their neighbours easily.

VOCABULARY: *stilt – Pfahl

2 Read the text again and answer the questions.

1. How many Americans live in trailer homes?
2. When do the Mongolian people move their homes?
3. Why do people build their houses on stilts?
4. What do the Uros use to build their houses?
5. How do the people in Costa Rican tree houses visit their neighbours?

Vocabulary Inside a room

3 Listen and look at the picture. Then number the words.

7 wardrobe	4 fridge	2 sink	6 radiator
10 bed	1 cooker	5 cupboard	16 sofa
15 table	9 bedside table	13 carpet	3 curtains
12 chair	14 armchair	11 rug	8 lamp

Get talking Memory game

4 Work in pairs. One of you closes your book. Test each other.

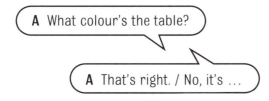

A What colour's the table?

A That's right. / No, it's …

B It's …

Sounds right /juː/ /ʊ/

5 Listen and say the poem.

New curtains for the window,
new cupboards for my books.
A wardrobe for my clothes,
and how nice my bedroom looks!

Get talking Remembering

 Work in pairs. Look at the plan of the house. Close your book. Say what's in each room.

In the living room, there's a television, and …
In the kitchen, there are …

living room
kitchen
bathroom
Mike and Nick's room
Joanna's room

  Listen. Which room are the people in?

Conversation 1: Joanna's room
Conversation 2: Mike and Nicks room
Conversation 3: bathroom/~~kitchen~~
Conversation 4: living rooms

  Listen again and complete. Use the words in the box.

mine
yours
hers
his
whose
ours
theirs
whose

Mum ¹ whose school bag is this?
Mike It's Joanna's.
Mum Well, it shouldn't be on the sofa. Take it to her room, please.
Mike Why me? It's ² hers , not ³ mine !

Simon I like your room.
Nick Thanks. I share it with my brother. This is my bed, and that's ⁴ his .
Simon Right. Is this your computer?
Nick Yes and no – I mean, it's ⁵ ours !

Mum ⁶ whose trainers are those? Are they ⁷ yours ?
Joanna No – they're Mike's! I borrowed them, and they got dirty – so now I'm cleaning them.
Mum OK – but don't clean them here, in the bathroom! Wash them in the kitchen!

Mike Mum – why is there a dictionary here on the fridge?
Mum Oh, that – yes, can you take it to Mr and Mrs Smith next door, please?
Mike OK. Is it ⁸ theirs ?
Mum No, it's ours, but they want to borrow it.

WB p. 101, 102, 103

UNIT 14   101

Listen to the dialogue. Then act out similar dialogues using the things in the pictures.

Susan Whose pen is this? Is it yours?
Mark No. It's hers.

  Listen and complete. Then repeat.

Whose is it? Is it yours?
No, it isn't [1].......................... .
Whose is it? Is it Mike's?
No, it isn't [2].......................... .
Whose is it? Is it Sue's?
No, it isn't [3].......................... .
Whose is it? Jane and Paul's?
No, it isn't [4].......................... .

Whose is it? Whose is it?
Give it to us.
It's ours!
And it's so good!
Mmm!

Writing for your Portfolio

 Read Emily's text and answer the questions.

- Which is her favourite room?
- Why does Emily like this room best?

The best place in my house

The best place in my house is the kitchen. There's a big table and four chairs where we have breakfast and dinner. There's a big window and we can look into the garden. There's a sink and a fridge, but no washing machine (that's in the garage). Our cat's basket is in the kitchen, too, and she sleeps there at night.
I like the kitchen because it's a place for all the family. It's always warm in there, too!

 Write a text about the best place in your house or flat. Write 60–80 words.
Think about:

- where the place is
- what it looks like
- what you do there
- why it is your special place

GRAMMAR

Whose ... ?

Wenn du fragen willst, wem etwas gehört, fragst du mit *Whose ... ?*

Whose school bag is this?   **Whose** trainers are those?

Possessive *'s*

Wenn du sagen willst, wem etwas gehört, hängst du an den Namen der Person oder das Nomen *'s* an:

Whose bag is this? – It's **Joanna's**.   They're **Mike's** trainers.
This is **my brother's** bed.

Wenn der Name oder das Nomen im Plural steht oder auf *-s* endet, setzt du ans Ende des Wortes ein ' (Apostroph):

This is my **parents'** room.   It's our **neighbours'** dog.   That's **Les'** mum.

Bei Wörtern mit unregelmäßiger Pluralform setzt du *'s* ans Ende des Wortes:

That's the **children's** school.   Don't take other **people's** things!

Possessive pronouns

Du verwendest ein *possessive pronoun*, wenn du sagen willst, wem etwas gehört – ohne dass du den Namen der Person verwendest.

Complete with he / I / they / she.

(¹.............) It's **mine**.
(² ..you..) Are they **yours**?
(³.............) This is my bed, and that's **his**.
(⁴.............) The bag is **hers**.
(⁵ ..we..) The computer is **ours**.
(⁶.............) The dictionary isn't **theirs**.

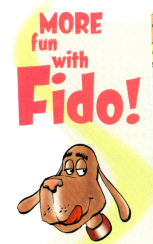

The Twins 5
DEVELOPING SPEAKING COMPETENCIES

Language function
- describing an object (*einen Gegenstand beschreiben*)

Speaking strategy
- checking what someone says (*bei jemandem nochmal nachhaken*)

Leo's watch

Vocabulary   Materials and patterns

1 Match the materials **and** the patterns with the pictures.

Materials:
1 made of leather
2 made of plastic
3 made of cotton

Patterns:
A spotted
B plain
C striped

sunglasses

jacket

watch strap

2 Watch or listen to the dialogue. Then read it. What's Leo's problem?

Leo	Hello. I'm looking for my watch. I think I lost it at school this morning.
Secretary	OK, let's see what we can do. What's it like?
Leo	Well, it's white. It's made of plastic.
Secretary	OK, so it's plain white, is it?
Leo	No, sorry. The watch face is white with some orange on it, but the strap is different.
Secretary	OK. So what's the strap like?
Leo	It's striped. Orange, green, purple and … erm … red.
Secretary	Are you certain?
Leo	Yes, it's orange, green, purple and red.

Secretary	And what's the strap made of?
Leo	It's made of metal. No, sorry. It's made of plastic.
Secretary	Are you sure?
Leo	Yes, yes. It's made of plastic, and it's striped orange, green, purple and red.
Secretary	OK, so let's see what we've got.

3 Cover up the dialogue in **2**. Try to answer the questions. Then check.

1 Where does Leo think he lost his watch?
2 What's the watch strap like?
3 What's the watch face like?

Useful phrases Describing an object

 Write two sentences to describe each object.

1

2

3

It's made of plastic.
It's ……………………

? What do you think? Answer the questions.

- Where did Leo lose his watch?
- How does he find it?

Mobile homework

Watch part 2 of the video. Read the sentences and correct them.

1 The secretary hasn't got any lost and found watches. ………………
2 The librarian shows Leo a watch, but it's not his. ………………
3 Leo goes to the gym to do some exercise there. ………………
4 Leo talks to his friends. They don't want to help him. ………………
5 In the end Leo finds the watch. He is wearing it. ………………

Speaking strategy Checking what someone says

 Fill in the correct words. Then check with the dialogue in .

1 **Leo** It's striped. Orange, green, purple and … erm … red.
  Secretary A……………… you c……………… ?

2 **Leo** It's made of metal. No, sorry. It's made of plastic.
  Secretary A……………… you s……………… ?

6 CHOICES

A Work in pairs. A says what he/she can't find and describes it. B checks what A says.

> A I can't find my T-shirt. It's … erm … blue.
> B Are you sure?
> A Yes, I am. It's blue.

B ROLE PLAY: You are in a lost and found office. One of you is the assistant in the office. The other one lost something a few days ago (a watch, a camera, a pen, etc.). Work in pairs and extend it into a longer dialogue. Take 2 or 3 minutes to practise it. Don't write it down. Act it out in class.

UNIT 15 Feeling better

You learn
- about the present perfect and past participles
- words for aches and pains

You can
- ask what has happened to someone
- write a message to someone who has had an accident

   1 Listen to the jokes. Then read them and colour 1–5 stars to give a score for each joke.

Jenny's Jokes!

Hi! My name's Jenny and welcome to my joke pages. Every week I choose a topic and ask you to send me your favourite jokes. Last week I chose "doctor, doctor" jokes. You sent me hundreds. Here are my favourite six. What do you think? Vote for each joke on the star chart and let's find out which is the greatest "doctor, doctor" joke in the world.

Patient Doctor, doctor, every time I drink a cup of hot chocolate I get a pain in the eye.
Doctor Try taking the spoon out first.
Vote now:

Patient Doctor, doctor, I've only got 59 seconds to live.
Doctor OK. Give me a minute and I'll call you back.
Vote now:

Patient Doctor, doctor, I've lost my memory.
Doctor When did this happen?
Patient When did what happen?
Vote now:

Patient Doctor, doctor, I've broken my arm in two places.
Doctor Don't go back to either of them.
Vote now:

Patient Doctor, doctor, I couldn't drink my medicine after my bath like you told me.
Doctor Why not?
Patient Well, after I drank my bath, I didn't have room for the medicine.
Vote now:

Patient Doctor, doctor, please come to my house quickly. My son has swallowed* my pen. What should I do?
Doctor Use a pencil until I arrive.
Vote now:

VOCABULARY: *swallow – hinunterschlucken

2 Here are three more "doctor, doctor" jokes. In pairs, think of an ending for each one. Then listen and check.

1 **Patient** Doctor, doctor, I think I need glasses.
  Doctor You certainly do. I'm not doctor

2 **Patient** Doctor, doctor, I think I'm a sheep.
  Doctor How do you feel?
  Patient I feel baaad

3 **Patient** Doctor, doctor, what's the quickest way to get to hospital?
  Doctor Hit an ambulance on the way here

3 Write the names of the people under the pictures.

Emily — William — Jacob — Sue — Jessica — Tim

Sue has got a pain in her ankle.
Tim's head hurts.
Jacob's knee hurts.

Emily has got a pain in her back.
William's throat hurts.
Jessica has got stomach ache.

> **Note:**
> I've got stomach ache.
> (or stomachache).
> I've got earache.
> I've got toothache.
> I've got backache.
> But we usually say
> "I've got **a** headache."

Sounds right /p/ /b/ /æ/ /e/

  4 Listen and repeat.

A **pa**in in your **ha**nd?   A **pa**in in your **le**g?
A **pa**in in your **ba**ck?   A **pa**in in your **he**ad?
That's too **ba**d!   Then st**a**y in **be**d!

Get talking Aches and pains

 5 Work in groups of three. Act out a problem and talk about it.

6 Listen and number the pictures in the order you hear them.

7 Complete the dialogues with the words in the box. Practise the dialogues in pairs.

dropped
cut
broken
walked
fallen
hurt

1 Does your head hurt?
   Yes, I've just ...walked... into a lamp post.

2 What's the matter?
   I think I've ...broken... my toe.

3 Come quickly!
   Why? What's the matter?
   Kevin has ...fallen... out of the tree!

4 Why is he walking like that?
   He has ...hurt... his ankle.

5 Why is she crying?
   She has just ...dropped... a heavy box on her foot.

6 There's blood on your shirt.
   Yes, I've just ...cut... my hand.

8 Look at the conversations again and find the past participles of these verbs. Write them.

walk	break	cut	hurt	fall	drop
walked	broken	cut	hurt	fallen	dropped

9 Here are some more past participles. What do you think the base forms of the verbs are? Write them.

eaten	loved	thought (think)	hit	told	played
eat	loved	thought	hit	tell	played

put	met	known	wanted	rung	read
put	met	known	want	ring	read

10 Read the text about the Amazon Rainforest.

The world's new gold

The Amazon Rainforest is very important for our planet. It's the largest rainforest in the world and it produces more than 20% of our oxygen*. But the Amazon is in danger. People are cutting down the trees to sell the wood and make money quickly. Big companies are clearing away the trees so they can have more land for their huge farms.

The Amazon is also home to a lot of wildlife and many of the world's animals, birds, insects and fish live there. There are also more than 430,000 different types of plants in the forest and some of them are very special. These plants can help sick people. Scientists have found more than 2,000 plants in the Amazon Rainforest that can help the fight against cancer. There are also many other plants there that can help the fight against different illnesses. These plants are really valuable* for medical science. They are the world's new gold.

Five hundred years ago, more than 10,000,000 Indians* lived in the Amazon Rainforest. Now there are less than 200,000. The Indian medicine men know a lot about these special plants. They know what illnesses the plants can fight against and they know how to use them. But many of the medicine men are now very old. We must listen to what they can tell us. It is important for the world that we learn what they know!

VOCABULARY: *oxygen – Sauerstoff; valuable – wertvoll; Indians – Indios (Ureinwohner Südamerikas)

11 How many of these tasks can you do?

1. The Amazon Rainforest produces *20%* / *100%* of our oxygen.
2. People cut down lots of trees to make *big fires* / *big money*.
3. You can find lots of animals, birds, fish and plants in the Amazon *River* / *Rainforest*.
4. There are more than 430,000 types of plants – they can all help sick people.   T / F
5. Scientists are interested in plants that can help people with cancer.   T / F
6. The Indians don't know much about the special plants in the rainforest.   T / F
7. There are fewer Indians living in the rainforest than in the past. Why is this, do you think?

8. If more and more of the rainforests are cut down, what will the consequences be?
   The population of animals living there will digrepte decrease

9. Why is it important to listen to the medicine men?
   They know how to use plants as medicine

12 Check your answers with a partner.

Grammar chant Present perfect

13 A chant. Listen and repeat.

I've hurt my head.
I've hurt my back.
I've hurt both of my knees.
I've hurt my arm.
I've hurt my leg.
Please, call a doctor, please.

She's hurt her head.
She's hurt her back.
She's hurt both of her knees.
She's hurt her arm.
She's hurt her leg.
Please, call a doctor, please.

14 CHOICES

Writing for your Portfolio

Read this text message and answer the questions.

- Where is the writer?
- What's the problem?
- Who gets the message?

> Hi guys, I'm in hospital. No school for ten days :'-((Want to know why? I had a bike accident!!! Both knees badly injured. I've broken my ankle. Terrible headache. I've got to stay in bed for a week. Boooooooring! C u soon!

A Imagine the writer of the text message is your friend. Write a text message (30–40 words) to make him/her feel better. Think of the following points:

- say how you feel about the fact that he/she can't come to school
- make suggestions what he/she could do to make the time in hospital less boring
- say you are going to phone him/her soon

B Imagine the writer of the text message above is your friend. Write an email (about 150 words).

- try to make him/her feel better
- tell him/her about something funny/interesting that happened in school since he/she has been in hospital
- make suggestions what he/she could do while in hospital so it's less boring

GRAMMAR

Present perfect

Du verwendest das Present perfect, um jemandem eine Neuigkeit zu erzählen. Dabei wird nicht erwähnt, wann dies geschehen ist.

I**'ve lost** my cat. We**'ve bought** a new car. She **has cut** her finger.
David **has broken** his leg. They**'ve gone** on holiday.

Wenn du betonen willst, dass etwas gerade geschehen ist, verwendest du *just*.

I**'ve just passed** my English test.
He **has just walked** into a lamp post.

Bildung: have/has + *past participle* (3. Form) of the verb

He **has fallen** off his bike.
We**'ve** just **moved** house.

They've just scored a goal.

Past participles

Das *past participle* findest du in der dritten Spalte der Verblisten. Bei regelmäßigen Verben hat das *past participle* die gleiche Form wie das Past simple. Hänge einfach **-ed** (oder **-d**) an die Nennform an.

pass	pass**ed**	pass**ed**
walk	walk**ed**	walk**ed**
move	move**d**	move**d**

Die Formen der unregelmäßigen Verben solltest du am besten auswendig lernen (siehe auch S. 144):

go	went	**gone**	lose	lost	**lost**
buy	bought	**bought**	cut	cut	**cut**
fall	fell	**fallen**	hurt	hurt	**hurt**
break	broke	**broken**	win	won	**won**
find	found	**found**	see	saw	**seen**

Kids in NYC 3

The city quiz

Before you watch

1 Write the words under the pictures.

an internet café
a library
a prize
a quiz

1 .... 2 .... 3 .... 4 ....

2 In what order do you think these pictures come in the DVD? Write 1–4 in the boxes.

Watch the story

  Check your answers to .

 Circle T (*True*) or F (*False*).

1 The children have written a quiz.   T / F
2 There are 20 questions in the quiz.   T / F
3 The children can win a prize in the quiz.   T / F
4 The children have three hours to do the quiz. T / F

5 Complete the dialogue.

with
idea
way
off
crazy
together

Jenny Come on – let's all do the quiz ¹........................ .
Gerry No ².......................... ! I'm going to the internet café over here. I'm going to get all my answers ³.......................... the internet.
Emma Great ⁴.......................... , Gerry. Can I come ⁵.......................... you?
Gerry Sure. We can get a coffee too.
Steve You're ⁶.......................... . What if the teacher sees you?
Gerry Ah! Who cares?
Jenny Come on, Steve. Let's start. Bye, you guys. See you at two!

6 Answer the questions.

1 What time do the children have to be back at the park?
....

2 What does Gerry order at the internet café?
....

3 Which street is the New York Public Library on?
....

7 Complete the list of places that Steve and Jenny see.

St Patrick's Cathedral, ...
....

Everyday English

8 Complete the dialogues.

Let's see
have fun
Who cares?
I have no clue.

OK? I want you back here at two o'clock and .... , everybody!

You're crazy! What if the teacher sees you?

Ah! ....

What did she mean?

....

What's the lunch special number four on the menu at Flor's Kitchen?

.... – grilled chicken over salad.

UNIT 16 Light rain in the north

You learn
- about the future with *will*
- weather words

You can
- talk about the weather
- talk about your hopes and expectations
- express a spontaneous decision
- write an email about the weather

1 Look at the map and read the text. Change the Fahrenheit temperatures into Celsius. Use this scale to help you.

F	0	10	20	30	40	50	60	70	80	90	100
C	-18	-12	-7	-1	4	10	16	21	27	32	38

Note:
To change Fahrenheit to Celsius, use this formula:
(°F - 32) × $\frac{5}{9}$ = °C
0°F = -18°C

The weather today

The good weather continues. Early morning clouds give way to lots of sunshine. Nicely cool and dry at the coast with lower temperatures in the North. Very hot in the South with temperatures in the 100s Fahrenheit.

Vocabulary Weather

2 Listen and look. Then fill in the numbers. Test your partner.

☐ hot ☐ cold ☐ cloudy ☐ thunderstorm ☐ snowy ☐ foggy ☐ rainy ☐ sunny ☐ windy

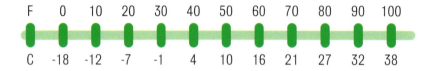

What's "neblig" in English?

Listen to the weather forecast. Then read it and draw the missing symbols on the maps.

Note: ° = degrees

Today:
Sunny, some clouds north of Leicester. Thick fog in the Stoke area will clear up later. Temperatures between 3°C and 12°C. Winds 10–20 mph.

Outlook for tomorrow:
Light rain in the Stoke area. Sunny in the Leicester area. More rain in the Malverns and thunderstorms coming from the north in the evening. Strong winds. Temperatures between 8°C and 15°C.

  Look at the maps of the UK. Listen to the weather forecasts and draw the symbols.

UNIT 16   115

5 CHOICES

Listen to the dialogues. Then read them. Make some changes and act them out.

A DIALOGUE 1: Weather small talk

Monica	Nice day today.
Robert	That's right. It's really nice. But …
Monica	But what?
Robert	They say it'll rain later.
Monica	Oh, really. That's bad.
Robert	Why's that?
Monica	I wanted to go for a walk with you.
Robert	Really? Let's go. But …
Monica	But what?
Robert	I'll get an umbrella.

B DIALOGUE 2: Planning a trip

Receptionist	Highland Hotel Aviemore. Can I help you?
Tourist	Yes, I'd like to ask you about a hiking holiday*.
Receptionist	Yes.
Tourist	What's the weather like at your place right now?
Receptionist	Well, it's raining, and it's pretty cold.
Tourist	What about next week?
Receptionist	They say it'll be a bit warmer.
Tourist	But are you sure?
Receptionist	Well, I can't promise, of course. They say it'll be warmer and less windy. And towards the end of the week it'll be very sunny.
Tourist	Lovely. Thank you.

VOCABULARY: *hiking holiday – Wanderurlaub

Get talking Asking about the weather

6 Work in pairs. Look at the map and say what the weather is like in an area. Your partner tries to guess the place.

A There is thick fog and the temperature is 10°C.

B You're in London.

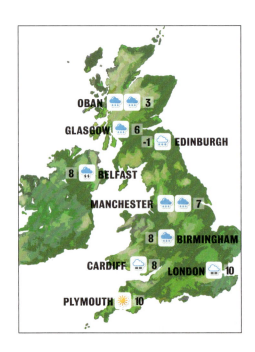

Time for a sketch

  7 Read the sketch.

"And the weather for tomorrow ..."

Dad OK, have we finished packing? Has everybody got their swimming trunks and bathing suits?
Jane Yes, Dad. Do I need a sweater?
Dad I don't think so. It won't be very cold in the evenings. *(Turns to Jamie.)* Jamie, turn off the TV. We're leaving in a few minutes.
Jamie Just a second, Dad. The weather report is coming on. Hey, Dad, listen to this.
(He turns up the volume.)
Weatherman ... In the south of England showers will be quite heavy and the sun won't come out for another few days. Temperatures will drop to 10° Celsius during the night and only go up to 17° Celsius during the day. There might also be a few thunderstorms. The weather situation will only get better after the weekend – and that's all from us for today.
Mum Turn it down, Jamie. Come here, and help with the unpacking.
Jane Oh, Mum. Why do we have to unpack?
Dad Your mum's right. We have to take out all the swimming things and put in a few sweaters. Come on, kids, it's a long way to the coast.
(They start unpacking.)
Jane What about my sweater? Will I need it?

Mum Yes, of course. And the raincoat too.
(15 minutes later.)
Dad Right. Have we got everything? And Jamie!!! Turn off the TV!
Jamie But Dad ...
Dad Turn it off!
Jamie Look, the weatherman is on again.
Mum Let's hear what he's got to say.
(Jamie turns up the volume.)
Weatherman ... have to apologise. I'm very sorry, but I gave you last week's weather report. I'm very sorry. Now here's the correct weather report for the next few days. Sunshine wherever we look, with temperatures going up to 25 to 30° Celsius. Some light cloud in the evenings, but there's nothing to worry about.
Dad OK! Let's start again!

8 How many of these tasks can you do?

1 The family are packing for a holiday. (T)/ F
2 Dad thinks Jane doesn't need a sweater. (T)/ F
3 The family are leaving tomorrow. T /(F)
4 Mum asks Jamie to ☑ help pack. ☑ turn down the TV. ☐ watch the weather forecast.
5 The family are going to the ☐ mountains. ☑ seaside. ☐ countryside.
6 After the first weather report, Jane asks if she needs to take
☐ a bathing suit. ☐ an umbrella. ☑ a sweater.
7 Why doesn't Jamie want to turn off the TV? Because the weather report was on.
8 Why does Jamie turn up the volume? Because his mom asked him to.
9 What mistake did the weatherman make? He told that weather report for the last week.

 9 Check your answers with a partner. Then listen to the sketch and act it out.

10 Read the two texts and convert the numbers from Fahrenheit to Celsius, feet to metres and inches to centimetres.

Note:
1 ft (foot) = 30.48 centimetres
1 inch = 2.54 centimetres

The hottest place in the USA

Death Valley is generally sunny, dry and clear throughout the year. The winters are mild, but summers are very hot and dry. In fact, Death Valley is one of the hottest places on earth. The highest temperature ever recorded in the USA was 134°F on July 10th, 1913. Summer high temperatures are usually around 120°F. The average rainfall each year is two inches.
Death Valley has the lowest point in the western world – 282 feet below sea level near Badwater – as well as many high mountains such as Telescope Peak at over 11,000 feet.

The wettest place in England

The wettest place in England is in the Lake District. It is a small village called Seatoller. Seatoller is the starting point for some great walks. But bring good clothes against the rain. The average rainfall each year is 120 inches. Some people say there is even more rainfall in Seathwaite (one mile away): 130 inches.
Seatoller doesn't have more rainy days than other places – but when it rains, it rains more.

Writing for your Portfolio

11 Read Carina's email to Tony. Draw a line where she should start a new paragraph.

To: tony@home.uk
Subject: bad weather :(

Hi Tony,
I'm sitting at the computer in the hotel lobby – guess why? No swimming, no lying in the sun. Outside it's raining, raining, raining. It all started with a thunderstorm yesterday. Then it got colder and then the heavy rain came. No tan* when I come back! ☹ And the outlook? More rain!! How boring. Hope I can catch a movie in town. How are things with you? Alright? Write back. Maybe we can chat a bit.
Love,
Carina

VOCABULARY: *tan – Bräune

12 Think back on your holidays and write an email about what it was like. Write as much as possible about the weather (60–80 words).

Sounds right /l/

 13 Listen. Number the sentences as you hear them.

- [ ] I do it every day.
- [ ] I'll speak English to her.
- [ ] We tell jokes a lot.
- [ ] I speak English quite well.
- [ ] They see us on Fridays.
- [ ] We'll tell you a joke.
- [ ] They'll see us on Friday.
- [ ] I'll do it my way.

GRAMMAR *will*-future

Mithilfe der *will*-future drückst du Erwartungen, Vermutungen und Hoffnungen für die Zukunft aus:

*We **will meet** again. (We'**ll meet** again.)*
*I **will not go** away for a very long time. (I **won't go** away for a very long time.)*

Du verwendest die *will*-future auch dann, wenn du etwas vorhersagen willst:

*Some heavy rain **will come** in from Northern Scotland.*
*The south of England **will have** quite a lot of fog near the coast.*
*The sun **won't come** out for another few days.*

Du verwendest die *will*-future auch dann, wenn du dich spontan entschließt oder spontan versprichst, etwas zu tun:

*Maybe **I'll try** sailing, too.*
***I'll help** you with your homework tonight.*

Complete with 'll / will / won't.

Bildung: person + ¹...................... (not) + base form of the verb
Kurzformen: I will = I ²......................
                       I will not = I ³......................

There'll be some showers today.

MORE fun with **Fido!**

I love rainy days!

I love really hot days!

But only on TV!

UNIT 17 Get active!

You learn
- about the present perfect with *ever / never / yet / already*
- sports words

You can
- talk about your favourite sport
- write a text about your favourite sport

Vocabulary Sports

1 Write the numbers of the sports in each picture.

| play | 1 football
2 tennis
3 basketball
4 volleyball | go | 5 mountain climbing
6 cycling
7 mountain biking
8 roller-skating | 9 ice skating
10 skateboarding
11 swimming
12 snowboarding | 13 surfing
14 windsurfing
15 skiing
16 running |

A 14
B 9
C 12
D 5

E 16
F 1
G 2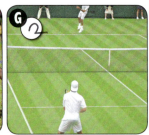
H 11

I 7
J 10
K 6
L 8

M 13
N 4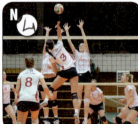
O 3
P 15

2 Listen and check your answers.

Get talking Sports

 Ask and answer questions about some of the sports in .

Do you like … ?   How often do you … ?
What's your favourite … team?   Do you like watching … on TV?
Do you play/go … ?   Who's your favourite sportsman/sportswoman?

  Listen to the interviews with these two American teenagers and complete the profiles.

This is 14-year-old Danni from California. Her favourite sport is surfing. She started surfing when she was ¹ 5 years old. She lives near the ² beach in Santa Barbara. She goes surfing ³ twice a day.

This is 14-year-old Ricky from Colorado. His favourite sport is mountain climbing. He started climbing when he was ⁴ 10 years old. He always goes climbing with his ⁵ dad. They go about ⁶ 3 times a month. They usually go climbing in the Rocky Mountains. They live ⁷ 10 miles away from the Rocky Mountains National Park.

 Look at the questions below from the interviews. Which questions do you think are for Danni and which are for Ricky? Write D or R in the boxes.

1 Have you ever won any competitions? **D** Yes
2 Have you ever got lost in the mountains? **R** No
3 Have you ever seen a shark? **D** No
4 Have you ever had an accident? **R D** No No
5 Have you ever climbed the Matterhorn? **R** No
6 Have you ever been to Australia? **D** Yes 2 times

  Listen and check. Then listen again. Are their answers to the questions yes or no?

Get talking Asking questions with *Have you ever ... ?*

7 Work in small groups. Ask and answer questions to find someone who has ...

1 met a famous person.
2 won a competition.
3 appeared on television.
4 found some money.
5 lived in another country.
6 been to a pop concert.
7 fallen asleep in a lesson.
8 written a poem.

Have you ever met a famous person?

A Have you ever met a famous person?
B Yes, I have.
A Who?

B ...
A When was that?
B ...

8 Listen to the poem. Then read it.

The game

Eleven of us were on the field.
The other team looked scared.
"We're going to win," our trainer said.
"We're really well prepared."

Then Johnny kicked the ball to Paul
and Paul kicked it to Sue,
when Sue's mum shouted, "Come home,
Sue, there's work for you to do."

Ten of us were on the field
and Helen tackled Eddie.
Then Mr Sutton arrived and said,
"Triplets, your dinner's ready."

Seven of us were on the field.
The other team then scored.
And Tom and Helen said, "We're off,
we're getting really bored."

Five of us were on the field,
when Roland hurt his knee.
He left. And Lisa went with him.
And then we were only three.

Three of us were on the field.
The score was twenty – nil.
"I've had enough. It's a waste of time."
And off the field went Phil.

Two of us were on the field
and we tried our very best.
But then Johnny turned to me and said,
"I'm off, I need a rest."

So there I was all on my own,
a goalie without a team.
Then Dad called out, "Wake up! You're late."
Thank God – it was just a dream.

Sounds right /ɔː/ /əʊ/

9 Which is the odd one out? Listen and check.

1. a) m**o**re   b) b**oa**rd   c) c**oa**t
2. a) d**oo**r   b) g**o**   c) sl**ow**
3. a) f**our**   b) kn**ow**   c) s**aw**
4. a) sp**or**t   b) b**ough**t   c) t**oe**

10 CHOICES

A Read the text and match the sentence halves.

Extreme sports profile
ACTION WOMAN

Who is she?
Emma Sanderson, from England.

What does she do?
She's a yachtswoman.

Tell me more.
She sails a yacht, in team races or alone.

What competitions has she won?
She won the Round Britain and Ireland Race in 2000 at the age of 25 and also the Europe 1 New Man Star from Plymouth to Rhode Island, USA.

What is she most famous for?
She won the Around Alone race in 2002/03. She was the youngest woman and first British person to complete the 29,000 mile solo around-the-world yacht race. She was at sea for over 135 days. She had to face a hurricane, pirates and the extreme weather of the Southern Ocean – and, of course, she was alone at sea for four and a half months.

What does she say about her sport?
"I love the challenge. I don't really like being alone for a long time – I'm a people person. But I really wanted to be in the Around Alone race. I'm also in a global education programme and now I can tell kids about my sailing. I really enjoy that."

1. Emma Sanderson is an — 4 complete the 29,000 mile solo race.
2. She sails in — 6 about her sailing.
3. She won many team races, — 2 team races or alone.
4. She was the youngest woman to — 1 English yachtswoman.
5. She doesn't like being — 3 but she's really famous for the Around Alone race.
6. Now she enjoys telling kids — 5 alone for such a long time, but she loves the challenge.

B Read the text and complete the sentences.

Sports profile
Tommy Caldwell, Master of Rock

Who is he?
Tommy Caldwell (born August 11th, 1978 in Estes Park, Colorado) is an American rock climber.

What does he do?
traditional climbing, big wall speed-climbing, big wall free climbing

What is a big wall?
A big wall is a huge cliff usually around 300 metres high. But there are some much higher ones, such as El Capitan or Dawn Wall in Yosemite National Park. They are 900 metres. Climbers often go up in pairs; sometimes it takes a few days to get to the top.

So what has he already climbed?
He has already climbed walls like The Nose several times. He climbed it with his former wife in four days. He has also speed-climbed it in less than twelve hours. For many years his greatest challenge was to climb the Dawn Wall of the El Capitan Mountain in Yosemite National Park in California. In January 2015, after several attempts, he finally managed to get to the top.

How important is climbing for him?
Very important, of course. He likes the adventure and the thrill. But he also likes the fact that it has given him a chance to travel and to see the world. He has already been to so many beautiful places and he thinks he's living a full and exciting life. Climbing has also taught him to live without fear.

What does he think about his sport?
He loves it. He enjoys pushing himself, and he enjoys the freedom. He thinks life doesn't get any better than this. But he also sees the dangers. One danger is to become too obsessed and forget your friends and family. He says: "I've learned that I love climbing, but I love people more."

What are his goals for the future?
To be a good husband and a good dad and to share his love of climbing with others all over the world.

1 Tommy Caldwell is from _Colorado US_.
2 His sports are _rock climbing_.
3 Caldwell has already climbed _The Nose, the Dawn Wall_
4 He doesn't only like the adventure of climbing, but also _sees the dangers in it_.
5 He loves climbing, but he says it's more important _than his family and friends_
6 One goal for his future is _to be a good husband and a good dad to share his love of climbing with_

Writing for your Portfolio

 Read the text about someone's favourite sport.

I love volleyball. I love playing it and I love watching it on TV too. There are some great teams like Brazil and Italy. I like playing it because it's a fantastic team sport. It's also a brilliant way to make friends. I play in the school team. We're very good. Last year we won 18 out of 20 games. Once I broke my arm playing volleyball. I couldn't play for three months. My dream is to play professional volleyball.

Write a text about your favourite sport (60–80 words). Think about:

- what sport it is
- why you like it
- where / when / how often you play it
- how good you are / how good your team is

GRAMMAR

Present perfect with *already* and *yet*

Zur Erinnerung: Du verwendest das Present perfect oft dann, wenn du nicht über einen bestimmten Zeitpunkt in der Vergangenheit sprichst.

I've heard about it. (= Ich hab davon gehört, jemand hat mir irgendwann davon erzählt.)
She **has gone** home. (= Sie ist nach Hause gegangen, aber es ist unwichtig oder unbekannt, wann das war.)

Wenn du sagen willst, dass jemand etwas schon gemacht hat, kannst du das Present perfect mit dem Wort *already* verwenden. Das Wort *already* steht zwischen *has / have* und dem *past participle* (3. Form des Verbs).

He **has already climbed** walls like The Nose several times.
He **has already been** to so many beautiful places.

Wenn du sagen willst, dass etwas noch nicht geschehen ist, verwendest du *not yet* mit Present perfect. Das Wort *yet* kommt an das Satzende.

He **hasn't reached** the top **yet**.
There's a new film at the cinema, but I **haven't seen** it **yet**.

Present perfect with *ever* and *never*

**Wenn du fragen willst, ob jemand *irgendwann* in der Vergangenheit etwas getan oder erlebt hat, dann verwendest du meist das Present perfect.
Du verwendest es auch um auszudrücken, dass du etwas *nie* getan oder erlebt hast.
Häufig verwendest du in diesen Situationen die Wörter *ever* und *never*.**

Have you **ever seen** a shark?
Have you **ever won** a competition?

I've never had an accident.
I've never met a famous person.

I've never seen a giant octopus.

The Twins 6
DEVELOPING SPEAKING COMPETENCIES

Language function
- making requests and offers (*einen Wunsch äußern und Vorschläge machen*)

Speaking strategy
- responding to requests and offers (*auf Wünsche und Vorschläge reagieren*)

The sports party

Vocabulary Sports

1 Match the sports and the pictures. Listen and check.

- football
- rugby
- tennis
- cricket
- golf
- swimming

2 Watch or listen to the dialogue. Then read it. What sports do Lucy and Leo want at their party?

Lucy So we're having a sports party for our birthday this year.
Leo Yeah. Football and tennis. It's going to be cool.
Lucy Why don't I write the invitations?
Leo That's great. And I'll organise the equipment.
Lucy Fantastic. What else do we need to do?
Leo Well, Mum has already booked the sports centre.
Lucy What about food? Can you make a list of the food?
Leo Sure, no problem. And could you organise the drinks?
Lucy Of course.
Leo Football, tennis, food and drink. This is going to be the best party ever.
Lucy I just hope the weather's good.
Leo Don't be so silly. I checked the forecast. It's going to be sunny all day.

3 **Read the to-do list for Lucy and Leo's party and tick (✓) for 'done' or cross (X) for 'to do'.**

1 Decide what kind of party to have. ☐
2 Write the invitations. ☐
3 Organise the equipment. ☐
4 Hire the sports centre. ☐
5 Make a list of food and drink. ☐
6 Check the weather forecast. ☐

Useful phrases Making requests and offers

4 **Read the sentences. Write R (*Request*) or O (*Offer*).**

1 I'll organise the equipment. ☐
2 Can you make a list of the food? ☐
3 Could you organise the drinks? ☐
4 Why don't I write the invitations? ☐

? **What do you think? Answer the questions.**

- Is the party a success?
- Why (not)?

Mobile homework

Watch part 2 of the video and answer the questions.

1 What other sports does Lucy suggest? ....
2 What does Leo think about these suggestions? ....
3 What's the weather like on the day of the party? ....
4 What sports do they play at the party? ....
5 Is the party a success? ....

Speaking strategy Responding to requests and offers

5 **Match the responses with sentences 1–4 in 4. Check with the dialogue in 2.**

- Of course.
- Fantastic.
- Sure, no problem.
- That's great.

6 CHOICES

A Work in pairs. Use the prompts.

A Make a request or offer. → B Respond.

request	offer
make me / sandwich	play tennis / you
take me to / party	do / washing up
help me with / homework	wash / car

A Can you make me a sandwich?
B Of course.

B ROLE PLAY: Work in pairs.

You are organising a party.

- Make a list of all the things you need to organise (e.g. what kind of party, food, drink, music, invitation, etc.).
- Discuss the list. Make offers and requests.

DEVELOPING SPEAKING COMPETENCIES

UNIT 18 Caring for animals

You learn
- words for looking after a pet
- how to use *so do/have I* and *neither do/have I*

You can
- ask about pets
- agree/disagree with someone

Vocabulary Looking after your pet

1 Listen and look at the pictures. Then number the words.

8 play with your pet	7 brush your pet	10 stroke your pet	9 take your pet to the vet
1 clean out your pet's cage	5 feed your pet	2 walk your pet	3 clean out the litter tray
	4 dry your pet	6 give your pet a bath	

2 Play a memory game.

— What did you do yesterday?
— 5, 2, 9.
— Ah, you fed your pet, you walked your pet and you took your pet to the vet.
— That's right.

3 Listen to the interviews and tick the correct answers.

Megan

1. What is Megan's pet? ✓ a cat ☐ a hamster ☐ a dog
2. What colour is she? ✓ black and white ☐ black and grey ☐ black, grey and brown
3. Where does she sleep? ☐ in Megan's room ☐ in the bathroom ✓ in the living room
4. How often does she feed her? ☐ once a day ✓ twice a day ☐ three times a day
5. How much time a day does she spend on her? ✓ 15 minutes ☐ 50 minutes ☐ 90 minutes

David

6. What is David's pet? ☐ a cat ☐ a hamster ✓ a dog
7. What colour is he? ☐ black ✓ brown ☐ brown and white
8. How often does he feed him? ✓ once a day ☐ twice a day ☐ three times a day
9. How much time a day does he spend on him? ☐ 15 minutes ☐ 50 minutes ✓ 90 minutes
10. Where does he sleep? ✓ in the hall ☐ in David's room ☐ in the living room

4 Listen to the interviews again and complete the sentences.

1. Megan doesn't often …
2. When Megan does her homework, Princess …
3. Megan doesn't like to …
4. When it rains, David has to …
5. David's sister doesn't …
6. David plays a lot with Buddy when he …

Get talking Asking about pets

5 Hold interviews. Ask two classmates. Take notes.

Questions:

Have you got a pet?
What is it?
What colour is it?
How often do you feed it?
Where does it sleep?
How much time a day do you spend on it?

What would you like?

Answers:

Yes, I have. A mouse / …

No, I don't. A …

6 Report to the class.

Nathalie has got a … . It's … . It sleeps … . She feeds it … . She spends … minutes on it.

Story time

7 Read the picture story. Then listen to it.

A new pet

1
Bob Do you know what this house needs, Alice?
Alice What does it need, Bob?
Bob A pet. This house needs a pet. A pet to keep us company.
Alice That's a great idea. Let's get one.

2
Alice "The Animal Shelter". I think we're going to find something in here.
Bob So do I. Something very special to make our house the perfect home.

3
Alice How about a dog? They've got some lovely dogs here.
Bob Hmm, I'm not too sure. Think of the mess they make and the noise. Then we need to take them for walks …
Alice Yes, that's a good point. Let's look at the cats.

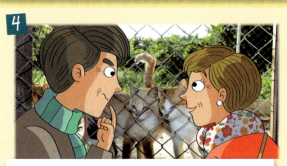

4
Bob Cats. They're cleaner than dogs, but they're not very good company. I don't really like cats.
Alice Neither do I. Let's forget about cats and look for something else.
Bob Let's go to the pet shop.

5
Bob "The Perfect Pet". The best pet shop in town. What are these?
Alice Rats! No way. I've got a fear of rats.
Bob So have I. There's no way I want a rat in the house.

6
Alice What about a budgie? They're easy to look after and they're great company.
Bob No. I don't really like the idea of birds in cages. Birds need to fly.

Bob Snakes. Hmm. Interesting. They're easy to look after, for sure. And they'll keep the house safe. Nobody's going to break into a house with a snake like this in it. It's going to need a big glass cage, but we've got lots of space in the living room.
Alice No way! I'm scared of snakes.
Bob So what are we going to get, Alice?
Alice Come with me. I think I've got the perfect pet for us.

Bob A goldfish. Perfect.
Alice Isn't it beautiful?
Bob I haven't thought of a name for it yet.
Alice Neither have I. But we've got all day to think of one.

8 Read the picture story again and answer the questions.

1 Why does Bob say they need a pet?
2 Why doesn't Bob want a dog?
3 Why don't Bob and Alice want a cat?
4 Why don't Bob and Alice want a rat?
5 Why doesn't Bob want a bird?
6 Why does Bob think a snake might be a good idea?

A Song 4 U

9 Listen and sing.

Getting a pet

*We've got to get a pet,
something for our home.
We've got to get a pet.
Don't want to be alone.*

*Shall we get a cat?
Or shall we get a dog?
Shall we get a snake?
Or shall we get a frog?
Hmmmmmmmmm ...*

*A dog is too much work.
A cat is much too proud.
A snake's too dangerous.
A frog is much too loud.*

*We've got to get a pet,
something for our home.
We've got to get a pet.
Don't want to be alone.*

*Shall we get a bird?
Or shall we get a rat?
Or shall we get a goldfish, dear?
What do you say to that?
Hmmmmmmmmmmm ...*

*Bird in a cage? No way!
I've got a fear of rats.
I'd really love a goldfish, dear.
So would the neighbours' cats.*

Story time

  10 Read the story.

The story of Happy Feet

In June 2011, some people found an emperor penguin on a beach in New Zealand. It was really unusual because there are no emperor penguins in New Zealand. The penguin was more than 2,500 kilometres from home! Penguins are excellent swimmers, but that's a very long way to swim, even for a penguin. The people saw that the penguin ate sand. They also saw that the bird was quite sick. Why did he eat sand? Because the poor bird thought it was snow.

They took the penguin to the zoo in Wellington, the capital of New Zealand. They called the emperor penguin "Happy Feet". Happy Feet soon became a star. Lots of people wanted to see him. At the zoo they fed Happy Feet fish and after some months Happy Feet was fine again. They decided to take him back home.

> **Did you know?**
> The emperor penguin is the tallest and heaviest of all penguins. They can be 120 cm tall and weigh up to 45 kilos. They eat fish and other small animals that live in the Arctic Sea.

They fixed a transmitter* to the bird and put him on a ship. They took him about 600 km south. Then they said goodbye to him and put him in the sea to swim home.

But what happened to Happy Feet? After five days there was no signal from the transmitter any more. Did he get home? Did a shark eat him? We will never know.

VOCABULARY: *transmitter – Sender

11 How many of these tasks can you do?

1. The penguin wasn't a very long way from home.   T / F
2. Penguins often swim more than 2,500 km.   T / F
3. The penguin was trying to eat sand.   T / F

4. The penguin was quite sick because he ....
5. The penguin stayed .... for a while.
6. Before they let Happy Feet go, they .... on him.

7. Where did they release Happy Feet? ....
8. What happened to Happy Feet? ....
9. How are emperor penguins different from other penguins? ....

   12 Check your answers with a partner. Then listen to the story.

13 CHOICES

Writing for your Portfolio

Read the texts. Then write your own text.

A
I haven't got a pet. We live in a flat and my parents always say no. I'd like a dog. My parents say dogs are a lot of work, but I don't think so. One of my friends has got a dog. He doesn't spend a lot of time on it. We sometimes play with it in the park.

B
My pet is a rat. He's brown and his name is Fluff. I often play with Fluff. He likes it when I put him inside my shirt. Some of my friends are scared of Fluff. When I take Fluff out of my shirt or jacket, they run away. I don't understand that. I clean the cage every second day and I put in clean water twice every day. At night, Fluff sleeps in his cage. When I get up at the weekend, I put him in the pocket of my pyjamas. Then I go into the kitchen and hug my mum. When she feels Fluff, she screams.

GRAMMAR   So do/have I. – Neither do/have I.

Read the examples.

A Rats! No way. I**'ve got** a fear of rats.
B **So have** I.

A I **haven't thought** of a name for her yet.
B **Neither have** I.

A I **think** we're going to find something in here.
B **So do** I.

A I **don't** really **like** cats.
B **Neither do** I.

Complete the sentences with *neither* or *so*.

Du verwendest ¹............................. *do/have I*, um einer positiven Aussage zuzustimmen.
Du verwendest ²............................. *do/have I*, um einer negativen Aussage zuzustimmen.

MORE fun with Fido!

"Why doesn't she clean my bowl?"

"Why doesn't he tidy up my basket?"

"I have to do everything myself."

Kids in NYC 4

The missing cat

Before you watch

1 Write the words under the pictures.

> market
> cell phone
> reward

1 .... 2 .... 3 ....

2 In what order do you think these pictures come in the DVD? Write 1–4 in the boxes.

Note:
cell phone = American English
mobile (phone) = British English

3 In pairs, invent a story that goes with the pictures in **2**.

Watch the story

  4 Check your answers to .

5 Complete the sentences.

1 Steve and Jenny see ....
2 They want to ....
3 First they want to look .... and ....
4 Then Jenny has an idea. She wants to look for the cat ....
5 She thinks they might find the cat there because ....

6 Complete the dialogue.

| think |
| look |
| see |
| get |
| check |

Jenny ¹..................................... that cat? Doesn't it ²..................................... like Tiger?
Steve No. I don't ³..................................... so. But look. There, behind that box. Let's ⁴..................................... with the picture.
Jenny Yeah, it looks a bit like Tiger. ⁵..................................... him.
Steve Here, kitty, kitty. Here, kitty. Got you, Tiger.

7 Circle T (*True*) or F (*False*).

1 Jenny and Steve find Tiger at the fish market.   T / F
2 They find Tiger under a car.   T / F
3 They put Tiger in a bag.   T / F
4 The man at the fish market has a cat and a dog.   T / F
5 Jenny and Steve give Tiger to the man.   T / F
6 The woman gives Jenny and Steve a $20 reward.   T / F

Everyday English

8 Complete the dialogues.

I don't get it.
Got you,
What for?
Right here.

Take a photo of the cat.

Have you got the photo?

I'm hungry

The Fulton Fish Market?
....

Hungry! That's it! We have to go to the Fulton Fish Market.

.... Tiger.

Extra UNIT Holidays

1 Everybody is waiting for the holidays. So is Marcus White. Read his diary. What day of the week do these things happen?

1 Marcus wants a new best friend.
2 Marcus runs a race.
3 Marcus gets told off in the school assembly.
4 Marcus makes a list.
5 Marcus is late for school.
6 Marcus gets his test results.

Sunday

Fantastic. Great. Wonderful. Finally – it's here!
The last week of school for six weeks.
Six weeks of holiday!
Oh, what a happy week!
Things to do for my holidays
- Paint my bedroom black.
- Do karate lessons.
- Beat my dad at chess.
- Read all the Percy Jackson books – again!
- Get fit!
- Build a new go-kart with Sam (my best friend this week).
- Spend time with Jenny – this might be difficult because I've never spoken to her in my life. I'll definitely need a plan for this.

Monday

School was a bit boring.
I got my test results. 'C' for everything.
'C' isn't so bad. It's better than 'D'.
I explained this to Dad. He didn't really understand. I don't think he's very happy at the moment.
I think he has got problems at work.
I forgot to ask Jenny for her phone number.
I must do this tomorrow.
Four days to go!

Tuesday

I had a big argument with my dad at breakfast today. He says I can't paint my bedroom black. It has got to be blue. Blue!
My dad doesn't understand teenagers.
I'm not going to speak to him for a week.
School was better. We played games all day. I think our teachers are very tired. There was one bad thing. Sam had some news for me – Jenny is going to live in London. She's not going to be at our school next term. "What!?" I screamed.
Then Sam said it was a joke.
I think I need a new best friend.

That's me! :(

Wednesday

Another bad breakfast. I asked my dad for £10 to buy some wood for my go-kart. Dad said "Have you forgotten? You're not speaking to me." He's so smart. So I asked Mum because I'm still speaking to her. She said "Ask your dad." Parents are complicated.

It was Sports Day at school today. I was in the 2,000 metres – five times around the running track! I got a new school record – the slowest time in the history of Sports Day. It was the last race of the day. When I finished, nobody was there. That was a shame because I wanted to ask Jenny for her phone number. I must do this tomorrow.

Thursday

I got up half an hour late today because I didn't want to see Dad at breakfast. The plan worked. I didn't see him. The only problem was I was half an hour late for school.
My teacher wasn't happy.
We had the school play this afternoon.
I don't really remember what the story was about. But Jenny was in it. She was great. After the play everybody wanted to talk to her. I couldn't ask her for her phone number. There were too many people. I'm going to be in the school play next year.

Friday

Today we had the final assembly with Mr Hill, the headmaster. He read out all the names of the best students. The best students at Maths, the best students at Science, at Sport, at French, etc. Then he shouted out my name – not because I'm best at anything (unfortunately), but because I was talking to my friend. Everyone looked at me. Jenny looked at me. I think she smiled. I went red. I didn't ask Jenny for her phone number, but I've got a new plan. I'm going to talk to Jenny next term. I'll be thirteen then. I read in a book that talking to girls is easier when you're thirteen! But I wrote a holiday song for her and uploaded it on the internet. I hope Jenny likes it.

Life in the USA

School life in the USA

1 Read about the different methods of schooling in the USA.

The American school system

School	Age
Elementary school (Grades 1–8)	6–13
High school (Grades 9–12)	14–17

Home schooling

In the United States, there are thousands of children who don't go to school but learn from home. In 2012, there were 1.8 million children 'home schooling'.

The school system

Hi, my name's Susannah and I'm American. There are five types of schools in America: public schools, charter schools, private schools, religious schools and home schooling. I go to a charter school. Charter schools are run by* a private organization and you don't pay. There are over 6,100 of these schools in America now.

VOCABULARY
*run by – geführt von

Home schooling

Hello, my name is Mark and I have home schooling. It's fantastic! I do all my lessons at home on the computer. I don't have to wear a uniform and I don't have to catch the school bus. And of course I don't have homework after school!

2 Listen to Amy talk about her high school prom and answer the questions.

The high school prom

Did you know?

* In American schools, there is a junior and a senior prom.
* The senior prom is at the end of the last year of high school.
* Traditionally, boys wear suits and ties and girls wear ball gowns*.
* The girl's date* for the evening gives her flowers to wear.

VOCABULARY: *ball gown – Ballkleid; **date** – Verabredung

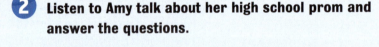

1 What did Amy wear to the prom?
2 Who asked her to the prom?
3 How did she travel to her date's house?
4 Was the tar* on the driveway* dry?
5 How much did her shoes cost?
6 How long did it take her mother to get the tar out of her hair?

VOCABULARY: *tar – Teer; **driveway** – Auffahrt/Einfahrt

3 Write a short email to Susannah or Mark about your school.

POPULAR AMERICAN SPORTS

1 Match the sports to the correct pictures.

1 baseball 2 American football 3 basketball

 2 Do the quiz. Then listen and check your answers.

1 Which sport is the oldest?
   a) American football
   b) basketball
   c) baseball

2 Which sport are these terms from: a pitcher, a home run and a pennant?
   a) baseball   b) football   c) rounders

3 There are ... players in a basketball team.
   a) 5   b) 6   c) 7

4 How long does a baseball match usually last?
   a) 50 minutes
   b) 90 minutes
   c) more than three hours

5 What is a baseball field called?
   a) a star   b) a diamond   c) a square

6 The Cincinnati Red Stockings were the first professional ... team.
   a) basketball
   b) baseball
   c) American football

7 How many points do you score for a 'touchdown' in American football?
   a) 5   b) 6   c) 1

3 Read about the two kids' favourite sports.

> Note:
> favorite = American English; favourite = British English

 Swimming is my favorite sport. I learnt to swim when I was five years old. My parents and my two brothers also like swimming. We have a cabin at a lake in Wisconsin and in summer we spend three weeks there. We swim before breakfast and in the afternoon. I also love swimming in the lake when there is a full moon. I love swimming because it is good for my body. And there is another thing: when I swim slowly in our lake, good ideas often come to my mind.

 My favorite sport is badminton. I love badminton because it is good exercise and a lot of my best friends play. I also love to watch badminton matches on TV. Unfortunately, the US have not won any medals in badminton at the Olympic Games. We have a school team that plays against other schools, but I'm not on it. I train hard so maybe I will be on the team next year.

4 Now write a short text about your favourite sport.

LIFE IN THE USA 139

Life in the USA

American national parks

1 Listen to Emma talking about her visit to the Redwood National Park. Complete the information about the trees.

2 Read about the Colorado Rockies and Yellowstone National Park. Then answer the questions.

1 Who lived in the Rocky Mountains?
2 How many mountains are there in the Rocky Mountain chain?
3 Why are the Colorado Rockies called 'the roof of America'?
4 What is Yellowstone famous for?
5 How often does Yellowstone erupt?

THE REDWOOD NATIONAL PARK

The Redwood Trees

Height:

Number of years to grow:

Age:

Did you know?
The first national park in the USA was Yellowstone Park. It opened in 1872 and was the first national park in the world.

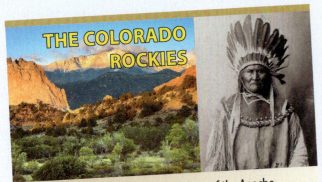

THE COLORADO ROCKIES

The Rocky Mountains were the home of the Apache, Blackfoot and Sioux, and stretch from* Alaska to New Mexico. The Rockies are high! There are 107 mountains in the range* which are over 3,000 meters. The Colorado Rockies are the tallest. People call them 'the roof of America' because the tops of the mountains here are more than 4,000 meters. The Colorado Rockies are a popular area to go mountain climbing, fishing, hunting and skiing.

VOCABULARY: *stretch from – erstrecken sich von; range – Gebirgskette

YELLOWSTONE NATIONAL PARK

This park is in Wyoming and is older than the other national parks in America. It is famous for its hot springs* and for its grizzly bears. Some of the bears are huge. They can weigh 700 kg. There are also wolves and bison in the park.

The park is 8,980 square km. Before human history, a huge volcanic eruption* covered* the area with ash*. Yellowstone is the name of a volcano too and it usually erupts every 600,000 years. The last eruption was 640,000 years ago!

VOCABULARY: *hot springs – heiße Quellen; volcanic eruption – Vulkanausbruch; covered – bedeckt; ash – Asche

3 Work in groups. Choose an Austrian national park. Collect pictures and information and do a poster presentation.

Extreme weather

1 Which photograph shows a hurricane and which a tornado?

A

B

HURRICANES
– THE FACTS –

- Hurricanes come from the sea.
- They travel at 119 km per hour.
- They can be from 100 to 1,600 km wide.
- Hurricanes are given girls' and boys' names, for example Hurricane Andrew.

TORNADOES
– THE FACTS –

- There are about 800 to 1,200 tornadoes a year in America.
- They are usually in Northwest Texas, Oklahoma and Kansas.
- They circle around* at speeds of 320 to 800 km per hour.
- They are a dark grey colour because they pick up* soil and other objects.

VOCABULARY: *circle around – sich drehen; **pick up** – aufheben/mitnehmen

2 Read Mary Ann's story and answer the questions.

1. When did Hurricane Katrina hit Florida?
2. What happened after the rooms were filled with water?
3. What happened to the building?
4. How fast was the wind?
5. How far did the water carry Mary Ann?

Mary Ann's Story

In 2005, Hurricane Katrina hit my three-storey block of flats near Hallandale Beach in Florida. First, the sea hit the building and all the windows broke. Then the room filled with water. Five minutes later, my bed was up by the ceiling. Then it went out of the window. It was dark and the wind was making a really loud noise. I was terrified. The building was falling down* all around me. The wind was awful. It reached a speed* of more than 300 km per hour. I was cut and bleeding* from head to toe. Finally, someone found me 8 km from my house and they took me to hospital.

VOCABULARY
*was falling down – stürzte ein; reach a speed – eine Geschwindigkeit erreichen; was bleeding – blutete

3 Listen and circle T (*True*) or F (*False*). (CD4 30)

The Storm Chasers!
Most people run away or hide from hurricanes and tornadoes but some people in America chase them! You can even go on a storm-chasing holiday!

1. The storm-chasing tours are not safe.   T / F
2. There is a good chance you will see a tornado. T / F
3. The tornadoes are always far from the hotel.   T / F
4. You can't take photos of the tornadoes.   T / F
5. If there aren't any tornadoes, they go sightseeing. T / F

LIFE IN THE USA   141

GRAMMAR

TENSES (ZEITEN)

PRESENT TENSE

Present simple (Einfache Gegenwartsform)

Die Form des Present simple ist für alle Personen gleich.
Ausnahme: In der 3. Person Singular wird ein **-s** angehängt.

Positive Aussagen	Negative Aussagen	Fragen	Kurzantworten	
I **like** London.	I **don't (do not) like** London.	**Do/Don't** I **like** London?	Yes, I **do**.	No, I **don't**.
You **like** London.	You **don't (do not) like** London.	**Do/Don't** you **like** London?	Yes, you **do**.	No, you **don't**.
He **likes** London.	He **doesn't (does not) like** London.	**Does/Doesn't** he **like** London?	Yes, he **does**.	No, he **doesn't**.
She **likes** London.	She **doesn't (does not) like** London.	**Does/Doesn't** she **like** London?	Yes, she **does**.	No, she **doesn't**.
It **likes** fish.	It **doesn't (does not) like** fish.	**Does/Doesn't** it **like** fish?	Yes, it **does**.	No, it **doesn't**.
We **like** London.	We **don't (do not) like** London.	**Do/Don't** we **like** London?	Yes, we **do**.	No, we **don't**.
You **like** London.	You **don't (do not) like** London.	**Do/Don't** you **like** London?	Yes, you **do**.	No, you **don't**.
They **like** London.	They **don't (do not) like** London.	**Do/Don't** they **like** London?	Yes, they **do**.	No, they **don't**.

Present continuous / progressive (Verlaufsform, -ing-Form)

Das Present continuous wird mit der richtigen Form von **be** und der **-ing**-Form des Verbs gebildet.

Positive Aussagen	Negative Aussagen	Fragen	Kurzantworten	
I'm (I am) **playing** golf.	I'm not (I am not) **playing** golf.	**Am / Am** I not **playing** golf?	Yes, I **am**.	No, **I'm not**.
You're (You are) **playing** golf.	You **aren't** (You're not) **playing** golf.	**Are/Aren't** you **playing** golf?	Yes, you **are**.	No, you **aren't**. / No, **you're not**.
He's (He is) **playing** golf.	He **isn't** (He's not) **playing** golf.	**Is/Isn't** he **playing** golf?	Yes, he **is**.	No, he **isn't**. / No, **he's not**.
She's (She is) **playing** golf.	She **isn't** (She's not) **playing** golf.	**Is/Isn't** she **playing** golf?	Yes, she **is**.	No, she **isn't**. / No, **she's not**.
It's (It is) **raining**.	It **isn't** (It's not) **raining**.	**Is/Isn't** it **raining**?	Yes, it **is**.	No, it **isn't**. / No, **it's not**.
We're (We are) **playing** golf.	We **aren't** (We're not) **playing** golf.	**Are/Aren't** we **playing** golf?	Yes, we **are**.	No, we **aren't**. / No, **we're not**.
You're (You are) **playing** golf.	You **aren't** (You're not) **playing** golf.	**Are/Aren't** you **playing** golf?	Yes, you **are**.	No, you **aren't**. / No, **you're not**.
They're (They are) **playing** golf.	They **aren't** (They're not) **playing** golf.	**Are/Aren't** they **playing** golf?	Yes, they **are**.	No, they **aren't**. / No, **they're not**.

Present perfect – Regular verbs (Regelmäßige Verben)

Das Present perfect wird gebildet mit **has / have** und der dritten Form (*past participle* Form) des Verbs (siehe "irregular verbs").

Positive Aussagen	Negative Aussagen			Fragen			Kurzantworten	
I've (I have)	I	**haven't (have not)**	finished.	Have/ Haven't	I	finished?	Yes, I **have**.	No, I **haven't**.
You've (You have)	You				you		Yes, you **have**.	No, you **haven't**.
He's (He has)	He	**hasn't (has not)**		Has/ Hasn't	he		Yes, he **has**.	No, he **hasn't**.
She's (She has)	She				she		Yes, she **has**.	No, she **hasn't**.
It's (It has)	It				it		Yes, it **has**.	No, it **hasn't**.
We've (We have)	We	**haven't (have not)**		Have/ Haven't	we		Yes, we **have**.	No, we **haven't**.
You've (You have)	You				you		Yes, you **have**.	No, you **haven't**.
They've (They have)	They				they		Yes, they **have**.	No, they **haven't**.

Present perfect + *already / yet*

Already stellst du zwischen **have / has** und die dritte Form des Verbs, **yet** stellst du an das Satzende.

| I've **already washed** the car. | We've **already seen** this film. | I **haven't done** my homework **yet**. | She **hasn't told** him **yet**. |

Present perfect + *ever / never*

Ever und **never** stellst du zwischen **have / has** und die dritte Form des Verbs.

| **Have** you **ever been** to Hollywood? | **Has** she **ever met** a famous person? | I've **never been** to Hollywood. | She **has never met** a famous person. |

PAST TENSE

Past simple – *was / were* (Einfache Vergangenheitsform)

Das Past simple von **be** wird wie folgt gebildet:

Positive Aussagen	Negative Aussagen	Fragen	Kurzantworten	
I **was** tired.	I **wasn't (was not)** tired.	**Was/Wasn't** I tired?	Yes, I **was**.	No, I **wasn't (was not)**.
You **were** tired.	You **weren't (were not)** tired.	**Were/Weren't** you tired?	Yes, you **were**.	No, you **weren't (were not)**.
He **was** nice.	He **wasn't (was not)** nice.	**Was/Wasn't** he nice?	Yes, he **was**.	No, he **wasn't (was not)**.
She **was** nice.	She **wasn't (was not)** nice.	**Was/Wasn't** she nice?	Yes, she **was**.	No, she **wasn't (was not)**.
It **was** blue.	It **wasn't (was not)** blue.	**Was/Wasn't** it blue?	Yes, it **was**.	No, it **wasn't (was not)**.
We **were** busy.	We **weren't (were not)** busy.	**Were/Weren't** we busy?	Yes, we **were**.	No, we **weren't (were not)**.
You **were** busy.	You **weren't (were not)** busy.	**Were/Weren't** you busy?	Yes, you **were**.	No, you **weren't (were not)**.
They **were** busy.	They **weren't (were not)** busy.	**Were/Weren't** they busy?	Yes, they **were**.	No, they **weren't (were not)**.

Past time markers

Bei diesen Wörtern verwendest du beim Erzählen das Past simple:

| then | ago | later | after | one day | finally |

Past simple – Regular verbs (Regelmäßige Verben)

Das Past simple wird bei regelmäßigen Verben mit **-ed** gebildet, bei unregelmäßigen Verben mit der zweiten Form (siehe "irregular verbs").

Positive Aussagen	Negative Aussagen
I **liked** London.	I **didn't (did not) like** London.
You **laughed** a lot.	You **didn't (did not) laugh** a lot.
He **walked** home.	He **didn't (did not) walk** home.
She **looked** good.	She **didn't (did not) look** good.
It **turned** around.	It **didn't (did not) turn** around.
We **jumped** into the water.	We **didn't (did not) jump** into the water.
You **cooked** dinner.	You **didn't (did not) cook** dinner.
They **loved** the film.	They **didn't (did not) love** the film.

Irregular verbs (Unregelmäßige Verben)

Hier findest du eine Liste mit einer Auswahl der wichtigsten unregelmäßigen Verben:

Present	Past simple	Past participle	Übersetzung
be	was/were	been	sein
become	became	become	werden
begin	began	begun	beginnen
blow	blew	blown	blasen
break	broke	broken	brechen
bring	brought	brought	bringen
build	built	built	bauen
buy	bought	bought	kaufen
catch	caught	caught	fangen
choose	chose	chosen	(aus-)wählen
come	came	come	kommen
cut	cut	cut	schneiden
dig	dug	dug	graben
do	did	done	tun, machen
draw	drew	drawn	zeichnen
dream	dreamt (dreamed)	dreamt (dreamed)	träumen
drink	drank	drunk	trinken
drive	drove	driven	fahren; treiben
eat	ate	eaten	essen
fall (asleep)	fell (asleep)	fallen (asleep)	fallen (einschlafen)
feel	felt	felt	fühlen
fight	fought	fought	kämpfen
find	found	found	finden
fly	flew	flown	fliegen
forget	forgot	forgotten	vergessen
get	got	got	bekommen; werden
get up	got up	got up	aufstehen
give	gave	given	geben
go	went	gone	gehen, fahren
hang	hung	hung	hängen
have	had	had	haben
hear	heard	heard	hören
hide	hid	hidden	(sich) verstecken
hit	hit	hit	schlagen
hold	held	held	(fest-)halten
hurt	hurt	hurt	(sich) verletzen, schmerzen
know	knew	known	wissen; kennen

Present	Past simple	Past participle	Übersetzung
lay	laid	laid	legen
learn	learnt (learned)	learnt (learned)	lernen
leave	left	left	verlassen
let	let	let	lassen
lie	lay	lain	liegen
lose	lost	lost	verlieren
make	made	made	machen
meet	met	met	treffen
put	put	put	legen; setzen; stellen
read	read [red]	read [red]	lesen
ride	rode	ridden	reiten; fahren
ring	rang	rung	läuten
run	ran	run	laufen
say	said	said	sagen
see	saw	seen	sehen
send	sent	sent	senden, schicken
shoot	shot	shot	schießen
show	showed	shown (showed)	zeigen
sing	sang	sung	singen
sink	sank (sunk)	sunk	untergehen, sinken
sit	sat	sat	sitzen, sich setzen
sleep	slept	slept	schlafen
smell	smelt (smelled)	smelt (smelled)	riechen
speak	spoke	spoken	sprechen, sagen
spend	spent	spent	verbringen; ausgeben
stand	stood	stood	stehen
steal	stole	stolen	stehlen
swim	swam	swum	schwimmen
take off	took off	taken off	ausziehen
take	took	taken	nehmen
teach	taught	taught	lehren, unterrichten
tell	told	told	sagen, erzählen
think	thought	thought	denken
wake (up)	woke (up)	woken (up)	(auf-)wachen
win	won	won	gewinnen
write	wrote	written	schreiben

FUTURE TENSE

going to-future (Zukunft mit going to)

Die *going to*-future wird mit einer Form von **be** und **going to** und der Grundform des Vollverbs gebildet.

Positive Aussagen		Negative Aussagen		Fragen		Kurzantworten
I'm	going to play football.	I'm not	going to play football.	Am I / Aren't I	going to play football?	Yes, I am. / No, I'm not.
You're		You aren't (You're not)		Are/Aren't you		Yes, you are. / No, you aren't (you're not).
He's		He isn't (He's not)		Is/Isn't he		Yes, he is. / No, he isn't (he's not).
She's		She isn't (She's not)		Is/Isn't she		Yes, she is. / No, she isn't (she's not).
We're		We aren't (We're not)		Are/Aren't we		Yes, we are. / No, we aren't (we're not).
You're		You aren't (You're not)		Are/Aren't you		Yes, you are. / No, you aren't (you're not).
They're		They aren't (They're not)		Are/Aren't they		Yes, they are. / No, they aren't (they're not).

will-future

Die *will*-future verwendest du, wenn du etwas vorhersagen möchtest oder versprichst.

Positive Aussagen	Negative Aussagen	Fragen	Kurzantworten	
I'll (I will) see you tomorrow.	I won't (will not) see you tomorrow.	Will I see you tomorrow?	Yes, I will.	No, I won't (will not).
You'll (You will) see me tomorrow.	You won't (will not) see me tomorrow.	Will you see me tomorrow?	Yes, you will.	No, you won't (will not).
He'll (He will) see her tomorrow.	He won't (will not) see her tomorrow.	Will he see her tomorrow?	Yes, he will.	No, he won't (will not).
She'll (She will) see him tomorrow.	She won't (will not) see him tomorrow.	Will she see him tomorrow?	Yes, she will.	No, she won't (will not).
It'll (It will) rain tomorrow.	It won't (will not) rain tomorrow.	Will it rain tomorrow?	Yes, it will.	No, it won't (will not).
We'll (We will) see you tomorrow.	We won't (will not) see you tomorrow.	Will we see you tomorrow?	Yes, we will.	No, we won't (will not).
You'll (You will) see me tomorrow.	You won't (will not) see me tomorrow.	Will you see me tomorrow?	Yes, you will.	No, you won't (will not).
They'll (They will) see you tomorrow.	They won't (will not) see you tomorrow.	Will they see you tomorrow?	Yes, they will.	No, they won't (will not).

BESONDERE VERBEN

to be – affirmative, negative

Das Verb **be** wird wie das deutsche Verb **sein** verwendet.

Positive Aussagen	Negative Aussagen
I'm (I am) tired.	I'm not tired.
You're (You are) clever.	You aren't/You're not clever.
He's (He is) nice.	He isn't/He's not nice.
She's (She is) in class 3B.	She isn't/She's not in class 3B.
It's (It is) blue.	It isn't/It's not blue.
We're (We are) busy.	We aren't/We're not busy.
We're (We are) busy.	We aren't/We're not busy.
They're (They are) twelve.	They aren't/They're not twelve.

Questions with *to be*

Fragen	Kurzantworten	
Am I tired?	Yes, I **am**.	No, I**'m not**.
Are/Aren't you tired?	Yes, you **are**.	No, you **aren't**. / No, you**'re not**.
Is/Isn't he nice?	Yes, he **is**.	No, he **isn't**. / No, he**'s not**.
Is/Isn't she in class 3B?	Yes, she **is**.	No, she **isn't**. / No, she**'s not**.
Is/Isn't it blue?	Yes, it **is**.	No, it **isn't**. / No, it**'s not**.
Are/Aren't we busy?	Yes, we **are**.	No, we **aren't**. / No, we**'re not**.
Are/Aren't you busy?	Yes, you **are**.	No, you **aren't**. / No, you**'re not**.
Are/Aren't they twelve?	Yes, they **are**.	No, they **aren't**. / No, they**'re not**.

have got / haven't got

Have got wird wie das deutsche Verb **haben** (besitzen) verwendet.
Die richtige Form für die 3. Person der Gegenwart (**he/she/it**) ist **has got**.

Positive Aussagen	Negative Aussagen	Fragen	Kurzantworten	
I**'ve got** (I have got) a dog.	I **haven't got** (have not got) a dog.	**Have/Haven't** I **got** a dog?	Yes, I **have**.	No, I **haven't**.
You**'ve got** (You have got) a dog.	You **haven't got** (have not got) a dog.	**Have/Haven't** you **got** a dog?	Yes, you **have**.	No, you **haven't**.
He**'s got** (He has got) a dog.	He **hasn't got** (has not got) a dog.	**Has/Hasn't** he **got** a dog?	Yes, he **has**.	No, he **hasn't**.
She**'s got** (She has got) a dog.	She **hasn't got** (has not got) a dog.	**Has/Hasn't** she **got** a dog?	Yes, she **has**.	No, she **hasn't**.
It**'s got** (It has got) big ears.	It **hasn't got** (has not got) big ears.	**Has/Hasn't** it **got** big ears?	Yes, it **has**.	No, it **hasn't**.
We**'ve got** (We have got) a dog.	We **haven't got** (have not got) a dog.	**Have/Haven't** we **got** a dog?	Yes, we **have**.	No, we **haven't**.
You**'ve got** (You have got) a dog.	You **haven't got** (have not got) a dog.	**Have/Haven't** you **got** a dog?	Yes, you **have**.	No, you **haven't**.
They**'ve got** (They have got) a dog.	They **haven't got** (have not got) a dog.	**Have/Haven't** they **got** a dog?	Yes, they **have**.	No, they **haven't**.

there is / there are

There is / **there are** wird verwendet, um auszudrücken, dass etwas vorhanden ist, oder dass es etwas gibt.

There's a monster in the tree. (= **There is** a monster in the tree.)
There are three frog**s** on the table.

Modal verbs (Modalverben)

Die wichtigsten Modalverben sind **should / shouldn't**, **have to / don't have to**, **might / might not**, **must / mustn't**, **can / can't**, **could / couldn't**, **will / won't**, **would / wouldn't**, **shall / shall not**, and **may / may not**.

I	can/can't (cannot)	come today.	I	have to/don't have to	go to school.
You			You		
He	must/mustn't		He	has to/doesn't have to	
She			She		
It	should/shouldn't		It		
We	might/might not (mightn't)		We	have to/don't have to	
You			You		
They			They		

can / can't

Can ist ein Modalverb und wird deshalb immer in Verbindung mit einem Vollverb verwendet.
Die Verneinung wird gebildet als **cannot** oder **can't**.

Positive Aussagen	Negative Aussagen	Fragen	Kurzantworten	
I **can speak** French.	I **can't (cannot) speak** French.	**Can/Can't** I speak French?	Yes, I **can**.	No, I **can't**.
You **can speak** French.	You **can't (cannot) speak** French.	**Can/Can't** you speak French?	Yes, you **can**.	No, you **can't**.
He **can speak** French.	He **can't (cannot) speak** French.	**Can/Can't** he speak French?	Yes, he **can**.	No, he **can't**.
She **can speak** French.	She **can't (cannot) speak** French.	**Can/Can't** she speak French?	Yes, she **can**.	No, she **can't**.
It **can run** fast.	It **can't (cannot) run** fast.	**Can/Can't** it run fast?	Yes, it **can**.	No, it **can't**.
We **can speak** French.	We **can't (cannot) speak** French.	**Can/Can't** we speak French?	Yes, we **can**.	No, we **can't**.
You **can speak** French.	You **can't (cannot) speak** French.	**Can/Can't** you speak French?	Yes, you **can**.	No, you **can't**.
They **can speak** French.	They **can't (cannot) speak** French.	**Can/Can't** they speak French?	Yes, they **can**.	No, they **can't**.

like (doing)

Mit **like doing** sagst du, ob jemand gerne etwas macht oder sich gerne mit etwas beschäftigt. Gebildet wird es mit der einfachen Gegenwartsform von **like** + der **-ing**-Form des folgenden Verbs.

Samantha **doesn't like reading**, but she **likes listening** to music.	James **likes running**, but he **doesn't like swimming**.

ADVERBS (ADVERBIEN)

Adverbs of manner (Adverbien der Art und Weise)

Mit Adverbien der Art und Weise beschreibst du, wie jemand etwas macht. Regelmäßige Adverbien werden mit **-ly** gebildet.

Regular (+ -ly) (Regelmäßig)			**Irregular** (Unregelmäßig)	
bad – bad**ly**	quiet – quiet**ly**	happy – happi**ly**	fast – fast	good – well

Adverbs of frequency (Häufigkeitsadverbien)

0%	→	→	→	100%
never	sometimes	often	usually	always

We **sometimes** go to the cinema on Fridays.
She's **always** happy.

IMPERATIVES (IMPERATIV / BEFEHLSFORMEN)

Die Befehlsform ist immer gleich wie die Grundform des Verbs (ohne **to**).
Die Verneinung wird mit **do not** (**don't**) + Grundform gebildet.

Run!	Don't run!
Sit down.	Don't sit down.
Open the window.	Don't open the window.

ARTICLES (ARTIKEL)

Indefinite article (Unbestimmter Artikel)

Der unbestimmte Artikel **a** wird vor einem zählbaren Hauptwort verwendet, **an** wird vor Selbstlauten verwendet.

a bike		**Vor den Vokalen (Selbstlauten): a, e, i, o, u**
a teacher		**an** egg [ən ˈeg]
a dog		**an** apple [ən ˈæpl]

Definite article (Bestimmter Artikel)

Der bestimmte Artikel, der wie **der/die/das** im Deutschen verwendet wird, ist im Englischen immer **the**.

the bike	**the** teacher	**the** dog

NOUNS (HAUPTWÖRTER)

Plural nouns – Irregular plurals (Pluralformen)

Regelmäßige Pluralformen werden gebildet, indem ein **-s** angehängt wird.
Bei unregelmäßigen Formen wird am Wortende **-y** zu **-ies** (Vokal vor **-y** bleibt **-y**) und **-f** oder **-fe** zu **-ves**.
Aber es gibt auch Ausnahmen, die ganz andere Formen haben und keiner Regel folgen. Diese lernst du am besten auswendig, um sie dir gut zu merken.

Regelmäßig		
dog – dog**s**	snake – snake**s**	cat – cat**s**

Unregelmäßig						
baby – bab**ies**	leaf – lea**ves**	woman – women	person – people	mouse – mice	foot – feet	child - children

whose + possessive *'s* (Genitiv)

Wenn du fragen willst, wem etwas gehört, verwendest du **whose**.
Wenn du mit einem Namen oder Nomen antwortest, fügst du das Possessive **'s** an.
Wenn der Name oder das Nomen im Plural steht oder auf *-s* endet, setzt du ans Ende des Wortes ein **'** (Apostroph).
Bei Wörtern mit unregelmäßiger Pluralform hängst du ebenfalls das Possessive **'s** an.

Whose is this book?	It's **Amanda's** (book).	**Whose** is this room?	It's the **teachers'** (room).
Whose book is this?	It's **Les'** (book).	**Whose** is this room?	It's the **children's** (room).

PRONOUNS (PRONOMEN)

Personal pronouns – Subject and object pronouns (Personalpronomen)

Personalpronomen können als Subjekt oder Objekt eines Satzes verwendet werden.
Das unpersönliche deutsche **man** kann im Englischen durch **you**, **they** oder **one** ausgedrückt werden.

Subjekt	I	you	he	she	it	we	you	they

Objekt	me	you	him	her	it	us	you	them

Possessives

Possessives stehen immer vor dem Hauptwort und zeigen an, wem oder zu wem etwas gehört.

I	you	he	she	it	we	you	they
my	your	his	her	its	our	your	their

Possessive pronouns (Possessivpronomen)

Besitzanzeigende Fürwörter zeigen an, wem etwas gehört.

It's my book. It's **mine**.	It's his book. It's **his**.	It's our book. It's **ours**.
It's your book. It's **yours**.	It's her book. It's **hers**.	It's their book. It's **theirs**.

Question words (Fragewörter)

Who	What	Where	How often
Who is she?	**What**'s your name?	**Where** are you now?	**How often** do you go to the cinema?
Who are you?	**What** eats insects?	**Where** do you live?	
Who likes ice cream?	**What** does your dog eat?		
Who do you like?			

this / that – these / those

This / that, **these / those** sind Demonstrativpronomen, die verwendet werden, um Nähe oder Ferne auszudrücken.
This / these beschreibt etwas in der Nähe, **that / those** etwas weiter Entferntes.

I like **this** sweater here.	I like **that** sweater over there.	I like **these** shoes here.	I like **those** shoes over there.

one – ones

Wenn du ein Hauptwort nicht wiederholen willst, kannst du es durch **one / ones** ersetzen.

What **book** are you reading? **One** about a man travelling around Africa.
What **kind of books** do you like? **Ones** about travel.

some – any

Wenn du etwas Unzählbares beschreibst oder nach etwas fragst, von dem du weißt, dass es vorhanden ist, verwendest du **some**.
Wenn du fragen willst, ob es etwas gibt, oder wenn du sagen willst, dass es etwas nicht gibt, verwendest du **any**.

some	any	
We've got **some** cheese.	We haven't got **any** cheese.	Is there **any** milk in the fridge?
I've got **some** money.	I haven't got **any** money.	Have we got **any** strawberries?
Can I have **some** soup?	There aren't **any** onions in the kitchen.	Do they sell **any** sweets?

PREPOSITIONS (PRÄPOSITIONEN)

Präpositionen stehen vor einem Hauptwort oder Pronomen und zeigen die Richtung, den Ort (siehe "prepositions of place"), oder die Zeit (siehe "time prepositions") an.

Time prepositions (Präpositionen der Zeit)

My birthday is **on** February 12th / May 28th / September 5th.	The film starts **at** 7 o'clock / half past eight / six forty-five.
The concert's **on** Thursday, July 15th.	We have Maths **in** the morning / **in** the afternoon.
My sister's birthday is **in** December / April / June.	We go to bed late **at** night.

Prepositions of place (Directions) (Präpositionen des Ortes)

at	by	behind	in	in front of	inside	near
next to	on	opposite	outside	over	round	under

ADJECTIVES (ADJEKTIVE)

as ... as

Wenn du sagen willst, dass etwas (nicht) gleich ist wie etwas anderes, verwendest du **(not) as ... as**.

I am **as** intelligent **as** my sister.	He is **not as** tall **as** his father.

Comparatives & Superlatives (Vergleiche & Steigerung der Adjektive)

Einsilbige Adjektive steigerst du mit **-er** und **-est**. Bei mehr als zwei Silben steigerst du mit **more** und **most**. Eine Auflistung der am häufigsten verwendeten Adjektivsteigerungen findest du hier.

My bike is big**ger** than your bike.	My mum is **the most intelligent** person in our family.

Adjective	Comparative	Superlative
bad	**worse**	**worst**
big	big**ger**	big**gest**
cold	cold**er**	cold**est**
fast	fast**er**	fast**est**
good	**better**	**best**
hot	hot**ter**	hot**test**
long	long**er**	long**est**
new	new**er**	new**est**
old	old**er**	old**est**
rich	rich**er**	rich**est**
safe	saf**er**	saf**est**
small	small**er**	small**est**
strong	strong**er**	strong**est**
tall	tall**er**	tall**est**
young	young**er**	young**est**

Adjective	Comparative	Superlative
easy	eas**ier**	eas**iest**
funny	funn**ier**	funn**iest**
happy	happ**ier**	happ**iest**
heavy	heav**ier**	heav**iest**
pretty	prett**ier**	prett**iest**
ugly	ugl**ier**	ugl**iest**
beautiful	**more** beautiful	**most** beautiful
boring	**more** boring	**most** boring
dangerous	**more** dangerous	**most** dangerous
difficult	**more** difficult	**most** difficult
exciting	**more** exciting	**most** exciting
expensive	**more** expensive	**most** expensive
handsome	**more** handsome	**most** handsome
important	**more** important	**most** important
intelligent	**more** intelligent	**most** intelligent
poisonous	**more** poisonous	**most** poisonous
popular	**more** popular	**most** popular
relaxing	**more** relaxing	**most** relaxing

CONJUNCTIONS (KONJUNKTIONEN)

Linking words (*and, but, because*)

Konjunktionen verbinden Hauptsätze und Nebensätze miteinander.

We went to the cinema **and** watched a great film.	
but it was closed.	
because we had free tickets.	

So do/have I – Neither do/have I

Wenn du jemandem zustimmen willst („ich auch"), verwendest du **So do I**. Bei einer negativen Aussage, der du zustimmst („ich auch nicht"), verwendest du **Neither do I**.
Bei Modalverben und **have** wiederholst du das Verb, ansonsten verwendest du **do**.

I **like** rap. – **So do I.**	I **don't like** rock. – **Neither do I.**
I've **got** a laptop. – **So have I.**	I **haven't got** a laptop. – **Neither have I.**
I **can** play the piano. – **So can I.**	I **can't play** the piano. – **Neither can I.**
I **went** to the cinema last night. – **So did I.**	I **didn't go** to the cinema last night. – **Neither did I.**

why – because

Um die Ursache von etwas zu erfragen bzw. zu begründen, verwendest du **why** bzw. **because**.

Why did you go to the store? – **Because** I needed bread.

QUANTITY / MEASUREMENT (MENGENANGABEN)

How much is / are … ?

Mit **how much** wird nach der Menge (bei nicht zählbaren Hauptwörtern) oder nach dem Preis gefragt.

How much ice cream do you eat every day?	**How much** is the ice cream?	**How much** money have you got?	**How much** are the trainers?

Ordinal numbers

Cardinal		Ordinal
1	one	**first**
2	two	**second**
3	three	**third**
4	four	fourth
5	five	fifth
6	six	sixth
7	seven	seventh
8	eight	eighth
9	nine	ninth
10	ten	tenth
11	eleven	eleventh
12	twelve	twelfth
13	thirteen	thirteenth
14	fourteen	fourteenth
15	fifteen	fifteenth

Cardinal		Ordinal
16	sixteen	sixteenth
17	seventeen	seventeenth
18	eighteen	eighteenth
19	nineteen	nineteenth
20	twenty	twentieth
21	twenty-one	twenty-**first**
30	thirty	thirtieth
40	forty	fortieth
50	fifty	fiftieth
60	sixty	sixtieth
70	seventy	seventieth
80	eighty	eightieth
90	ninety	ninetieth
100	hundred	hundredth
101	a/one hundred and one	**the (one) hundred and first**

CLASSROOM LANGUAGE

Can you understand your teacher?

We have plenty of time.
Have a go.
Have a guess.
Don't worry about your pronunciation.
Don't worry, it'll get better.
Maybe this will help you.
Can anybody correct this sentence?
That's very good.
Well done.
That's nice.
I like that.
You did a great job.
That's correct.
That's quite right.
Yes, you've got it.
That's much better.
That's a lot better.
You didn't make a single mistake.
Your pronunciation is very good.
You're getting better all the time.
Work in pairs/threes/fours/fives.
Work in groups of two/three/four.

Stand up and find another partner.
Have you finished?
Do the next activity.
Let's check the answers.
Come out and write it on the board.
Repeat after me.
Again, please.
Would you like to answer question 3?
Right. Now we will go on to the next exercise.
Next one, please.
You have ten minutes to do this.
Your time is up.
Are you ready?
Any questions?
I'm afraid it's time to finish now.
We'll have to stop here.
Hang on a moment.
Just a moment, please.
One more thing before you go.
This is your homework.
Do exercise 11 on page 22 for your homework.
There is no homework today.

When you have a problem, say this:

Sorry? / Pardon?
Can you help me, please?
What's … in English, please?
I don't understand this.
Sorry, I've forgotten my … .
Sorry, what's our homework?

ENGLISH SOUNDS

[ɑː]	arm	[eə]	there	[ŋ]	song, long
[ʌ]	fun	[eɪ]	take, they	[p]	present, top
[e]	desk	[ɪə]	here	[r]	red, right
[ə]	a, an	[ɔɪ]	boy	[s]	sister, class
[ɜː]	girl, bird	[əʊ]	go, old	[t]	time, cat
[æ]	apple	[ʊə]	tourist	[z]	nose, dogs
[ɪ]	in, it	[b]	bag, club	[ʒ]	television
[i]	every	[d]	duck, card	[dʒ]	orange
[iː]	easy, eat	[f]	fish, laugh	[ʃ]	sure, English
[ɒ]	orange, sorry	[g]	get, dog	[tʃ]	child, cheese
[ɔː]	all, call	[h]	hot	[ð]	these, mother
[ʊ]	look	[j]	you	[θ]	think, mouth
[u]	February	[k]	can, duck	[v]	very, have
[uː]	food	[l]	lot, small	[w]	what, word
[aɪ]	eye, buy	[m]	more, mum		
[aʊ]	our	[n]	now, sun		

The English alphabet:

A	[eɪ]	**Q**	[kjuː]
B	[biː]	**R**	[ɑː]
C	[siː]	**S**	[es]
D	[diː]	**T**	[tiː]
E	[iː]	**U**	[juː]
F	[ef]	**V**	[viː]
G	[dʒi]	**W**	[ˈdʌbəljuː]
H	[eɪtʃ]	**X**	[eks]
I	[aɪ]	**Y**	[waɪ]
J	[dʒeɪ]	**Z**	[zed/ziː]
K	[keɪ]		
L	[el]		
M	[em]		
N	[en]		
O	[əʊ]		
P	[piː]		

WORDLIST

U6/10 = Unit 6 Exercise 10; **EU** = Extra Unit; **S1** = Story of the Stones Episode 1; **NYC2** = Kids in NYC 2;
G = Grammar; **F** = Fido; **DSC1** = Developing speaking competencies (The Twins 1); **C** = Culture (Life in the USA);
MORE 1 = Wörter, die schon in MORE 1 vorgekommen sind

A

a / an MORE 1	[ə, eɪ / ən]	ein/e
above MORE 1	[əˈbʌv]	(dar-)über, oberhalb
absent-minded U12/15	[ˌæbsntˈmaɪndɪd]	zerstreut
absolutely U9/10	[ˌæbsəˈluːtli]	absolut
accident MORE 1	[ˈæksɪdənt]	Unfall
ache U15/3	[eɪk]	Schmerz/en
acrobat U11/3	[ˈækrəbæt]	Akrobat/in
across MORE 1	[əˈkrɒs]	quer durch/über
active U17	[ˈæktɪv]	aktiv
activity MORE 1	[ækˈtɪvəti]	Aktivität
actually U11/2	[ˈæktʃuəli]	eigentlich; tatsächlich
add U3/9	[æd]	hinzufügen
address (pl -es) MORE 1	[əˈdres]	Adresse, Anschrift
adopt U12/3	[əˈdɒpt]	adoptieren
adult MORE 1	[ˈædʌlt]	Erwachsene/r
adventure MORE 1	[ədˈventʃə]	Abenteuer, Erlebnis
advice U3/6	[ədˈvaɪs]	Rat(schlag)
aeroplane U8/2	[ˈeərəpleɪn]	Flugzeug
a few U3/1	[ə fjuː]	ein paar
be afraid (of) U13/8	[biː əˈfreɪd əv]	Angst haben (vor)
I'm afraid (so/not) U13/S6	[aɪm ˌəˈfreɪd səʊ / nɒt]	leider / leider nicht
Africa U12/3	[ˈæfrɪkə]	Afrika
(be) after U9/S4	[biː ˈɑːftə]	her sein hinter
after all U7/9	[ɑːftər ˈɔːl]	schließlich
against MORE 1	[əˈgenst]	gegen
age MORE 1	[eɪdʒ]	Alter
aged (11) U4/3	[eɪdʒd]	(11) Jahre alt
(two days) ago MORE 1	[əˈgəʊ]	vor (zwei Tagen)
agree (with sb) U18	[əˈgriː wɪð ˈsʌmbədi]	(jemandem) zustimmen
air MORE 1	[eə]	Luft
airplane U9/9	[ˈeəpleɪn]	Flugzeug
airport U6/6	[ˈeəpɔːt]	Flughafen
alarm U2/2	[əˈlɑːm]	Angst; hier: Alarm
alien U3/4	[ˈeɪliən]	Außerirdische/r
alive U4/S2	[əˈlaɪv]	lebendig, am Leben
all day U1/12	[ˈɔːl deɪ]	den ganzen Tag
all the time U5/1	[ˈɔːl ðə ˈtaɪm]	die ganze Zeit
all over U12/3	[ɔːl ˈəʊvə]	überall auf/in
almost U2/S1	[ˈɔːlməʊst]	fast, beinahe
alone MORE 1	[əˈləʊn]	alleine
along U3/DSC1	[əˈlɒŋ]	entlang
the Alps U17/6	[ði ælps]	die Alpen
already U2/2	[ɔːlˈredi]	schon
altar U11/2	[ˈɔːltə]	Altar
amazing MORE 1	[əˈmeɪzɪŋ]	erstaunlich
Amazon U11/2	[ˈæməzən]	Amazonas
America C/p.138	[əˈmerɪkə]	Amerika
American U12/3	[əˈmerɪkən]	Amerikaner/in; amerikanisch
American football C/p.139	[əˈmerɪkən ˈfʊtbɔːl]	(American) Football
anaconda U5/13	[ˌænəˈkɒndə]	Anakonda
ancient U11	[ˈeɪnʃənt]	alt, antik
anecdote U12/15	[ˈænɪkdəʊt]	Anekdote
Angola U12/9	[æŋˈgəʊlə]	Angola
angry MORE 1	[ˈæŋgri]	verärgert, zornig, wütend
animal shelter U18/7	[ˈænɪməl ˌʃeltə]	Tierheim
ankle MORE 1	[ˈæŋkl]	Fußgelenk, Knöchel
anorak U7/3	[ˈænəræk]	Anorak
another MORE 1	[əˈnʌðə]	ein/e andere/r/s; weitere/r/s
answer MORE! 1	[ˈɑːnsə]	antworten; Antwort
Antarctic U18/10	[æntˈɑːktɪk]	Antarktis
antelope U5/11	[ˈæntɪləʊp]	Antilope
any MORE 1	[ˈeni]	irgendein/e; etwas
(not) any longer U13/S6	[nɒt ˈeni lɒŋə]	nicht mehr
(not) any more U7/7	[nɒt ˈeni ˈmɔː]	nicht mehr
anyone U3/6	[ˈeniwʌn]	irgendjemand
anyway MORE 1	[ˈeniweɪ]	jedenfalls; sowieso
apologise U3/DSC1	[əˈpɒlədʒaɪz]	sich entschuldigen
appear U17/7	[əˈpɪə]	erscheinen
applause U2/2	[əˈplɔːz]	Beifall
Arctic Sea U18/10	[ˈɑktɪk siː]	Arktischer Ozean
area U7/3	[ˈeəriə]	Gebiet, Region
argument EU/1	[ˈɑːgjʊmənt]	Wortwechsel; Streit
armchair U14/3	[ˈɑːmtʃeə]	Sessel, Lehnstuhl
(eight-)armed U1/11	[ɑːmd]	(acht-)armig
arrest U2/2	[əˈrest]	verhaften
arrive MORE 1	[əˈraɪv]	ankommen
art U1/2	[ɑːt]	Kunst
article MORE 1	[ˈɑːtɪkl]	(Zeitungs-)Artikel
as ... as MORE 1	[əz əz]	(genau)so ... wie

as much as U16/12	[əz mʌtʃ əz]	so viel wie
as soon as U1/4	[əz suːn əz]	so bald (wie)
as well as U16/10	[əz wel əz]	so wie; als auch
as well U16/10	[əz wel]	auch, ebenfalls
ash C/p.140	[æʃ]	Asche
be ashamed U8/7	[əˈʃeɪmd]	sich schämen
Asia U5/10	[ˈeɪʒə]	Asien
(fall) asleep U17/7	[fɔːl əsliːp]	einschlafen
assembly MORE 1	[əˈsembli]	Versammlung
assistant U2/1	[əˈsɪstənt]	Assistent/in, Mitarbeiter/in
astronaut U9/4	[ˈæstrənɔːt]	Astronaut/in
(not) at all U3/DSC1	[ət ɔːl]	gar nicht
Atlantian U5/6	[ətˈlæntɪən]	Bewohner/in von Atlantis
at least U13/12	[ət liːst]	mindestens
attack U1/9	[əˈtæk]	angreifen
attacker U1/8	[əˈtækə]	Angreifer/in
attempt U17/10	[əˈtempt]	Versuch, Anlauf
aunt MORE 1	[ɑːnt]	Tante
Austrian U17/6	[ˈɒstriːən]	österreichisch
avenue U15/NYC3	[ˈævənjuː]	(breite) Straße, Allee
average U16/10	[ˈævərɪdʒ]	durchschnittlich
away MORE 1	[əˈweɪ]	weg
awesome U3/8	[ˈɔːsəm]	beeindruckend
awful MORE 1	[ˈɔːfl]	schrecklich, scheußlich

B

back MORE 1	[bæk]	zurück
back U1/10	[bæk]	Rücken
backache U15/3	[ˈbækeɪk]	Rückenschmerzen
background U2/2	[ˈbækgraʊnd]	Hintergrund
backside (informal) C/p.138	[ˈbæksaɪd]	Hintern, Hinterteil
bad MORE 1	[bæd]	schlecht, böse
badly U15/4	[ˈbædli]	schwer, schlimm
badminton C/p.139	[ˈbædmɪntən]	Federball
ball gown C/p.138	[ˈbɔːl ˌgaʊn]	Ballkleid
bandage U11/8	[ˈbændɪdʒ]	Verband
bank MORE 1	[bæŋk]	Bank
bank U7/S3	[bæŋk]	Ufer, Böschung
bar U7/7	[bɑː]	Tafel, Riegel
barefoot U11/3	[ˈbeəfʊt]	barfuß
bark U9/1	[bɑːk]	bellen
baseball U10/NYC2	[ˈbeɪsbɔːl]	Baseball
basket U10/3	[ˈbɑːskɪt]	Korb
bat U10/NYC2	[bæt]	Schläger
bath U11/2	[bɑːθ]	Bad
bathing suit U16/7	[ˈbeɪðɪŋ suːt]	Badeanzug
bathroom MORE 1	[ˈbɑːθruːm]	Bad, Badezimmer
(be) like U1/12	[biː laɪk]	wie etwas sein
be lucky MORE 1	[biː ˈlʌki]	Glück haben
be scared MORE 1	[biː skeəd]	Angst haben
be worried U3/1	[biː ˈwʌrid]	sich Sorgen machen
beach MORE 1	[biːtʃ]	Strand
bear MORE 1	[beə]	Bär
beat U12/S5	[biːt]	schlagen
because of U3/6	[bɪkəz əv]	wegen, aufgrund
become MORE 1	[bɪˈkʌm]	werden
bedside table U14/3	[ˈbedsaɪd ˈteɪbl]	Nachttisch
beef MORE 1	[biːf]	Rindfleisch
beer U13/7	[bɪə]	Bier
begin MORE 1	[bɪˈgɪn]	anfangen, beginnen
beginner U2/F	[bɪˈgɪnə]	Anfänger/in
behaviour U3/6	[bɪˈheɪvjə]	Benehmen, Verhalten
behind MORE 1	[bɪˈhaɪnd]	hinter
believe MORE 1	[bɪˈliːv]	glauben
belong U14	[bɪˈlɒŋ]	zugehören; hingehören
below MORE 1	[bɪˈləʊ]	unten; darunter
belt U2/S1	[belt]	Gürtel
beside U6/G	[bɪˈsaɪd]	neben
between MORE 1	[bɪˈtwiːn]	zwischen
bike MORE 1	[baɪk]	Fahrrad
bird MORE 1	[bɜːd]	Vogel
bison C/p.140	[ˈbaɪsən]	Bison
bite MORE 1	[baɪt]	Biss; beißen
bleed C/p.141	[bliːd]	bluten
block U11/6	[blɒk]	Block, Klotz
blog U3/6	[blɒg]	Blog
blonde U10/NYC2	[blɒnd]	blond
blood U2/2	[blʌd]	Blut
blue whale U5/10	[bluː weɪl]	Blauwal
blue-ringed U1/7	[bluːrɪŋd]	blau beringt
board MORE 1	[bɔːd]	an Bord gehen
apple bobbing U4/1	[ˈæpl ˌbɒbɪŋ]	Apfeltauchen (traditionelles Halloween-Spiel)
body MORE 1	[ˈbɒdi]	Körper
bone U4/F	[bəʊn]	Knochen
book U17/DSC6	[bʊk]	buchen
bookshop U15/2	[ˈbʊkʃɒp]	Buchhandlung
(car) boot U13/6	[ˈkɑː buːt]	Kofferraum
bored MORE 1	[bɔːd]	gelangweilt
(be) born MORE 1	[bɔːn]	geboren
borrow (from) U4/4	[ˈbɒrəʊ]	ausleihen (von)
both MORE 1	[bəʊθ]	beide
bother U6/DSC2	[ˈbɒðə]	stören
Botswana U12/9	[bɒtˈswɑːnə]	Botswana

bottle MORE 1	[ˈbɒtl]	Flasche
bottom U7/2	[ˈbɒtəm]	untere/r/s
bowl U4/3	[bəʊl]	Schüssel
boyfriend MORE 1	[bɔɪfrend]	fester Freund
branch MORE 1	[brɑːntʃ]	Zweig; Ast
brave U4/2	[breɪv]	tapfer
Brazil U17/11	[brəˈzɪl]	Brasilien
break MORE 1	[breɪk]	(zer-)brechen
break U1/2	[breɪk]	Pause
break into U2/2	[ˈbreɪkˌɪntə]	einbrechen in
breathe U12/5	[briːð]	atmen
bridge MORE 1	[brɪdʒ]	Brücke
bright U1/9	[braɪt]	hell, leuchtend
brilliant MORE 1	[ˈbrɪliənt]	genial, toll
bring MORE 1	[brɪŋ]	(mit-)bringen
Britain MORE 1	[ˈbrɪtən]	Großbritannien
British MORE 1	[ˈbrɪtɪʃ]	britisch
brochure C/p.141	[ˈbrəʊʃə]	Broschüre, Prospekt
broom U9/1	[bruːm]	Besen
brush U18/1	[brʌʃ]	(ab-)bürsten
budgie MORE 1	[ˈbʌdʒi]	Wellensittich
build U7/3	[bɪld]	bauen
building MORE 1	[ˈbɪldɪŋ]	Gebäude
bully U3/7	[ˈbʊli]	tyrannisieren, mobben
bumblebee bat U5/10	[ˈbʌmblbiː bæt]	Hummelfledermaus
bun U5/16	[bʌn]	Semmel, Brötchen
burn U12/5	[bɜːn]	(ver-)brennen
on business U6/7	[ɒn ˈbɪznɪs]	geschäftlich, auf Dienstreise
busy MORE 1	[ˈbɪzi]	beschäftigt
button MORE 1	[ˈbʌtn]	Knopf, Taste
buy MORE 1	[baɪ]	kaufen
by MORE 1	[baɪ]	an; bei; mit
by U12/12	[baɪ]	bis (spätestens)
by accident U2/3	[baɪ ˈæksɪdnt]	versehentlich, zufällig
by the way U10/NYC2	[baɪ ðə weɪ]	übrigens
bye MORE 1	[baɪ]	tschüss, tschau

C

cabbage U10/1	[ˈkæbɪdʒ]	Kohl, Kraut
cabin C/p.139	[ˈkæbɪn]	Hütte
cache U7/7	[kæʃ]	Versteck
cage MORE 1	[keɪdʒ]	Käfig
cake MORE 1	[keɪk]	Kuchen
California U17/4	[kælɪˈfɔːnjə]	Kalifornien
call MORE 1	[kɔːl]	(an-)rufen
call U18/10	[kɔːl]	nennen
call back U15/1	[kɔːl bæk]	zurückrufen
called MORE 1	[kɔːld]	genannt
calm U2/7	[kɑːm]	ruhig
calm down U9/S4	[kɑːm ˈdaʊn]	sich beruhigen
Cambodia U12/3	[kæmˈbəʊdiə]	Kambodscha
camera MORE 1	[ˈkæmərə]	Kamera, Fotoapparat
camp U7/3	[kæmp]	Zeltlager
canary U11/8	[kəˈneəri]	Kanarienvogel
cancer U15/10	[ˈkænsə]	Krebs (Krankheit)
candle U4/3	[ˈkændl]	Kerze
canoeing U7/3	[kəˈnuːɪŋ]	Paddeln, Kanufahren
capital MORE 1	[ˈkæpɪtl]	Hauptstadt
care about U11/3	[ˈkeərəˌbaʊt]	sich aus … etw. machen
care for somebody U18	[keə fə ˈsʌmbədi]	sich um jemanden kümmern
I don't care. U2/2	[aɪ dəʊnt ˈkeə]	Ist mir egal.
careful MORE 1	[ˈkeəfl]	vorsichtig
carpet U14/3	[ˈkɑːpɪt]	Teppich
carry U5/10	[ˈkæri]	(über-)tragen
carry U9/1	[ˈkæri]	befördern, transportieren
case MORE 1	[keɪs]	Fall; Hülle
castle MORE 1	[ˈkɑːsl]	Schloss, Burg
catch MORE 1	[kætʃ]	fangen, festnehmen
cathedral U11/2	[kəˈθiːdrəl]	Kathedrale, Dom
cattle U11/3	[ˈkætl]	Vieh
ceiling C/p.141	[ˈsiːlɪŋ]	(Zimmer-)Decke
cell phone U18/NYC4	[sel fəʊn]	Handy
cellar U14/1	[ˈselə]	Keller
centimetre U5/10	[ˈsentɪˌmiːtə]	Zentimeter
Central Asia U14/1	[ˈsentrəl ˈeɪʒə]	Zentralasien
certain U14/DSC5	[ˈsɜːtn]	sicher, gewiss
certainly MORE 1	[ˈsɜːtnli]	sicherlich, bestimmt
chain U13/1	[tʃeɪn]	Kette
challenge U17/10	[ˈtʃælɪndʒ]	Herausforderung
chance U2/S1	[tʃɑːnts]	Chance
change MORE 1	[tʃeɪndʒ]	(sich) (ver-)ändern
change trains U6/6	[tʃeɪndʒ treɪns]	umsteigen
change one's mind U12/DSC4	[tʃeɪndʒ wʌnz maɪnd]	seine Meinung ändern
character U2/2	[ˈkærɪktə]	Charakter; hier: Person
chase MORE 1	[tʃeɪs]	verfolgen, jagen
chaser C/p.141	[ˈtʃeɪsə]	Jäger/in
chart U15/1	[tʃɑːt]	Tabelle, Karte
charter school C/p.138	[ˈtʃɑːtə ˌskuːl]	Charterschule
chat U12/5	[tʃæt]	plaudern, chatten; Unterhaltung, Plauderei
cheap MORE 1	[tʃiːp]	billig
cheek U11/8	[tʃiːk]	Wange, Backe
cheesecake U10/1	[ˈtʃiːzkeɪk]	Käsekuchen
cheetah U5/10	[ˈtʃiːtə]	Gepard

chef U10/7	[ʃef]	Koch, Köchin
chemist's U6/2	[ˈkemɪsts]	Apotheke, Drogerie
chess EU/1	[tʃes]	Schach(spiel)
chief U4/9	[tʃiːf]	Haupt-, Chef-
child (pl children) MORE 1	[tʃaɪld, ˈtʃɪldrən]	Kind
chimpanzee U5/6	[ˌtʃɪmpænˈziː]	Schimpanse
chips MORE 1	[tʃɪps]	Pommes
chocolates U3/1	[ˈtʃɒklǝts]	Pralinen
choose MORE 1	[tʃuːz]	(aus-)wählen
chop U10/7	[tʃɒp]	Kotelett
(household) chores U1/2	[ˈhaʊshəʊld ˌtʃɔːz]	Aufgaben im Haushalt
church U6/2	[tʃɜːtʃ]	Kirche
cigar U13/7	[sɪˈɡɑː]	Zigarre
city MORE 1	[sɪti]	Stadt
class MORE 1	[klɑːs]	(Schul-)Klasse
classmate U18/5	[ˈklɑːsmeɪt]	Klassenkamerad/in, Mitschüler/in
clean (up) MORE 1	[kliːn ʌp]	sauber machen; putzen
clean U2/2	[kliːn]	sauber
cleaning lady U3/3	[ˈkliːnɪŋ ˈleɪdi]	Putzfrau
clear U16/10	[klɪər]	hier: wolkenlos
clear away U15/10	[klɪər əˈweɪ]	wegräumen, entfernen
clear up U16/3	[klɪər ˈʌp]	(auf-)klären; hier: sich aufhellen
cliff U17/10	[klɪf]	Klippe, Felsen
climb MORE 1	[klaɪm]	(hinauf-)steigen; klettern
climber U17/4	[ˈklaɪmə]	Kletterer/in
clock tower U6/DSC2	[klɒk taʊə]	Uhrturm
close MORE 1	[kləʊz]	schließen, zumachen
closed U9/DSC3	[kləʊzd]	geschlossen, zu
clothes (no pl) MORE 1	[kləʊðz]	Kleider, Kleidung
cloud U9/9	[klaʊd]	Wolke
cloudy U16/2	[ˈklaʊdi]	bewölkt
clue MORE 1	[kluː]	Hinweis, Tipp
I have no clue. U15/NYC3	[aɪ həv nəʊ ˈkluː]	Ich habe keine Ahnung.
coast U16/1	[kəʊst]	Küste
coat U8/G	[kəʊt]	Mantel
coffee MORE 1	[ˈkɒfi]	Kaffee
coin U7/7	[kɔɪn]	Münze, Geldstück
coke U12/DCS4	[kəʊk]	Cola
collect MORE 1	[kəˈlekt]	sammeln
come after U4/2	[kʌm ˈɑːftə]	jagen, verfolgen
come along U7/3	[kʌm əˈlɒŋ]	mitkommen
come over MORE 1	[kʌm ˈəʊvə]	vorbeikommen
comfortable U9/11	[ˈkʌmftəbl]	bequem
command U2/2	[kəˈmɑːnd]	Befehl
comment U8/7	[ˈkɒment]	kommentieren
communication U8/7	[kəˌmjuːnɪˈkeɪʃn]	Kommunikation
company U15/10	[ˈkʌmpəni]	Firma, Unternehmen
company U18/7	[ˈkʌmpəni]	Gesellschaft
compare U5	[kəmˈpeər]	vergleichen
competition U17/5	[ˌkɒmpəˈtɪʃn]	Wettbewerb
complain U13/8	[kəmˈpleɪn]	sich beschweren
complete MORE 1	[kəmˈpliːt]	vervollständigen
complicated EU/1	[ˈkɒmplɪkeɪtɪd]	kompliziert; schwierig
compliment U10/F	[ˈkɒmplɪmənt]	Kompliment
conference U6/6	[ˈkɒnfrnts]	Konferenz, Tagung
confused U3/1	[kənˈfjuːzd]	verwirrt
confusing U3/8	[kənˈfjuːzɪŋ]	verwirrend
connect U14/1	[kəˈnekt]	anschließen; verbinden
consequence U15/11	[ˈkɒntsɪkwənts]	Folge, Konsequenz
contact MORE 1	[ˈkɒntækt]	kontaktieren
continue U16/1	[kənˈtɪnjuː]	andauern; weitergehen
conversation MORE 1	[ˌkɒnvəˈseɪʃn]	Gespräch, Unterhaltung
convert U16/10	[kənˈvɜːt]	umwandeln
cook MORE 1	[kʊk]	Koch, Köchin; kochen
cooker U13/6	[ˈkʊkə]	Herd
cool U11/10	[kuːl]	kühl
coordinate U7/7	[kəʊˈɔːdɪnət]	Koordinate
corner MORE 1	[ˈkɔːnər]	Ecke
corridor U11/11	[ˈkɒrɪdɔː]	Flur, Gang, Korridor
cost C/p.138	[kɒst]	kosten
Costa Rica U14/2	[ˌkɒstə ˈriːkə]	Costa Rica
Costa Rican U14/1	[ˌkɒstə ˈriːkən]	costa-ricanisch
costume U4/1	[ˈkɒstjuːm]	Tracht; Kostüm
cotton U14/DSC5	[ˈkɒtn]	Baumwolle
could MORE 1	[kʊd]	könnte/n, könntest
couldn't (could not) U2/G	[ˈkʊdnt]	könnte/n nicht; konnte/n nicht
count MORE 1	[kaʊnt]	zählen
count to MORE 1	[kaʊnt ˈʌp]	hochzählen, zusammenzählen
country MORE 1	[ˈkʌntri]	Land; Staat
countryside U12/5	[ˈkʌntrisaɪd]	Land, Landschaft
couple U10/8	[ˈkʌpl]	Paar
courage U13/S6	[ˈkʌrɪdʒ]	Mut, Tapferkeit
course U12/5	[kɔːs]	Kurs, Lehrgang
main course U10/7	[ˈmeɪn kɔːs]	Hauptgericht, Hauptgang
cousin U12/1	[ˈkʌzn]	Cousin/e
cover MORE 1	[ˈkʌvər]	bedecken, verdecken
cover U6/6	[ˈkræk]	hier: Titelseite
Crack! U9/1	[kræk]	Knack!
crash U8/10	[kræʃ]	zu Bruch fahren
crazy MORE 1	[ˈkreɪzi]	verrückt
create MORE 1	[kriˈeɪt]	erstellen, entwerfen
creature U5/18	[ˈkriːtʃə]	Kreatur, Lebewesen
cricket U17/DSC6	[ˈkrɪkɪt]	Kricket
crocodile MORE 1	[ˈkrɒkədaɪl]	Krokodil

cross U6/1	[krɒs]	durchqueren, überqueren	
cross U11/2	[krɒs]	Kreuz	
cruise (ship) U1/1	[kruːz ʃɪp]	Kreuzfahrt(schiff)	
cry MORE 1	[kraɪ]	weinen; schreien	
cry U7/S3	[kraɪ]	Schrei	
cup U5/15	[kʌp]	Tasse	
cupboard U14/3	[ˈkʌbəd]	Schrank	
curse U11/1	[kɜːs]	Fluch	
curtain U14/3	[ˈkɜːtən]	Vorhang	
customer MORE 1	[kʌstəmər]	Kunde, Kundin	
cut MORE 1	[kʌt]	schneiden	
cut down U15/10	[kʌt daʊn]	fällen	
cycle U3/DSC1	[ˈsaɪkl]	Rad fahren	

D

daily U1/3	[ˈdeɪli]	täglich	
damn (informal) U12/15	[dæm]	verdammt	
dance MORE 1	[dɑːnts]	tanzen	
dancer U11/3	[ˈdɑːnsə]	Tänzer/in	
danger U4/S2	[ˈdeɪndʒə]	Gefahr	
dangerous MORE 1	[ˈdeɪndʒərəs]	gefährlich	
dark MORE 1	[dɑːk]	dunkel, finster	
dark U4/3	[dɑːk]	Dunkelheit	
date C/p.138	[deɪt]	Verabredung	
daughter MORE 1	[ˈdɔːtə]	Tochter	
dead U2/S1	[ded]	tot	
decide MORE 1	[dɪˈsaɪd]	entscheiden	
decision U12/5	[dɪˈsɪʒən]	Entscheidung	
deckchair U13/6	[ˈdektʃeə]	Liegestuhl	
deep MORE 1	[diːp]	tief	
definitely U13/10	[ˈdefənətli]	eindeutig, definitiv; auf jeden Fall	
degree (°) U16/3	[dɪˈɡriː]	Grad (°)	
delete U12/13	[dɪˈliːt]	streichen, löschen	
delicious U3/DSC1	[dɪˈlɪʃəs]	köstlich	
delta U11/2	[ˈdeltə]	Delta, Flussmündung	
demon U4/S2	[ˈdiːmən]	Dämon	
depend U5/NYC1	[dɪˈpend]	abhängen von	
describe MORE 1	[dɪˈskraɪb]	beschreiben	
desert U5/10	[ˈdezət]	Wüste	
design U5/18	[dɪˈzaɪn]	gestalten, entwerfen	
design and technology U1/4	[dɪˈzaɪn ənd tekˈnɒlədʒi]	Design und technisches Zeichnen	
desk MORE 1	[desk]	Schreibtisch	
dessert MORE 1	[dɪˈzɜːt]	Nachtisch, Dessert	
destroy U9/10	[dɪˈstrɔɪ]	zerstören	
detail U6/11	[ˈdiːteɪl]	Detail, Einzelheit	

diamond U11/14	[ˈdaɪəmənd]	Diamant	
diary MORE 1	[ˈdaɪəri]	Tagebuch	
dictionary U14/8	[ˈdɪkʃənəri]	Wörterbuch	
die (from) MORE 1	[daɪ]	sterben (an/von)	
difference MORE 1	[ˈdɪfərənts]	Unterschied	
different MORE 1	[ˈdɪfrənt]	verschieden/e; anders	
difficult U3/8	[ˈdɪfɪklt]	schwierig, schwer	
dinner lady MORE 1	[ˈdɪnə ˈleɪdi]	Mitarbeiterin einer Schulkantine	
directions U6/5	[dɪˈrekʃns]	Anweisungen	
director U3/2	[daɪˈrektə]	Direktor/in	
dirty U2/2	[ˈdɜːti]	dreckig, schmutzig	
disagree with sb U18	[dɪsəˈɡriː]	jmd nicht zustimmen, nicht übereinstimmen	
disappear U4/7	[dɪsəˈpɪə]	verschwinden	
disappointment U9/DSC3	[ˌdɪsəˈpɔɪntmənt]	Enttäuschung	
disaster C/p.138	[dɪˈzɑːstə]	Katastrophe, Desaster	
discover U11/8	[dɪˈskʌvə]	herausfinden, entdecken	
discuss MORE 1	[dɪˈskʌs]	besprechen	
the dishes (pl) U2/5	[ðə ˈdɪʃɪz]	das Geschirr	
disk U9/9	[dɪsk]	Scheibe	
dismay U3/DSC1	[dɪˈsmeɪ]	Bestürzung	
doctor U2/2	[ˈdɒktə]	Arzt, Ärztin	
document U11/3	[ˈdɒkjʊmənt]	Dokument	
dollar U12/3	[ˈdɒlə]	Dollar	
dolphin U5/11	[ˈdɒlfɪn]	Delphin	
done MORE 1	[dʌn]	fertig	
doorbell U13/7	[ˈdɔːbel]	Türklingel	
dos and don'ts U3/6	[duːz ænd dəʊnts]	was man tun und nicht tun sollte	
down MORE 1	[daʊn]	hinunter, hinab	
down the road U12/9	[daʊn ðə rəʊd]	in/von unserer Straße	
Down Under U1/1	[daʊn ˈʌndə]	Australien und Neuseeland	
dragon U5/6	[ˈdræɡən]	Drache	
draw MORE 1	[drɔː]	malen; zeichnen	
dream MORE 1	[driːm]	Traum; träumen	
dress MORE 1	[dres]	Kleid	
drink MORE 1	[drɪŋk]	trinken; Getränk	
drive MORE 1	[draɪv]	fahren; führen; Fahrt	
drive U4/5	[draɪv]	Auffahrt, Einfahrt	
driveway C/p.138	[ˈdraɪvweɪ]	Auffahrt, Einfahrt	
driving test U8/10	[ˈdraɪvɪŋ test]	Fahrprüfung	
drop MORE 1	[drɒp]	fallen lassen	
drop U16/7	[drɒp]	sinken	
dry U16/1	[draɪ]	trocken	
dry U18/1	[draɪ]	(ab-)trocknen	
duck U11/3	[dʌk]	Ente	
during U1/9	[ˈdjʊərɪŋ]	während	
dustbin U9/1	[ˈdʌstbɪn]	Mülleimer	

E

each other U14/4	[iːtʃ 'ʌðə]	einander, gegenseitig
eagle MORE 1	['iːgl]	Adler
earache U15/3	[',ɪəreɪk]	Ohrenschmerzen
early MORE 1	['ɜːli]	früh
earth MORE 1	[ɜːθ]	Erde
easily U11/12	['iːzɪli]	leicht, einfach
easy MORE 1	['iːzi]	einfach
east U5/10	[iːst]	östlich, Ost-; Osten
eat in U12/DSC4	[iːt ɪn]	hier essen
education U17/10	[edjʊ'keɪʃn]	(Aus-)Bildung
Egypt MORE 1	['iːdʒɪpt]	Ägypten
Egyptian U11/2	[ɪ'dʒɪpʃən]	Ägypter/in; ägyptisch
(not) either of them U15/1	['aɪðə əv ðəm]	keine/r/s von beiden
electricity U14/1	[ɪlek'trɪsəti]	Elektrizität, Strom
elementary school C/p.138	[elɪ'mentəri ˌskuːl]	Volksschule
something else U7/7	[sʌmθɪŋ'els]	noch etwas
embarrassed U3/1	[ɪm'bærəst]	verlegen
embarrassing U3	[ɪm'bærəsɪŋ]	peinlich, unangenehm
emergency MORE 1	[ɪ'mɜːdʒənsi]	Notfall, Notdienst
emperor U11/2	['empərə]	Kaiser
emperor penguin U18/10	['empərə ˌpeŋgwɪn]	Kaiserpinguin
empty MORE 1	['empti]	leer
in the end U3/DSC1	[ɪn ðiː end]	schließlich, am Ende
ending MORE 1	['endɪŋ]	Ende, Schluss
Englishman (pl -men) U11/8	['ɪŋglɪʃmən]	Engländer
enjoy MORE 1	[ɪn'dʒɔɪ]	genießen
enough MORE 1	[ɪ'nʌf]	genügend, genug
entrance U11/12	['entrəns]	Eingang
equipment U17/DSC6	[ɪ'kwɪpmənt]	Ausrüstung
erupt C/p.140	[ɪ'rʌpt]	ausbrechen
(volcanic) eruption C/p.140	[vɒlˌkænɪk ɪ'rʌpʃən]	(Vulkan-)Ausbruch
escape U9/S4	[ɪ'skeɪp]	(ent-)fliehen; entkommen
especially U7/7	[ɪ'speʃli]	besonders
Estuarine crocodile U5/10	['estjʊəriːn 'krɒkədaɪl]	Salzwasserkrokodil
etc. (et cetera) U4/3	[et 'setərə]	usw., etc.
Ethiopia U12/3	[ˌiːθi'əʊpiə]	Äthiopien
even U9/9	['iːvən]	sogar
even U16/10	['iːvən]	noch
ever MORE 1	['evə]	je
evergreen C/p.140	['evəgriːn]	immergrün
every MORE 1	['evri]	jede/r/s
everybody U6/6	['evribɒdi]	jede/r; alle
everyone U1/6	['evriwʌn]	jede/r; alle
everything MORE 1	['evriθɪŋ]	alles
everywhere MORE 1	['evriweə]	überall
evil U4/S2	['iːvəl]	das Böse
exactly U7/7	[ɪg'zæktli]	genau
for example U7/7	[fər ɪg'zɑːmpl]	zum Beispiel
excellent MORE 1	['eksələnt]	ausgezeichnet
excited MORE 1	[ɪk'saɪtɪd]	aufgeregt
exciting MORE 1	[ɪk'saɪtɪŋ]	aufregend; spannend
excuse U8/7	[ɪk'skjuːz]	Ausrede
(do) exercise U14/DSC5	['eksəsaɪz]	trainieren
exotic U5/6	[ɪg'zɒtɪk]	exotisch; fremdländisch
expectation U16	[ˌekspek'teɪʃn]	Erwartung
expensive U2/7	[ɪk'spensɪv]	teuer
experience C/p.141	[ɪk'spɪəriənts]	Erfahrung
experiment U2/2	[ɪk'sperɪmənt]	Experiment, Versuch
expert U9/9	['ekspɜːt]	Experte, Expertin
explain U3/1	[ɪk'spleɪn]	erklären
explode U9/1	[ɪk'spləʊd]	explodieren
expression U7/S3	[ɪk'spreʃn]	Ausdruck
extend U3/DSC1	[ɪk'stend]	erweitern
extra U3/1	['ekstrə]	mehr; besonders; Extra
extreme U17/10	[ɪk'striːm]	extrem

F

face MORE 1	[feɪs]	Gesicht
face U17/10	[feɪs]	sich etwas aussetzen; sich zuwenden
face U14/DSC5	[feɪs]	Ziffernblatt
fact U2/2	[fækt]	Tatsache, Fakt; Wirklichkeit
fail somebody U2/S1	['feɪl ˌsʌmbədi]	jemanden enttäuschen
(it isn't) fair U10/NYC2	[ɪt ɪznt feə]	(es ist nicht) fair
fake U9/9	[feɪk]	Fälschung
fall asleep U17/7	[fɔːl ə'sliːp]	einschlafen
fall off U8/11	[fɔːl ɒf]	herunterfallen
fall over U11/12	[fɔːl 'əʊvə]	hinfallen; umfallen
false MORE 1	[fɒls]	falsch
famous MORE 1	['feɪməs]	berühmt
fancy dress U8/13	[ˌfænsi 'dres]	Verkleidung, Kostüm
far away U4/5	[fɑːr ə'weɪ]	weit weg, fern
farewell U13/S6	[feə'wel]	Abschied
farm MORE 1	[fɑːm]	Bauernhof
farmer U11/3	['fɑːmə]	Bauer, Bäuerin
fast MORE 1	[fɑːst]	schnell
fat U5/G	[fæt]	dick, fett
fat U11/3	[fæt]	Fett
fault MORE 1	[fɔːlt]	Schuld

favour, favor (AE) U5/NYC1	[ˈfeɪvə]	Gefallen	
favourite MORE 1	[ˈfeɪvrɪt]	Lieblings-	
fear U4/2	[fɪə]	fürchten	
fear U17/10	[fɪə]	Furcht, Angst	
feather U13/6	[ˈfeðə]	Feder	
feed MORE 1	[fiːd]	zu essen geben, füttern	
fence U13/6	[fens]	Zaun	
(a) few U3/1	[ə fjuː]	ein paar; einige	
field U7/1	[fiːld]	Feld; Spielfeld	
fight MORE 1	[faɪt]	kämpfen; Kampf	
file U12/13	[faɪl]	Ordner; (Akten-)Hefter	
fill U11/10	[fɪl]	füllen	
final U13/S6	[ˈfaɪnəl]	letzte/r/s, End-	
finally MORE 1	[ˈfaɪnəli]	schließlich; endlich	
find out U7/8	[faɪnd ˈaʊt]	herausfinden	
fingerprint U2/2	[ˈfɪŋɡəprɪnt]	Fingerabdruck	
finish U1/2	[ˈfɪnɪʃ]	aufhören; beenden; vervollständigen	
fire MORE 1	[ˈfaɪə]	Feuer	
first name U12/1	[ˈfɜːst ˌneɪm]	Vorname	
first thing U14/DSC5	[ˈfɜːst θɪŋ]	gleich als erstes	
fishing rod MORE 1	[ˈfɪʃɪŋ rɒd]	Angelrute	
get fit EU/1	[ɡet ˈfɪt]	sich fit machen	
fix U18/10	[fɪks]	befestigen	
flag U10/7	[flæɡ]	Flagge, Fähnchen	
flat MORE 1	[flæt]	Wohnung	
flight U2/2	[flaɪt]	Flug	
float U13/1	[fləʊt]	schweben	
float U14/1	[fləʊt]	schwimmen, oben bleiben	
floor MORE 1	[flɔː]	Boden; Stockwerk	
flower C/p.138	[ˈflaʊə]	Blume	
fly MORE 1	[flaɪ]	fliegen	
fog U16/3	[fɒɡ]	Nebel	
foggy U16/2	[ˈfɒɡi]	neblig	
follow MORE 1	[ˈfɒləʊ]	folgen	
following MORE 1	[ˈfɒləʊɪŋ]	folgende/r/s	
food MORE 1	[fuːd]	Essen	
fool U3/DSC1	[fuːl]	Dummkopf, Narr	
fool U9/9	[fuːl]	hereinlegen, täuschen	
foot (pl. feet) MORE 1	[fʊt]	Fuß	
footprint U2/2	[ˈfʊtprɪnt]	Fußabdruck	
for example U7/7	[fə ɪɡˈzɑːmpl]	zum Beispiel	
for sure (informal) U11/S5	[fə ˈʃɔː]	bestimmt, ganz sicher	
forecast U16/3	[ˈfɔːkɑːst]	Vorhersage	
foreign language U12/5	[ˈfɒrən ˌlæŋɡwɪdʒ]	Fremdsprache	
forest U6/1	[ˈfɒrɪst]	Wald	
forever U4/S2	[fəˈrevə]	für immer	
forget MORE 1	[fəˈɡet]	vergessen	
forgive U2/S1	[fəˈɡɪv]	vergeben	
former U17/10	[ˈfɔːmə]	ehemalig, früher	
formula U16/1	[ˈfɔːmjələ]	Formel	
foundation U12/3	[faʊnˈdeɪʃən]	Stiftung	
fountain U6/DSC2	[ˈfaʊntɪn]	Springbrunnen	
free MORE 1	[friː]	befreien; frei, kostenlos	
free climbing U17/10	[ˈfriː ˌklaɪmɪŋ]	Freiklettern	
freedom U17/10	[ˈfriːdəm]	Freiheit, Unabhängigkeit	
French MORE 1	[frentʃ]	französisch; Französisch	
fridge U10/7	[frɪdʒ]	Kühlschrank	
friendly U5/6	[ˈfrendli]	freundlich	
front MORE 1	[frʌnt]	vorder-	
front door MORE 1	[frʌnt ˈdɔː]	Vordertür; Haustür	
full U11/8	[fʊl]	voll	
full U17/10	[fʊl]	erfüllt	
funny MORE 1	[ˈfʌni]	lustig, komisch	
furious U1/11	[ˈfjʊəriəs]	wütend	
furniture U14	[ˈfɜːnɪtʃə]	Möbel	
future U17/10	[ˈfjuːtʃə]	Zukunft	

G

galaxy U9/4	[ˈɡæləksi]	Galaxie	
gaming cards U5/6	[ˈɡeɪmɪŋ kɑːds]	Spielkarten	
garage MORE 1	[ˈɡærɑːʒ]	Garage	
garden shed 13/7	[ˈɡɑːdən ʃed]	Gartenhäuschen	
gas U9/S4	[ɡæs]	Gas	
gasoline C/p.138	[ˈɡæsəliːn]	Benzin	
gate U4/5	[ɡeɪt]	Tor	
generally U16/10	[ˈdʒenrli]	im Allgemeinen	
genius U12/15	[ˈdʒiːniəs]	Genie	
gentleman (pl gentlemen) U2/2	[ˈdʒentlmən, ˈdʒentlmən]	Gentleman; Herr	
geo-caching U7/7	[ˈdʒiːəʊkæʃɪŋ]	Geo-caching, GPS-Schnitzeljagd	
geography U1/4	[ˈdʒɒɡrəfi]	Erdkunde, Geografie	
German U9/DSC3	[ˈdʒɜːmən]	deutsch; Deutsch	
get MORE 1	[ɡet]	erhalten, bekommen; holen	
get dressed U1/2	[ɡet drest]	sich anziehen	
get home U1/2	[ɡet həʊm]	nach Hause kommen	
I don't get it. U4/S2	[aɪ dəʊnt ɡet ɪt]	Verstehe ich nicht.	
get in touch U2/S1	[ɡet ɪn tʌtʃ]	kontaktieren, sich in Verbindung setzen	
get into trouble U5/2	[ɡet ˈɪntuː ˈtrʌbl]	in Schwierigkeiten geraten	
get lost U6/7	[ɡet ˈlɒst]	sich verirren; sich verlaufen haben	
get on U12/5	[ɡet ɒn]	ein-/zusteigen	
get out (of) MORE 1	[ɡet ˈaʊt əv]	hinauskommen, herauskommen (aus)	

get stuck U13/2	[get 'stʌk]	festsitzen
get up MORE 1	[get ʌp]	aufstehen
ghost U4/1	[gəʊst]	Geist
giant U17/G	['dʒaɪnt]	Riesen-, riesig
giraffe U5/11	[dʒə'rɑːf]	Giraffe
girlfriend U2/2	['gɜːlfrend]	Freundin
give MORE 1	[gɪv]	geben
give directions U6/5	[gɪv daɪ'rekʃəns]	den Weg beschreiben
give up MORE 1	[gɪv ʌp]	aufgeben
give way to U16/1	[gɪv weɪ tu]	in etwas übergehen
glad U1/1	[glæd]	froh
glass U7/7	[glɑːs]	Glas
glasses U11/2	['glɑːsəz]	Brille
global U17/10	['gləʊbl]	weltweit, global
Go ahead! U6/9	[gəʊ ə'hed]	Komm schon!
go along U7/7	[gəʊ ə'lɒŋ]	mitgehen
go for a run U2/5	[gəʊ fɔː ə rʌn]	laufen gehen
go for a walk U16/5	[gəʊ fɔː ə wɔːk]	spazieren gehen
go off U2/2	[gəʊ 'ɒf]	losgehen, weggehen; abgehen; ausgehen
go past U6/1	[gəʊ pɑːst]	vorbeigehen
go red EU/1	[gəʊ 'red]	rot werden
go to sleep MORE 1	[gəʊ tə 'sliːp]	einschlafen
go up U16/4	[gəʊ 'ʌp]	steigen
go wrong U3/6	[gəʊ rɒŋ]	schief gehen
goal U15/G	[gəʊl]	Tor; Ziel
goalie (informal) U17/8	['gəʊli]	Tormann, Torfrau
goat U11/3	[gəʊt]	Ziege
god U11/8	[gɒd]	Gott
go-kart EU/1	['gəʊkɑːt]	Gokart
gold MORE 1	[gəʊld]	Gold; golden
goldfish U18/7	['gəʊldfɪʃ]	Goldfisch
golf U1/9	[gɒlf]	Golf
Good luck! U6/1	[gʊd lʌk]	Viel Glück!
Goodness me! U2/2	['gʊdnəs 'miː]	Du lieber Himmel!
Oh, my goodness! U11/S5	[əʊ maɪ 'gʊdnəss]	Ach du meine Güte!
goose (pl geese) U11/2	[guːs, giːs]	Gans
Got you! U18/NYC4	[gɒt jʊ]	Hab' dich!
grab U18/NYC4	[græb]	greifen, nehmen
gram U5/10	[græm]	Gramm
grandfather U12/1	['grændfɑːðə]	Großvater
grandmother U12/1	['grændmʌðə]	Großmutter
grandparents (pl) MORE 1	['grænpeərənts]	Großeltern
grade (AE) C/p.138	[greɪd]	Jahrgangsstufe
grape U10/1	[greɪp]	Traube
grilled U15/NYC3	[grɪld]	gegrillt
grizzly bear C/p.140	[ˌgrɪzli 'beə]	Grizzlybär
ground MORE 1	[graʊnd]	(Erd-)Boden, Erde
group MORE 1	[gruːp]	Gruppe
grow U5/14	[grəʊ]	wachsen; hier: werden
grow up U17/4	[grəʊ 'ʌp]	aufwachsen
guard U2/2	[gɑːd]	Wache, Wachposten
guard U11/8	[gɑːd]	bewachen
guess MORE 1	[ges]	(er-)raten
guide U7/3	[gaɪd]	(Reise-)Führer, Reiseleiter
guinea pig MORE 1	['gɪni pɪg]	Meerschweinchen
guys (informal) MORE 1	[gaɪz]	Leute
gym U14/DSC5	[dʒɪm]	Turnsaal; Fitnesscenter

H

hairdresser C/p.138	['heəˌdresə]	Friseur/in
hairy U5/4	['heəri]	haarig, stark behaart
half (pl halves) MORE 1	[hɑːf, hɑːvz]	Hälfte
half an hour MORE 1	[hɑːf ən aʊə]	eine halbe Stunde
Halloween U4/1	[hæləʊiːn]	Halloween
ham MORE 1	[hæm]	Schinken
handful U7/7	['hændfʊl]	eine Hand voll
hang around U12/5	[hæŋ ə'raʊnd]	herumlungern
hang on U3/DSC1	[hæŋ 'ɒn]	durchhalten; hier: warten
happen U2/2	[hæpən]	geschehen
happy MORE 1	['hæpi]	glücklich, fröhlich
hard MORE 1	[hɑːd]	schwierig
hard U7/3	[hɑːd]	hart
hard hat U7/3	['hɑːd hæt]	Schutzhelm
harm U10/NYC2	[hɑːm]	Schaden, Unheil
haunted U4/1	['hɔːntɪd]	heimgesucht; Spuk-
have (food/drinks) MORE 1	[hæv]	zu sich nehmen
Have fun! U15/NYC3	[hæv 'fʌn]	Viel Spaß!
head MORE 1	[hed]	Kopf
headache U15/3	['hedeɪk]	Kopfschmerzen
headmaster EU/1	[hed'mɑːstə]	Schulleiter, Direktor
hear MORE 1	[hɪə]	hören
heavy MORE 1	['hevi]	schwer
heavy U16/4	['hevi]	stark
height C/p.141	[haɪt]	Höhe
helmet U3/DSC1	['helmət]	Helm
help MORE 1	[help]	helfen; Hilfe
Here we go! MORE 1	[hɪə wiː 'gəʊ]	Jetzt geht's los!
Here you are. MORE 1	[hɪə juː 'ɑː]	Hier, bitte!, Bitte schön!
hers U14/7	[hɜːz]	ihre/r/s

Hi there! MORE 1	[haɪ ðeə]	Hallo!	
hide MORE 1	[haɪd]	(sich) verstecken	
hieroglyphics U11/1	[haɪrə'glɪfɪks]	Hieroglyphen	
high MORE 1	[haɪ]	hoch	
high school C/p.138	['haɪ ˌskuːl]	höhere Schule, Highschool	
hiking U16/5	['haɪkɪŋ]	Wander-; Wandern	
hill U6/1	[hɪl]	Hügel; Anhöhe	
hire MORE 1	['haɪə]	mieten, ausleihen	
history U1/4	['hɪstəri]	Geschichte	
hit U1/6	[hɪt]	schlagen	
hoax U9/9	[həʊks]	Streich, Trick	
hobby U12/7	['hɒbi]	Hobby, Freizeitbeschäftigung	
hold U18/5	[həʊld]	abhalten	
hole MORE 1	[həʊl]	Loch	
holiday camp U7/7	['hɒlɪdeɪ]	Ferienlager	
home MORE 1	[həʊm]	Zuhause; zu Hause	
home run C/p.139	[ˌhəʊm 'rʌn]	Homerun (Baseball)	
home schooling C/p.138	['həʊm ˌskuːlɪŋ]	Unterricht zu Hause	
honestly MORE 1	['ɒnɪstli]	ehrlich; wirklich	
hop U2/2	[hɒp]	hüpfen	
hope MORE 1	[həʊp]	hoffen	
hope U16	[həʊp]	Hoffnung	
hopefully U11/S5	['həʊpfli]	hoffnungsvoll; hoffentlich	
horn U11/3	[hɔːn]	Horn	
horrible U12/18	['hɒrɪbl]	schrecklich	
horse MORE 1	[hɔːs]	Pferd	
hospital MORE 1	['hɒspɪtəl]	Krankenhaus	
hot U1/2	[hɒt]	heiß	
hot springs C/p.140	[ˌhɒt 'sprɪŋz]	heiße Quellen	
household U1/2	['haʊshəʊld]	Haushalt	
how MORE 1	[haʊ]	wie	
how about ... U11/S5	[haʊ ə'baʊt]	wie wär's mit ...	
how to U4/12	['haʊ tə]	wie man	
however U9/DSC3	[ˌhaʊ'evə]	aber; jedoch, allerdings	
hug U1/11	[hʌg]	umarmen	
huge MORE 1	[hjuːdʒ]	riesig, riesengroß	
human U11/2	['hjuːmən]	Mensch; menschlich	
hunt U1/9	[hʌnt]	jagen; Jagd	
hurray U13/2	[hʊ'reɪ]	hurra	
hurricane U17/10	['hʌrɪkən]	Orkan; Hurrikan	
hurry MORE 1	['hʌri]	sich beeilen	
hurt MORE 1	[hɜːt]	wehtun, schmerzen	
husband MORE 1	['hʌzbənd]	Ehemann	
hypnosis U2/G	[hɪp'nəʊsɪs]	Hypnose	
hypnotise U2/1	['hɪpnətaɪz]	hypnotisieren	
hypnotist U2/1	['hɪpnətɪst]	Hypnotiseur/in	

I

ice skating U17/1	['aɪsskeɪtɪŋ]	Schlittschuh laufen	
I'd like MORE 1	[aɪd laɪk]	ich möchte	
if MORE 1	[ɪf]	wenn	
ill MORE 1	[ɪl]	krank	
illness U15/10	['ɪlnəs]	Krankheit	
imagine U7/10	[ɪ'mædʒɪn]	sich vorstellen	
imaginary U5	[ɪ'mædʒɪnəri]	erfunden	
immediately U3/1	[ɪ'miːdiətli]	sofort	
important MORE 1	[ɪm'pɔːtənt]	wichtig	
in fact U4/2	[ɪn 'fækt]	genau genommen	
in one go MORE 1	[ɪn wʌn 'gəʊ]	auf einmal	
in this way U9/1	[ɪn ðɪs 'weɪ]	dadurch, auf diese Weise	
inch (pl inches) U16/10	[ɪntʃ, 'ɪntʃɪz]	Zoll (2,54 cm)	
indeed U9/S4	[ɪn'diːd]	in der Tat, wirklich	
India MORE 1	['ɪndiə]	Indien	
Indians U15/10	['ɪndiənz]	Indios (Ureinwohner Südamerikas)	
American Indian C/p.140	[əˌmerɪkən 'ɪndiən]	Indianer/in	
information U1/2	[ˌɪnfə'meɪʃn]	Information, Auskunft	
information technology (IT) U1/4	[ɪnfə'meɪʃn tek'nɒlədʒi]	Informatik	
injure U15/14	['ɪndʒə]	verletzen	
ink U1/11	[ɪŋk]	Tinte	
inside U1/6	[ɪn'saɪd]	innen; hinein	
instead U8/4	[ɪn'sted]	stattdessen	
intelligent U5/13	[ɪn'telɪdʒənt]	intelligent	
intention U8/1	[ɪn'tenʃn]	Vorhaben, Absicht	
interested (in) MORE 1	['ɪntrəstɪd]	interessiert (an)	
interesting MORE 1	['ɪntrəstɪŋ]	interessant	
interrupt U6/DSC2	[ˌɪntə'rʌpt]	unterbrechen	
intersect U15/NYC3	[ˌɪntə'sekt]	(sich) (über-)kreuzen	
interview MORE 1	['ɪntəvjuː]	Interview	
into MORE 1	['ɪntʊ]	in	
invent U11/2	[ɪn'vent]	erfinden	
invention U11/2	[ɪn'venʃn]	Erfindung	
investigation U9/9	[ɪnˌvestɪ'geɪʃn]	Untersuchung, Ermittlung	
invitation MORE 1	[ɪnvɪ'teɪʃn]	Einladung	
invite MORE 1	[ɪn'vaɪt]	einladen	
Italy U11/2	['ɪtəli]	Italien	
Italian U6/4	[ɪ'tæljən]	italienisch/e/r/s	
item U6/DSC2	['aɪtəm]	Punkt, Objekt	

J

jam U11/9	[dʒæm]	Marmelade	
Japan U1/6	[dʒəˈpæn]	Japan	
jewel U2/2	[ˈdʒuːəl]	Juwel	
jewellery U11/2	[ˈdʒuːəlri]	Schmuck	
job MORE 1	[dʒɒb]	Arbeit; Aufgabe	
join U3/DSC1	[dʒɔɪn]	sich anschließen/treffen	
join (in) MORE 1	[dʒɔɪn ˈɪn]	teilnehmen (an), mitmachen (bei)	
joke U7/7	[dʒəʊk]	Witz	
journey U9/1	[ˈdʒɜːni]	Reise	
juggle U11/9	[dʒʌgl]	jonglieren	
juggler U11/3	[ˈdʒʌglə]	Jongleur/in	
juice MORE 1	[dʒuːs]	Saft	
jump MORE 1	[dʒʌmp]	hüpfen; springen	
jungle U1/1	[ˈdʒʌŋgl]	Dschungel	
junior U17/6	[ˈdʒuːniə]	Junioren-, Jugend-	
junior prom C/p.138	[ˌdʒuːniə ˈprɒm]	Unterstufenabschlussball	
just U8/7	[dʒʌst]	gerade eben	

K

karate EU/1	[kəˈrɑːti]	Karate	
(be) keen on U4/13	[bi kiːn ɒn]	sich begeistern für	
keep MORE 1	[kiːp]	(be-)halten	
keep calm U12/5	[kiːp ˈkɑːm]	ruhig bleiben	
keep safe U18/7	[kiːp seɪf]	(ab-)sichern, sicher machen	
keep someone company U18/7	[kiːp ˈsʌmwʌn ˈkʌmpəni]	jdm. Gesellschaft leisten	
keep watch U7/S3	[kiːp ˈwɒtʃ]	Ausschau/Wache halten	
key MORE 1	[kiː]	Schlüssel	
kick U4/13	[kɪk]	Tritt, Stoß; treten, kicken	
kidnap U9/10	[ˈkɪdnæp]	entführen	
kill MORE 1	[kɪl]	töten	
kilogram U5/13	[ˈkɪləgræm]	Kilogramm	
what kind (of) MORE 1	[wɒt ˈkaɪnd]	was für	
kiss U2/2	[kɪs]	küssen	
kitchen MORE 1	[ˈkɪtʃən]	Küche	
kitty U18/NYC4	[ˈkɪti]	Kätzchen	
knife (pl knives) U4/4	[naɪf, naɪvz]	Messer	
knight U4/S2	[naɪt]	Ritter	
knock MORE 1	[nɒk]	Klopfen; klopfen	
know MORE 1	[nəʊ]	wissen; kennen	
kph (kilometres per hour) U5/8	[ˈkɪləˌmiːtəs pə aʊə]	Kilometer pro Stunde	

L

lab (informal) U14/DSC5	[læb]	Labor	
lake U7/1	[leɪk]	See	
lamb U10/1	[læm]	Lamm	
lamp U14/3	[læmp]	Lampe	
lamp post U6/F	[ˈlæmp pəʊst]	Laternenmast	
land U5/6	[lænd]	Land	
land U9/1	[lænd]	landen	
language MORE 1	[ˈlæŋgwɪdʒ]	Sprache	
large U2/7	[lɑːdʒ]	groß	
late MORE 1	[leɪt]	(zu) spät	
later MORE 1	[ˈleɪtə]	später	
laugh MORE 1	[lɑːf]	lachen	
laughter U2/2	[ˈlɑːftə]	Gelächter	
lay off sb (informal) U10/NYC2	[leɪ ˈɒf ˌsʌmbədi]	jemanden in Ruhe lassen	
lead U13/10	[liːd]	(an-)führen	
leaf (pl leaves) MORE 1	[liːf, liːvz]	Blatt	
leaflet U12/18	[ˈliːflət]	Broschüre	
learn MORE 1	[lɜːn]	lernen; herausfinden	
at least U13/12	[ət ˈliːst]	mindestens, wenigstens	
leather U11/3	[ˈleðə]	Leder	
leave MORE 1	[liːv]	verlassen, weggehen	
leave behind U12/DSC4	[ˌliːv bɪˈhaɪnd]	zurücklassen	
left U6/6	[left]	übrig	
left-hand U7/2	[ˈlefthænd]	linke/r/s	
less (than) U15/10	[les]	weniger (als)	
lesson MORE 1	[ˈlesən]	Unterrichtsstunde	
letter MORE 1	[ˈletə]	Brief; Buchstabe	
Let's see. U15/NYC3	[lets siː]	Schauen wir mal.	
librarian U14/DSC5	[laɪˈbreəriən]	Bibliothekar/in	
library MORE 1	[ˈlaɪbrəri]	Bibliothek, Bücherei	
lie MORE 1	[laɪ]	liegen; sich legen	
lie U8/7	[laɪ]	Lüge	
life (pl lives) MORE 1	[laɪf, laɪvz]	Leben	
life jacket U7/3	[ˈlaɪf dʒækɪt]	Schwimmweste	
lift (up) MORE 1	[lɪft]	(hoch-)heben	
light U9/6	[laɪt]	Licht	
light U11/3	[laɪt]	leicht	
lights U6/9	[laɪts]	Ampel	
(be) like 1/12	[laɪk]	wie etwas sein, ähnlich sein	
limo (informal) C/p.138	[ˈlɪməʊ]	Limousine	
line MORE 1	[laɪn]	Linie	
lion MORE 1	[ˈlaɪən]	Löwe	
Lisbon U1/1	[ˈlɪzbən]	Lissabon	
list U4/10	[lɪst]	Liste	
Listen up here. U15/NYC3	[ˌlɪsən ˈʌp hɪə]	Hör(t) mal zu.	

litter tray U18/1	['lɪtə treɪ]	Katzenklo
live MORE 1	[lɪv]	leben
lobby U16/11	['lɒbi]	Eingangshalle, Foyer
(door) lock U4/5	['dɔː lɒk]	(Tür-)Schloss
lock U13/2	[lɒk]	abschließen
look U11/3	[lʊk]	Aussehen; Blick
look after MORE 1	[lʊk 'aːftə]	sich kümmern um
look at MORE 1	['lʊk ət]	betrachten, sehen
look for MORE 1	['lʊk fɔː]	suchen nach
look forward to U9/DSC3	[lʊk fɔːwəd tu]	sich freuen auf
look like U7/7	[lʊk laɪk]	aussehen wie
lose U3/DSC1	[luːz]	verlieren
(get) lost U6/7	[get 'lɒst]	sich verirrt haben
lost and found office U14/DSC5	[lɒst ənd faʊnd 'ɒfɪs]	Fundbüro
a lot (of) MORE 1	[ə 'lɒt]	viel/e
lots of MORE 1	['lɒts‚əv]	viel, jede Menge
lots of love U3/1	[‚lɒts əv 'lʌv]	alles Liebe, liebe Grüße
loud MORE 1	[laʊd]	laut
lovely U16/5	['lʌvli]	schön
low U16/1	[ləʊ]	niedrig, schwach
luck MORE 1	[lʌk]	Glück
bad luck U14/DSC5	[‚bæd 'lʌk]	Pech, Unglück
luckily U3/1	['lʌkli]	glücklicherweise
be lucky MORE 1	[biː 'lʌki]	Glück haben

M

machine U3/4	[məˈʃiːn]	Maschine
madam MORE 1	['mædəm]	gnädige Frau (Anrede)
made of MORE 1	[meɪd əv]	aus … gemacht
magic U13	['mædʒɪk]	Magie, Zauber
main U10/7	[meɪn]	Haupt-
main course U10/7	[meɪn kɔːs]	Hauptgang
make friends U17/11	[meɪk frendz]	Freundschaft schließen
make sure U6/DSC2	[meɪk 'ʃɔː]	sich versichern, darauf achten
make up U5/18	[meɪk ʌp]	erfinden
malaria U5/10	[məˈleəriə]	Malaria
mammal U5/10	['mæml]	Säugetier
man (pl men) MORE 1	[mæn, men]	Mann
manage sth. U17/10	['mænɪdʒ]	etwas schaffen
many MORE 1	['meni]	viele
map U6/3	[mæp]	(Land-)Karte
marble U15/NYC3	['maːbl]	aus Marmor
market U18/NYC4	['maːkɪt]	Markt
market square U6/9	[‚maːkɪt skweə]	Marktplatz
married U12/9	['mærɪd]	verheiratet
mask U4/3	[maːsk]	Maske
master U2/S1	['maːstə]	Meister
match MORE 1	[mætʃ]	zuordnen
material U14/DSC5	[məˈtɪəriəl]	Stoff, Material
mathematician U12/15	[‚mæθəməˈtɪʃn]	Mathematiker/in
It doesn't matter. MORE 1	[ɪt dʌznt 'mætə]	Das ist nicht wichtig.
maximum U16/4	['mæksɪməm]	Maximum
maybe U2/2	['meɪbi]	vielleicht
mean U4/5	[miːn]	gemein
mean MORE 1	[miːn]	bedeuten; meinen
meat U10/2	[miːt]	Fleisch
medal U2/1	['medl]	Medaille
medical science U15/10	['medɪkl saɪəns]	medizinische Wissenschaft
medicine (no pl) U1/9	['medsən]	Medizin, Medikament/e
medicine man U15/10	['medsən mæn]	Medizinmann
meet up U8/7	[miːt ʌp]	(sich) treffen
melt U11/3	[melt]	schmelzen
memory MORE 1	['memri]	Gedächtnis; Erinnerung
mention MORE 1	['menʃən]	erwähnen
menu U10/7	['menjuː]	Speisekarte
mess U2/2	[mes]	Unordnung, Durcheinander
metal U14/DSC5	['metl]	Metall
metallic U9/9	[məˈtælɪk]	metallisch
metre MORE 1	['miːtə]	Meter
middle MORE 1	['mɪdl]	Mitte
midnight MORE 1	['mɪdnaɪt]	Mitternacht
might U8	[maɪt]	könnte; vielleicht (tun, sein)
mild U16/10	[maɪld]	sanft; mild
mile U16/10	[maɪl]	Meile
million MORE 1	['mɪljən]	Million
mine U14/7	[maɪn]	meine/r/s
mineral water MORE 1	['mɪnərəl 'wɔːtə]	Mineralwasser
miss U8/10	[mɪs]	verpassen
miss U12/5	[mɪs]	vermissen
missing MORE 1	['mɪsɪŋ]	vermisst
mission U13/S6	['mɪʃən]	Auftrag, Mission
mixed-up U8/7	[‚mɪkstˈʌp]	durcheinander
mobile (phone) MORE 1	[məʊbaɪl fəʊn]	Handy
modern U3/2	['mɒdn]	modern
mom (AE) C/p.138	[mɒm]	Mama, Mutti
Mongolian 14/1	[mɒŋˈgəʊliən]	mongolisch
monster U4/2	['mɒnstə]	Monster, Ungeheuer
monument U11/2	['mɒnjʊmənt]	Denkmal, Monument
moon U7/1	[muːn]	Mond

morph MORE 1	[mɔːf]	morphen, sich verwandeln	
mosquito (pl -es or -s) U5/10	[mɒˈskiːtəʊ]	Stechmücke, Moskito	
(the) most MORE 1	[ðə ˈməʊst]	am meisten; die meisten	
most of the time U6/6	[ˈməʊst əv ðə taɪm]	meistens	
mostly U11/2	[ˈməʊstli]	hauptsächlich	
motorway U7/1	[ˈməʊtəweɪ]	Autobahn	
mountain MORE 1	[ˈmaʊntɪn]	Berg	
mountain biking U17/1	[ˈmaʊntɪn ˌbaɪkɪŋ]	Mountainbiken	
mountain climbing U17/1	[ˈmaʊntɪn ˌklaɪmɪŋ]	Bergsteigen	
mountain climber U17/4	[ˈmaʊntɪn ˌklaɪmə]	Bergsteiger/in	
mouse (pl mice) MORE 1	[maʊs, maɪs]	Maus	
move U7/5	[muːv]	übersiedeln; (sich) bewegen	
move house U15/G	[muːv haʊs]	umziehen	
move in U12/9	[ˈmuːv ɪn]	einziehen	
moveable U14/1	[ˈmuːvəbl]	beweglich, transportierbar	
movie U16/11	[ˈmuːvi]	Film	
mph (miles per hour) U16/3	[ˌmaɪlz pə ˈaʊə]	Meilen pro Stunde	
Ms U5/NYC1	[məz]	Frau (Anrede)	
mummy U11/1	[ˈmʌmi]	Mumie	
museum U2/2	[mjuːˈziːəm]	Museum	
mushroom U10/4	[ˈmʌʃruːm]	Pilz	
music shop U6/2	[ˈmjuːzɪk ˌʃɒp]	Musikladen	
musician MORE 1	[mjuˈzɪʃn]	Musiker/in	
must MORE 1	[mʌst]	müssen	
mustn't U11/10	[ˈmʌsənt]	nicht dürfen	
myself U12/5	[maɪˈself]	mir, mich; hier: selbst	
mystery U18/NYC4	[ˈmɪstəri]	Rätsel; Geheimnis	

N

nail U13/6	[neɪl]	Nagel	
naked U11/3	[ˈneɪkɪd]	nackt, unbekleidet	
national park U17/4	[ˈnæʃnl pɑːk]	Nationalpark	
nearly MORE 1	[ˈnɪəli]	fast; beinahe	
need MORE 1	[niːd]	brauchen	
need to U6/9	[niːd tuː]	müssen	
neighbour MORE 1	[ˈneɪbə]	Nachbar/in	
Neither do I. U18/7	[ˈnaɪðə duː ˈaɪ]	Ich auch nicht.	
nervous MORE 1	[ˈnɜːvəs]	nervös	
network U13/10	[ˈnetwɜːk]	Netzwerk	

never MORE 1	[ˈnevə]	nie(mals)	
news (pl) MORE 1	[njuːz]	Nachrichten	
newspaper MORE 1	[ˈnjuːzpeɪpə]	Zeitung	
next door U14/7	[nekst ˈdɔː]	nebenan	
New Zealand U1/2	[ˌnjuːˈziːlənd]	Neuseeland	
nice MORE 1	[naɪs]	nett; schön, angenehm	
nightmare C/p.138	[ˈnaɪtmeə]	Alptraum	
nil U17/8	[nɪl]	nichts, null	
Nile U11/2	[naɪl]	Nil	
no longer U9/9	[ˌnəʊ ˈlɒŋgə]	nicht mehr	
No way! MORE 1	[nəʊ weɪ]	Auf keinen Fall!	
nobody MORE 1	[ˈnəʊbədi]	niemand	
noise MORE 1	[nɔɪz]	Lärm, Krach; Geräusch	
none U13/S6	[nʌn]	keine/r/s	
nonsense U9/10	[ˈnɒnsns]	Unsinn	
normally U18/10	[ˈnɔːməli]	normalerweise	
north U1/6	[nɔːθ]	nördlich, Nord-; Norden	
North Pole U1/1	[nɔːθ pəʊl]	Nordpol	
Northern Ireland U16/4	[ˈnɔːðən ˈaɪələnd]	Nordirland	
northwest C/p.141	[ˌnɔːθˈwest]	nordwestlich, Nordwest-; Nordwesten	
not any longer U13/S6	[nɒt ˈeni ˈlɒŋgə]	nicht mehr	
not any more U7/7	[nɒt ˈeni mɔː]	nicht mehr	
Not at all. U6/3	[nɒt æt ɔːl]	Nichts zu danken.	
no longer U13/S6	[nəʊ ˈlɒŋgə]	nicht mehr	
not feel well U8/7	[nɒt fiːl wel]	sich unwohl fühlen	
not only ... but also U3/6	[nɒt ˈəʊnli bʌt ˈɔːlsəʊ]	nicht nur ... sondern auch	
not that difficult U12/5	[nɒt ðæt ˈdɪfɪklt]	nicht so schwer	
not until U9/DSC3	[nɒt ənˈtɪl]	erst	
not yet U13/S6	[nɒt jet]	noch nicht	
note MORE 1	[nəʊt]	Notiz; Ankündigung	
notebook U12/13	[ˈnəʊtbʊk]	Notebook(-Computer)	
nothing MORE 1	[ˈnʌθɪŋ]	nichts	
notice MORE 1	[ˈnəʊtɪs]	bemerken	
number C/p.140	[ˈnʌmbə]	Anzahl	

O

object U7/8	[ˈɒbdʒɪkt]	Objekt, Gegenstand, Sache	
obsessed U17/10	[əbˈsest]	besessen	
ocean U17/10	[ˈəʊʃn]	Meer, Ozean	
octopus (pl -es) U1/6	[ˈɒktəpəs]	Tintenfisch	
the odd one out U9/5	[ðɪ ˈɒd wʌn ˈaʊt]	das fünfte Rad am Wagen; hier: das Wort, das nicht dazugehört	

WORDLIST 165

of course MORE 1	[əv 'kɔːs]	natürlich
off MORE 1	[ɒf]	aus; weg
be off U7/S3	[biː ɒf]	fortgehen, weggehen
Off you go. U2/2	[ˌɒf juː 'gəʊ]	Geh(t) schon., Gehen Sie schon.
offer U5/16	['ɒfə]	Angebot
office U2/2	['ɒfɪs]	Büro
officer U7/7	['ɒfɪsə]	Offizier/in; Beamter, Beamtin
often MORE 1	['ɒftən]	oft, häufig
older U1/2	['əʊldə]	älter
olive U10/4	['ɒlɪv]	Olive
the Olympic Games C/p.139	[ði əʊˌlɪmpɪk 'geɪmz]	die Olympischen Spiele
on his own U1/6	[ɒn hɪz 'əʊn]	allein, auf sich gestellt
on my own U17/8	[ɒn maɪ 'əʊn]	alleine
on time U9/DSC3	[ɒn 'taɪm]	pünktlich
once MORE 1	[wʌns]	einmal
once upon a time U4/S2	['wʌns əpɒn ə 'taɪm]	es war einmal
one by one U9/1	[wʌn baɪ wʌn]	nacheinander
onto MORE 1	['ɒntə]	auf
operation U3/1	[ˌɒpr'eɪʃn]	Operation
opposite U6/4	['ɒpəzɪt]	gegenüber
order MORE 1	['ɔːdə]	Reihenfolge
order U10/5	['ɔːdə]	bestellen
order U12/DSC4	['ɔːdə]	Bestellung
organise U3/1	['ɔːgnaɪz]	organisieren
organisation C/p.138	[ˌɔːgənaɪ'zeɪʃən]	Einrichtung, Organisation
ostrich U5/11	['ɒstrɪtʃ]	(Vogel) Strauß
other U1/6	['ʌðər]	andere/r/s
ours U14/7	['aʊəz]	unsere/r/s
outdoor U7/1	['aʊtˌdɔː]	im Freien
out loud U3/1	[aʊt laʊd]	laut, lauthals
out of MORE 1	['aʊt əv]	aus
outlook U16/3	['aʊtlʊk]	Aussicht
outside MORE 1	[aʊt'saɪd]	außen, außerhalb
out there U9/8	[aʊt ðeə]	da draußen
over MORE 1	['əʊvə]	über, herüber
own MORE 1	[əʊn]	eigene/r/s
owner MORE 1	['əʊnə]	Besitzer/in, Eigentümer/in
ox (pl oxen) U11/3	[ɒks, 'ɒksən]	Ochse
oxygen U15/10	['ɒksɪdʒən]	Sauerstoff

P

pack U16/7	[pæk]	packen
pain U15/1	[peɪn]	Schmerz
paint EU/1	[peɪnt]	malen, streichen
painting U11/3	['peɪntɪŋ]	Bild, Gemälde
pair MORE 1	[peər]	Paar
palm leaves U11/3	['pɑːm liːvz]	Palmenblätter
pancakes U10/1	['pænkeɪkz]	Palatschinken, Pfannkuchen
panic U12/5	['pænɪk]	in Panik geraten
paper MORE 1	['peɪpər]	Papier; Zeitung
papyrus U11/1	[pə'paɪrəs]	Papyrus
paragraph MORE 1	['pærəgrɑːf]	Absatz, Abschnitt
parents MORE 1	['peərənts]	Eltern
part MORE 1	[pɑːt]	Teil
partner U1/2	['pɑːtnə]	Partner/in
party MORE 1	['pɑːti]	Party
pass (a test) U15/G	[pɑːs]	(eine Prüfung) bestehen
pass on U3/6	[pɑːs ɒn]	weitergeben
pass through U13/1	[pɑːs 'θruː]	durchlaufen; hier: durchgehen durch
passenger C/p.141	['pæsəndʒə]	Passagier-
password U3/6	['pɑːswɜːd]	Passwort
past U6/1	[pɑːst]	nach; vorbei an
path U6/1	[pɑːθ]	Weg, Pfad
patient U15/1	['peɪʃənt]	Patient/in
pattern U14/DSC5	['pætn]	Muster
pay MORE 1	[peɪ]	bezahlen
peas MORE 1	[piː]	Erbsen
peach U10/1	[piːtʃ]	Pfirsich
peak U16/10	[piːk]	Gipfel, Bergspitze
pear U10/1	[peə]	Birne
penguin U18/10	['peŋgwɪn]	Pinguin
pennant C/p.139	['penənt]	Wimpel (dreieckige Flagge)
people (pl) MORE 1	['piːpl]	Leute, Menschen
people person U17/10	['piːpl pɜːsən]	geselliger Mensch
pepperoni U12/DSC4	[ˌpepə'rəʊni]	(scharfe) Salami
per U5/8	[pɜː]	pro
per cent (%) U11/2	[pə'sent]	Prozent (%)
perfect U1/12	['pɜːfekt]	perfekt
perfume U11/3	['pɜːfjuːm]	Parfüm
perfumed U11/3	['pɜːfjuːmd]	parfümiert
person U1/7	['pɜːsn]	Person, Mensch
Peru U14/1	[pə'ruː]	Peru
pet shop U18/7	['pet ˌʃɒp]	Tierhandlung
pharaoh U11/2	['feərəʊ]	Pharaoh
photo U3/DSC1	['fəʊtəʊ]	Foto
photograph U9/9	['fəʊtəgrɑːf]	Foto(grafie)
physical education (PE) U1/4	['fɪzɪkl ˌedjʊ'keɪʃn]	Sport(unterricht)
picture MORE 1	['pɪktʃə]	Bild
pick up MORE 1	[pɪk 'ʌp]	aufheben, abholen
picnic U3/DSC1	['pɪknɪk]	Picknick

pie U10/1	[paɪ]	Kuchen; Pastete
piece MORE 1	[piːs]	Stück
pig U5/1	[pɪg]	Schwein
pineapple U12/DSC4	[ˈpaɪnˌæpl]	Ananas
pitch (AE) U10/NYC2	[pɪtʃ]	werfen
pitcher (AE) C/p.139	[ˈpɪtʃə]	(Ball-)Werfer
pity U9/DSC3	[ˈpɪti]	hier: schade, dass
plain U14/DSC5	[pleɪn]	einfarbig, ungemustert; einheitlich
plan U3/1	[plæn]	planen
plan U14/6	[plæn]	(Lage-)Plan
plane U2/2	[pleɪn]	Flugzeug
planet U9/1	[ˈplænɪt]	Planet
plant U11/2	[plɑːnt]	Pflanze
plastic U14/DSC5	[ˈplæstɪk]	Plastik, Kunststoff
play MORE 1	[pleɪ]	Theaterstück; Spiel
play a trick/tricks on somebody U4/3	[pleɪ ə ˈtrɪk ɒn]	jemanden einen Streich spielen
player MORE 1	[ˈpleɪər]	Spieler/in
plenty of U4/12	[ˈplenti əv]	eine Menge von
plum U10/1	[plʌm]	Zwetschke, Pflaume
pocket U4/7	[ˈpɒkɪt]	(Hosen-)Tasche
point (at) U7/7	[pɔɪnt]	zeigen (auf)
point U15/14	[pɔɪnt]	Punkt; Argument
poison U1/9	[ˈpɔɪzn]	Gift
poisonous U1/6	[ˈpɔɪznəs]	giftig
police (no pl) MORE 1	[pəˈliːs]	Polizei
police station U2/2	[pəˈliːs ˌsteɪʃn]	Polizeiwache
policeman (pl -men) MORE 1	[pəˈliːsmən]	Polizist
policewoman (pl -women) U6/7	[pəˈliːsˌwʊmən]	Polizistin
politely U6/DSC2	[pəˈlaɪtli]	höflich
poor MORE 1	[pɔːr]	arm
Poor you! U7/S3	[pɔːr juː]	Du Armer/Arme!
pond U7/7	[pɒnd]	Teich
popular U5/6	[ˈpɒpjʊlə]	beliebt
pork U10/1	[pɔːk]	Schweinefleisch
Portuguese U12/9	[ˌpɔːtʃʊˈgiːz]	Portugiesisch
possible U16/12	[ˈpɒsɪbl]	möglich
post U3/6	[pəʊst]	posten, einen Beitrag verfassen (online)
posting U3/6	[ˈpəʊstɪŋ]	Posting, Beitrag (online)
post office U6/2	[ˈpəʊst ˌɒfɪs]	Postamt
pot U13/7	[pɒt]	Topf
pound (£) MORE 1	[paʊnd]	Pfund
power MORE 1	[ˈpaʊər]	Kraft; Macht
powerful U4/S2	[ˈpaʊəfəl]	mächtig
practice MORE 1	[ˈpræktɪs]	Übung
practise MORE 1	[ˈpræktɪs]	üben; Übung
prayer U1/2	[preə]	Gebet
prepare U1/2	[prɪˈpeə]	(vor-/zu-)bereiten
(be) prepared U17/8	[biː prɪˈpeəd]	vorbereitet sein
present MORE 1	[ˈpreznt]	Geschenk
presentation U8/2	[ˌprezənˈteɪʃən]	Präsentation
president MORE 1	[ˈprezɪdənt]	Präsident/in
press MORE 1	[pres]	drücken; klicken
pretty MORE 1	[ˈprɪti]	hübsch
pretty U7/7	[ˈprɪti]	ziemlich
priest U11/8	[priːst]	Priester/in
print out U12/13	[ˈprɪnt aʊt]	ausdrucken
prison U13/6	[ˈprɪzn]	Gefängnis
private U1/2	[ˈpraɪvət]	privat, Privat-
prize MORE 1	[praɪz]	Preis, Auszeichnung
probably U9/S4	[ˈprɒbəbli]	wahrscheinlich
produce U15/10	[prəˈdjuːs]	erzeugen
professional U17/6	[prəˈfeʃnl]	professionell, hauptberuflich
professor U11/7	[prəˈfesə]	Professor/in
profile U17/4	[ˈprəʊfaɪl]	Profil
project U8/2	[ˈprɒdʒekt]	Projekt
prom C/p.138	[prɒm]	(Abschluss-)Ball
promise MORE 1	[ˈprɒmɪs]	versprechen; Versprechen
prompt U6/DSC2	[prɒmt]	Hinweis
pronto (informal) U2/2	[ˈprɒntəʊ]	sofort
protect U4/S2	[prəˈtekt]	schützen
proud (of) U7/7	[praʊd]	stolz sein (auf)
public U15/NYC3	[ˈpʌblɪk]	öffentlich, staatlich
pull MORE 1	[pʊl]	ziehen
pumpkin U4/1	[ˈpʌmpkɪn]	Kürbis
push MORE 1	[pʊʃ]	schieben
push U9/11	[pʊʃ]	drücken
push yourself U17/10	[pʊʃ jɔːˈself]	sich selbst motivieren, anspornen
put MORE 1	[pʊt]	setzen, legen, stellen
put a spell on sb U13/6	[pʊt ə ˈspel ɒn ˈsʌmbədi]	jemanden verzaubern
put on U1/2	[pʊt ɒn]	anziehen
put out U13/7	[pʊt aʊt]	löschen
pyjamas (no pl) U18/13	[pəˈdʒɑːməz]	Pyjama, Schlafanzug
pyramid U11/1	[ˈpɪrəmɪd]	Pyramide

Q

quarter MORE 1	[ˈkwɔːtə]	Viertel(stunde)
quick MORE 1	[kwɪk]	schnell; kurz
quiet MORE 1	[ˈkwaɪət]	leise, ruhig
quite U1/11	[kwaɪt]	ziemlich

R

race	U17/10	[reɪs]	Wettfahrt; Wettkampf
radiator	U14/3	[ˈreɪdieɪtə]	Heizkörper
railway	U6/2	[ˈreɪlweɪ]	Gleise, Schienen; (Eisen)bahn
railway station	U6/2	[ˈreɪlweɪ ˈsteɪʃn]	Bahnhof
rain	MORE 1	[reɪn]	Regen; regnen
raincoat	U16/7	[ˈreɪnkəʊt]	Regenmantel
rainfall	U16/10	[ˈreɪnfɔːl]	Niederschlag
rainforest	U15/10	[ˈreɪnfɒrɪst]	Regenwald
rainy	U16/2	[ˈreɪni]	regnerisch
range	C/p.140	[reɪndʒ]	hier: Gebirgskette
rattle	U13/1	[ˈrætl]	klappern, rasseln
reach	U17/G	[riːtʃ]	erreichen, ankommen
react	U9/DSC3	[riˈækt]	reagieren
ready	MORE 1	[ˈredi]	fertig, bereit
real	MORE 1	[rɪəl]	wirklich; echt, real
really	MORE 1	[ˈrɪəli]	wirklich
reason	U3/8	[ˈriːzn]	Grund
receptionist	U16/5	[rɪˈsepʃənɪst]	Rezeptionist/in
recipe	U10/7	[ˈresəpi]	Rezept
record	U16/10	[ˈrekɔːd]	Rekord
record	EU/1	[rɪˈkɔːd]	aufzeichnen
the Red Cross	U12/9	[ðə ˌred ˈkrɒs]	das Rote Kreuz
reddish	U10/NYC2	[ˈredɪʃ]	rötlich
reed	U14/1	[riːd]	Schilf(rohr)
refugee	U12/3	[ˌrefjʊˈdʒiː]	Flüchtling
refugee camp	U12/3	[refjʊˈdʒiːkæmp]	Flüchtlingslager
region	C/p.140	[ˈriːdʒən]	Region, Gegend
religion	U11/2	[rɪˈlɪdʒən]	Religion
religious	C/p.138	[rɪˈlɪdʒəs]	religiös; Religions-
remember	MORE 1	[rɪˈmembər]	sich erinnern (an)
remind	U12/DSC4	[rɪˈmaɪnd]	erinnern
repeat	MORE 1	[rɪˈpiːt]	wiederholen
reply	MORE 1	[rɪˈplaɪ]	antworten
report	U16/4	[rɪˈpɔːt]	Bericht
reptile	U5/6	[ˈreptaɪl]	Reptil
request	U17/DSC6	[rɪˈkwest]	Bitte
rescue	MORE 1	[ˈreskjuː]	Rettung; retten
reservation	C/p.140	[ˌrezəˈveɪʃn]	Reservat
respond	MORE 1	[rɪˈspɒnd]	antworten
response	MORE 1	[rɪˈspɒnts]	Antwort
responsibly	U3	[rɪˈspɒntsɪbli]	verantwortungsvoll
rest	U13/7	[rest]	Rest
rest	U17/8	[rest]	Ruhe; Pause
result	EU/1	[rɪˈzʌlt]	Folge; Ergebnis
return	MORE 1	[rɪˈtɜːn]	zurückkehren
revenge	U9/DSC3	[rɪˈvendʒ]	Rache
revision	U1	[rɪˈvɪʒn]	Wiederholung
reward	U18/NYC4	[rɪˈwɔːd]	Belohnung
rhino (=rhinoceros)	U5/13	[ˈraɪnəʊ]	Nashorn, Rhinozeros
rhyme	MORE 1	[raɪm]	Reim
rice pudding	U10/1	[raɪs ˈpʊdɪŋ]	Milchreis
rich	MORE 1	[rɪtʃ]	reich
right away	U1/2	[raɪt əweɪ]	sofort
right-hand	U7/2	[ˈraɪthænd]	rechte/r/s
Right here.	U18/NYC4	[raɪt hɪə]	Hab' ich hier.
right now	U13/8	[raɪt naʊ]	jetzt gerade
ring	MORE 1	[rɪŋ]	anrufen
ring	U1/9	[rɪŋ]	Kreis
rise	U16/4	[raɪz]	steigen
river	MORE 1	[ˈrɪvər]	Fluss
road	MORE 1	[rəʊd]	Straße
roam	U9/8	[rəʊm]	wandern
roast	U13/7	[rəʊst]	rösten
roast potato	U13/6	[rəʊst pəˈteɪtəʊ]	Ofenkartoffel
robber	MORE 1	[ˈrɒbər]	Räuber/in
role	U3/DSC1	[rəʊl]	Rolle
roll	U11/12	[rəʊl]	rollen
roller-skating	U12/G	[ˈrəʊləskeɪtɪŋ]	inlineskaten
Roman	U7/7	[ˈrəʊmən]	römisch
Romania	U6/6	[rʊˈmeɪniə]	Rumänien
Romanian	U6/6	[rʊˈmeɪniən]	rumänisch
Rome	U1/1	[rəʊm]	Rom
roof	MORE 1	[ruːf]	Dach
room	U9/1	[ruːm]	Platz
rope	U2/S1	[rəʊp]	Seil
rose	U3/2	[rəʊz]	Rose
rotten	U13/7	[ˈrɒtən]	verfault, verdorben
round	U6/4	[raʊnd]	um ... herum
round	U9/1	[raʊnd]	rund
rounders	C/p.139	[ˈraʊndəz]	Schlagball (Sportart)
routine	U1/3	[ruːˈtiːn]	Routine
row	U9/DSC3	[rəʊ]	(Sitz-)Reihe
rubbish (informal)	U9/DSC3	[ˈrʌbɪʃ]	mies, schlecht
rug	U14/3	[rʌg]	Teppich
rugby practice	U1/2	[ˈrʌgbi ˈpræktɪs]	Rugbytraining
rule	MORE 1	[ruːl]	Regel; beherrschen
runaway	U18/NYC4	[ˈrʌnəweɪ]	entlaufen
running	U17/1	[ˈrʌnɪŋ]	Laufen

S

sacred U11/2	['seɪkrəd]	heilig	
safe U5/1	[seɪf]	sicher	
sail U16/G	[seɪl]	Segeln	
salad MORE 1	['sæləd]	Salat	
salt MORE 1	[sɔːlt]	Salz	
the same MORE 1	[ðə 'seɪm]	der-/die-/dasselbe	
sand U1/6	[sænd]	Sand	
sandal U11/3	['sændl]	Sandale	
sausage MORE 1	['sɒsɪdʒ]	Wurst, Würstchen	
save MORE 1	[seɪv]	retten	
say sorry U3/1	[seɪ 'sɒri]	sich entschuldigen	
scale U16/1	[skeɪl]	Skala, Maßstab	
scare U4/13	[skeə]	Angst machen, erschrecken	
be scared (of) MORE 1	[biː 'skeəd əv]	Angst haben (vor)	
scary U3/8	['skeəri]	furchterregend; unheimlich	
scene MORE 1	[siːn]	Szene	
science MORE 1	['saɪəns]	Naturwissenschaft	
scientist U9/9	['saɪəntɪst]	Wissenschaftler/in	
scooter MORE 1	['skuːtə]	Roller	
score U15/G	[skɔː]	erreichen, erzielen (Tore)	
score U15/1	[skɔː]	Punktestand, Spielstand	
Scotland U16/4	['skɒtlənd]	Schottland	
scream U13/1	[skriːm]	schreien; kreischen	
screen MORE 1	[skriːn]	Leinwand; Bildschirm	
sculpture U3/2	['skʌlptʃə]	Bildhauerei; Skulptur, Plastik	
sea MORE 1	[siː]	Meer	
sea level U16/10	['siː ˌlevəl]	Meeresspiegel	
seat U2/2	[siːt]	(Sitz-)Platz	
second U9/10	['sekənd]	Sekunde	
secret U2/2	['siːkrət]	geheim	
secretary U14/DSC5	['sekrətri]	Sekretär/in	
security U2/2	[sɪ'kjʊərəti]	Sicherheit	
seed U9/1	[siːd]	Same/n	
seem U10/NYC2	[siːm]	scheinen	
sell MORE 1	[sel]	verkaufen	
send MORE 1	[send]	senden, schicken	
senior prom C/p.138	[ˌsiːniə 'prɒm]	Maturaball	
sergeant U2/2	['sɑːdʒənt]	Sergeant; hier: Polizeimeister	
series MORE 1	['sɪəriːz]	Serie; Reihe	
serious U10/NYC2	['sɪəriəs]	ernst(haft)	
servant MORE 1	['sɜːvənt]	Diener/in	
serve U10/10	[sɜːv]	servieren	
several U7/7	['sevərəl]	einige, mehrere	
shall U3/DSC1	[ʃæl]	sollen; wollen	
shake U1/11	[ʃeɪk]	schütteln	
What a shame! U9/DSC3	[wɒt ə 'ʃeɪm]	Wie schade!	
That's a shame. U15/6	[ðæts ə 'ʃeɪm]	Wie schade! So ein Jammer!	
share U9/DSC3	[ʃeə]	teilen	
shed MORE 1	[ʃed]	Schuppen, Stall	
sheep (pl sheep) U11/3	[ʃiːp]	Schaf	
shell U1/6	[ʃel]	Schale; Muschel	
(animal) shelter U18/7	['ænɪməl ˌʃeltə]	Tierheim	
shock U2/2	[ʃɒk]	Schock	
shocked U11/11	[ʃɒkt]	schockiert, entsetzt	
shopping centre U6/6	['ʃɒpɪŋ 'sentə]	Einkaufszentrum	
short for U5/8	[ʃɔːt fɔːr]	kurz, kurz für	
should U4/5	[ʃʊd]	sollte/n, solltest	
show MORE 1	[ʃəʊ]	zeigen	
shower U16/7	[ʃaʊə]	Regenschauer	
showing U9/DSC3	['ʃəʊɪŋ]	Vorführung	
sick U15/10	[sɪk]	krank	
feel sick MORE 1	[fiːl 'sɪk]	sich schlecht fühlen	
side U4/5	[saɪd]	Seite	
sight U1/11	[saɪt]	Anblick	
go sightseeing C/p.141	[gəʊ 'saɪtˌsiːɪŋ]	Sehenswürdigkeiten besichtigen	
sign U6/3	[saɪn]	Zeichen, Schild	
signal U18/10	['sɪgnəl]	Signal; Zeichen	
silly MORE 1	['sɪli]	dumm, albern	
similar (to) MORE 1	['sɪmɪlə tʊ]	ähnlich (wie)	
simple U5/G	['sɪmpl]	einfach	
simply U6/9	['sɪmpli]	einfach	
since U15/14	[sɪnts]	seit	
sing MORE 1	[sɪŋ]	singen	
Singapore U2/2	[ˌsɪŋə'pɔː]	Singapur	
single parent U12/9	['sɪŋgl 'peərənt]	Alleinerziehende/r	
sink U14/3	[sɪŋk]	Waschbecken, Spüle	
sister MORE 1	['sɪstər]	Schwester	
sit up U2/2	[sɪt 'ʌp]	sich aufsetzen	
situation MORE 1	[sɪtʃu'eɪʃn]	Situation, Lage	
size U1/8	[saɪz]	Größe	
ski MORE 1	[skiː]	Skifahren	
sky U9/1	[skaɪ]	Himmel	
slave U11/3	[sleɪv]	Sklave, Sklavin	
sleep U9/11	[sliːp]	Schlaf	
slice U10/3	[slaɪs]	Scheibe	
slippers U3/9	['slɪpəs]	Hausschuhe	
slow MORE 1	[sləʊ]	langsam	
small talk U16/5	['smɔːl ˌtɔːk]	Small Talk, Plauderei	
smart EU/1	[smɑːt]	schlau	
smart phone U12/DSC4	['smɑːt ˌfəʊn]	Smartphone	

smell MORE 1	[smel]	riechen
smelly C/p.138	[ˈsmeli]	übelriechend
smile MORE 1	[smaɪl]	lächeln
smoke MORE 1	[sməʊk]	Rauch; rauchen
snack U7/7	[snæk]	Snack, Imbiss
snow U18/10	[snəʊ]	Schnee
snowy U16/2	[ˈsnəʊi]	verschneit
so-called U7/7	[ˌsəʊˈkɔːld]	sogenannt
So do I. U18/7	[səʊ du aɪ]	Ich auch.
So what? U1/6	[səʊ ˈwɒt]	Na und?
sofa U5/15	[ˈsəʊfə]	Sofa
soil C/p.141	[sɔɪl]	Erde, Boden
soldier U11/8	[ˈsəʊldʒə]	Soldat/in
sold out U9/DSC3	[səʊld aʊt]	ausverkauft
solo U17/10	[ˈsəʊləʊ]	Solo-
solve MORE I	[sɒlv]	lösen
somebody MORE 1	[ˈsʌmbədi]	jemand
someone MORE 1	[ˈsʌmwʌn]	jemand
something MORE 1	[ˈsʌmθɪŋ]	etwas
something else U7/7	[ˈsʌmθɪŋ els]	sonst etwas
sometimes MORE 1	[ˈsʌmtaɪmz]	manchmal
somewhere U1/6	[ˈsʌmweər]	irgendwo
son MORE 1	[sʌn]	Sohn
soon MORE 1	[suːn]	bald
sort MORE 1	[sɔːt]	Sorte, Art
sound U4/4	[saʊnd]	Geräusch
sound U8/5	[saʊnd]	klingen
south U1/2	[saʊθ]	südlich, Süd-; Süden
South East Asia U5/10	[saʊθ iːst ˈeɪʒə]	Südostasien
South Island U1/2	[saʊθ ˈaɪlənd]	Südinsel
southern U17/10	[ˈsʌðən]	südlich, Süd-
Southern Ocean U17/10	[ˈsʌðən ˈəʊʃn]	Südmeer, südlicher Ozean
spa U1/1	[spɑː]	Kurort
space U9	[speɪs]	Weltall
space U18/7	[speɪs]	Platz, Raum
spaceship U4/S2	[ˈspeɪsʃɪp]	Raumschiff
space station U9/4	[ˈspeɪs ˌsteɪʃən]	Raumstation
speak MORE 1	[spiːk]	sprechen
speed U17/10	[spiːd]	Geschwindigkeit, Tempo
spell MORE 1	[spel]	buchstabieren
spell U13/7	[spel]	Zauber, Bann
put a spell on sb U13/6	[pʊt ə ˈspel ɒn ˈsʌmbədi]	jemanden verzaubern
spend MORE 1	[spend]	ausgeben (Geld); verbringen (Zeit)
sphinx U11/1	[sfɪŋks]	Sphinx
spirit U11/8	[ˈspɪrɪt]	Geist
spontaneous U16	[spɒnˈteɪniəs]	spontan
spoon U15/1	[spuːn]	Löffel
sports centre U17/DSC6	[spɔts ˈsentə]	Sportzentrum
sportsman (pl -men) U17/3	[ˈspɔːtsmən, ˈspɔːtsmən]	Sportler
sportswoman (pl -women) U17/3	[ˈspɔːtswʊmən, ˈspɔːtswɪmɪn]	Sportlerin
spotted U14/DSC5	[ˈspɒtɪd]	gepunktet
sprinkle U13/6	[ˈsprɪŋkl]	sprenkeln, sprengen
square U6/8	[skweə]	Quadrat, Platz
stage MORE 1	[steɪdʒ]	Bühne
stain U13/1	[steɪn]	Fleck
staircase U14/1	[ˈsteəkeɪs]	Treppe
stairs U4/3	[steəz]	Treppe
stand up MORE 1	[stænd ˈʌp]	aufstehen
stand up (for) MORE 1	[stænd ˈʌp]	sich einsetzen (für)
star MORE 1	[stɑː]	Stern
starter U10/7	[ˈstɑːtə]	Vorspeise
starting point U16/10	[ˈstɑːtɪŋ pɔɪnt]	Ausgangspunkt
station U2/2	[ˈsteɪʃn]	Bahnhof; Station
statue U6/DSC2	[ˈstætʃuː]	Statue, Standbild
stay MORE 1	[steɪ]	bleiben
stay (at) U8/1	[steɪ]	übernachten (bei)
stay calm U12/5	[ˈsteɪ kɑːm]	ruhig bleiben
steal U2/3	[stiːl]	stehlen
step U6/9	[step]	Schritt
step U11/8	[step]	Stufe
stew U10/10	[stjuː]	Eintopf
sticker U4/3	[ˈstɪkə]	Sticker
stiff U2/2	[stɪf]	steif
still MORE 1	[stɪl]	(immer) noch
stilts U14/1	[stɪlts]	Stelzen
stolen U13/7	[ˈstəʊlən]	gestohlen
stomach U15/3	[ˈstʌmək]	Magen
stomachache U15/3	[ˈstʌmək ˌeɪk]	Magen-/Bauchschmerzen
storey C/p.141	[ˈstɔːri]	Stockwerk
storm C/p.141	[stɔːm]	Sturm
straight ahead U6/1	[streɪt əˈhed]	genau vor, geradeaus
straight on U6/3	[streɪt ɒn]	geradeaus
straightaway U10/7	[streɪtəˈweɪ]	sofort
strange MORE 1	[streɪndʒ]	sonderbar
strap U14/DSC5	[stræp]	Band
strawberry U10/1	[ˈstrɔːbəri]	Erdbeere
street MORE 1	[striːt]	Straße
stretch (from) C/p.140	[ˈstretʃ frəm]	sich erstrecken (von)
stripe MORE 1	[straɪp]	Streifen
striped U14/DSC5	[straɪpt]	gestreift
stroke U18/1	[strəʊk]	streicheln
strong MORE 1	[strɒŋ]	stark
strongest MORE 1	[ˈstrɒŋgəst]	stärkste/r/s
get stuck U13/2	[get ˈstʌk]	steckenbleiben

student U1/6	[ˈstjuːdnt]	Student/in; Schüler/in
study U1/2	[ˈstʌdi]	studieren; lernen
stuff (informal) U13/7	[stʌf]	Zeug
stupid MORE 1	[ˈstjuːpɪd]	dumm, blöd
subject U1/4	[ˈsʌbdʒekt]	(Schul-)Fach
success U3/1	[səkˈses]	Erfolg
such U3/6	[sʌtʃ]	solche/r/s
suddenly MORE 1	[ˈsʌdnli]	plötzlich, auf einmal
suggest MORE 1	[səˈdʒest]	vorschlagen
suggestion MORE 1	[səˈdʒestʃn]	Vorschlag
summary U7/S3	[ˈsʌmri]	Zusammenfassung
sun MORE 1	[sʌn]	Sonne
sunglasses U14/DSC5	[ˈsʌŋˌɡlɑːsɪz]	Sonnenbrille
sunshine MORE 1	[ˈsʌnʃaɪn]	Sonnenschein
superglue U4/5	[ˈsuːpəɡluː]	Superkleber
supermarket U6/2	[ˈsuːpəmɑːkɪt]	Supermarkt
superstar U12/3	[ˈsuːpəstɑː]	Superstar
supper U1/2	[ˈsʌpə]	Abendessen
be supposed to U5/NYC1	[biː səˈpəʊzd tʊ]	sollen
(be) sure U6/DSC2	[ʃɔː]	sicher (sein)
surf (the net) U12/13	[sɜːf ðə ˈnet]	surfen (im Internet)
surfer U17/6	[ˈsɜːfə]	Surfer/in
surprise MORE 1	[səˈpraɪz]	Überraschung
swallow U15/1	[ˈswɒləʊ]	(hinunter-)schlucken
swap U6/DSC2	[swɒp]	(ver-)tauschen
sweep U1/2	[swiːp]	kehren, fegen
sweet MORE 1	[swiːt]	süß
sweets (pl) MORE 1	[swiːts]	Süßigkeiten
swim MORE 1	[swɪm]	schwimmen
swimmer U5/1	[ˈswɪmə]	Schwimmer/in
swimming trunks U16/7	[ˈswɪmɪŋ trʌnks]	Badehose
swing U2/2	[swɪŋ]	(hin- und her-)schwingen
Swiss U17/6	[swɪs]	schweizerisch
switch off U12/13	[swɪtʃˈɒf]	abschalten
symbol U16/3	[ˈsɪmbəl]	Symbol, Zeichen
system C/p.138	[ˈsɪstəm]	System

T

table MORE 1	[ˈteɪbl]	Tisch
tackle U17/18	[ˈtækl]	attackieren (im Sport)
taipan U5/10	[ˈtaɪpæn]	Taipan-Schlange
take an order U12/DSC4	[teɪk ən ˈɔːdə]	eine Bestellung aufnehmen
take away U12/DSC4	[teɪk əˈweɪ]	mitnehmen
take down U14/1	[teɪk daʊn]	abbauen
take it easy U8/4	[teɪk ɪt ˈiːzi]	sich entspannen
take off U9/1	[teɪk ˈɒf]	abheben, starten
take off U13/1	[teɪk ˈɒf]	abnehmen
take out MORE 1	[teɪk ˈaʊt]	herausnehmen
take over U9/10	[teɪk ˈəʊvə]	übernehmen; erobern
take (time) MORE 1	[teɪk ˈtaɪm]	(Zeit) brauchen/dauern
take turns U8/12	[teɪk tɜːns]	sich abwechseln
tall MORE 1	[tɔːl]	groß
tan U16/11	[tæn]	Bräune
tar C/p.138	[tɑː]	Teer
task MORE 1	[tɑːsk]	Aufgabe
teach MORE 1	[tiːtʃ]	beibringen; unterrichten
team U5/G	[tiːm]	Team
teatime U5/15	[ˈtiːtaɪm]	Teestunde
technology U9/9	[tekˈnɒlədʒi]	Technologie
teen U12/5	[tiːn]	Teenager, Teenie
telegram U11/8	[ˈtelɪɡræm]	Telegramm
television MORE 1	[ˈtelɪvɪʒn]	Fernseher
tell a lie U8/7	[tel ə laɪ]	lügen
tell off EU/1	[tel ˈɒf]	ausschimpfen
temperature U16/1	[ˈtemprɪtʃə]	Temperatur
temple U11/1	[ˈtempl]	Tempel
term FU/1	[tɜːm]	Semester
terrible MORE 1	[ˈterəbl]	schrecklich, furchtbar
be terrified C/p.141	[biː ˈterəfaɪd]	große Angst haben
text U3/DSC1	[tekst]	eine SMS schicken, simsen
text message MORE 1	[ˈtekst mesɪdʒ]	Textnachricht, SMS
Thailand U5/10	[ˈtaɪlænd]	Thailand
(more) than U5/10	[ðæn]	(mehr) als
thank God U11/S5	[θæŋk ɡɒd]	Gott sei Dank
thank sb MORE 1	[θæŋk]	jemandem danken
their MORE 1	[ðeə]	ihr/e
theirs U14/7	[ðeəz]	ihre/r/s
them MORE 1	[ðem]	sie, ihnen
these MORE 1	[ðiːz]	diese
thick U16/3	[θɪk]	dicht; dick
thief (pl thieves) U2/2	[θiːf, θiːvz]	Dieb/in
though U10/NYC2	[ðəʊ]	aber, allerdings
thrill U17/10	[θrɪl]	Nervenkitzel
throat U15/3	[θrəʊt]	Hals
through U6/1	[θruː]	durch
throughout the year U16/10	[θruːˈaʊt ðə ˈjɪə]	das ganze Jahr (über)
throw MORE 1	[θrəʊ]	werfen
thunderstorm U16/2	[ˈθʌndəstɔːm]	Gewitter
tidy (up) U8/1	[ˈtaɪdi ˌʌp]	aufräumen
tight U1/11	[taɪt]	fest
till U12/12	[tɪl]	bis
time machine U9/4	[ˈtaɪm məʃiːn]	Zeitmaschine

Wort	Aussprache	Übersetzung
timetable U1/5	[ˈtaɪmteɪbl]	Stundenplan
tip U3/6	[tɪp]	Hinweis, Tipp
tired of U14/1	[taɪəd ɒv]	etwas satt haben; überdrüssig
today MORE 1	[təˈdeɪ]	heute
to-do list U17/DSC6	[təˈduː ˌlɪst]	Aufgabenliste
toe U15/6	[təʊ]	Zeh/e
together MORE 1	[təˈgeðə]	zusammen, gemeinsam
tomb U11/1	[tuːm]	Grab, Gruft
tomorrow MORE 1	[təˈmɒrəʊ]	morgen
ton U5/10	[tʌn]	Tonne (1000 kg)
tongue MORE 1	[tʌŋ]	Zunge
tongue-twister U11/9	[tʌŋ ˈtwɪstə]	Zungenbrecher
tonight MORE 1	[təˈnaɪt]	heute Abend
too MORE 1; U1/11	[tuː]	auch; zu
tool U12/7	[tuːl]	Werkzeug
tooth (pl teeth) MORE 1	[tuːθ, tiːθ]	Zahn
toothache U15/3	[ˈtuːθeɪk]	Zahnschmerzen
top U4/3	[tɒp]	ganz oben, Gipfel, Spitze
topic U15/1	[ˈtɒpɪk]	Thema
topping U12/DSC4	[ˈtɒpɪŋ]	Belag
torch U11/10	[tɔːtʃ]	Taschenlampe
tornado C/p.140	[tɔːˈneɪdəʊ]	Wirbelsturm
total U12/DSC4	[ˈtəʊtl]	gesamt; völlig
touch MORE 1	[tʌtʃ]	berühren
touchdown C/p.139	[ˈtʌtʃdaʊn]	Touchdown
tour U3/DSC1	[tʊə]	Tour
tourist MORE 1	[ˈtʊərɪst]	Tourist/in
tourist centre U11/10	[ˈtʊərɪst ˈsentə]	Touristenzentrum
tourist office U6/2	[ˈtʊərɪst ˈɒfɪs]	Fremdenverkehrsbüro
towards MORE 1	[təˈwɔːdz]	in Richtung, auf … zu
towel U5/1	[ˈtaʊəl]	Handtuch
tower U6/DSC2	[taʊə]	Turm
town MORE 1	[taʊn]	Stadt
(running) track EU/1	[træk]	Anlage; Laufbahn
tractor U12/5	[ˈtræktə]	Traktor
tradition U4/3	[trəˈdɪʃn]	Tradition
traditional U17/10	[trəˈdɪʃnl]	traditionell
traffic lights U6/DSC2	[ˈtræfɪk laɪts]	Verkehrsampel
trailer U14/1	[ˈtreɪlə]	Anhänger, Wohnwagen
train U6/6	[treɪn]	Zug
train U17/6	[treɪn]	trainieren
trainer MORE 1	[ˈtreɪnə]	Turnschuh
trainer U17/8	[ˈtreɪnə]	Trainer/in
translate U12/9	[trænsˈleɪt]	übersetzen
transmitter U18/10	[trænzˈmɪtə]	Sender
trap U7/S3	[træp]	fangen; in einer Falle
travel U1/1	[ˈtrævl]	reisen
tray U18/1	[treɪ]	Tablett
treasure MORE 1	[ˈtreʒə]	Schatz
treasure hunt U7/7	[ˈtreʒə ˌhʌnt]	Schatzsuche
treat U4/3	[triːt]	Vergnügen, Belohnung
tree house U7/3	[ˈtriː haʊs]	Baumhaus
trick or treat U4/3	[ˈtrɪk ə ˈtriːt]	Süßes oder Saures (Frage beim Halloween-Umzug)
tricky U11/2	[ˈtrɪki]	betrügerisch; schwierig, kompliziert
trip MORE 1	[trɪp]	Ausflug, Reise
triplets U17/8	[ˈtrɪpləts]	Drillinge
(it's no) trouble U10/NYC2	[ɪts nəʊ ˈtrʌbl]	keine Ursache
get into trouble U5/1	[get ˈɪntu ˈtrʌbl]	Probleme/Ärger bekommen
trust U9/S4	[trʌst]	Vertrauen
truth MORE 1	[truːθ]	Wahrheit
try MORE 1	[traɪ]	versuchen
turkey U10/1	[ˈtɜːki]	Truthahn
turn U1/9	[tɜːn]	werden; abbiegen
turn off MORE 1	[tɜːn ˈɒf]	abschalten
turn on MORE 1	[tɜːn ˈɒn]	einschalten
turn up U3/6	[tɜːn ˈʌp]	auftauchen
turn up/down U16/7	[tɜːn ˈʌp/daʊn]	lauter/leiser stellen
TV MORE 1	[ˌtiːˈviː]	Fernseher; Fernsehen
twice MORE 1	[twaɪs]	zweimal
twin U3/DSC1	[twɪn]	Zwilling, Zwillings-
type (of) MORE 1	[taɪp]	Art; Typ; Sorte

U

UFO (=unidentified flying object) U9/9	[juːefˈəʊ]	Ufo (unbekanntes Flugobjekt)
ufologist U9/9	[juːˈfɒlədʒɪst]	Ufologe, Ufologin
ugly U5/6	[ˈʌgli]	hässlich
uncle U12/1	[ˈʌŋkl]	Onkel
unconscious U9/S4	[ʌnˈkɒnʃəs]	bewusstlos
underground U6/6	[ˈʌndəgraʊnd]	U-Bahn
underline U10/11	[ˌʌndəˈlaɪn]	unterstreichen
underneath U14/1	[ˌʌndəˈniːθ]	unterhalb
understand MORE 1	[ˌʌndəˈstænd]	verstehen
understanding U6/DSC2	[ˌʌndəˈstændɪŋ]	Verständnis
unfair U4/4	[ʌnˈfeə]	unfair
unfortunately EU/1	[ʌnˈfɔːtʃənətli]	unglücklicherweise
unfriendly U13/7	[ʌnˈfrendli]	unfreundlich
unhappy MORE 1	[ʌnˈhæpi]	unglücklich
unidentified U9/9	[ˌʌnaɪˈdentɪfaɪd]	unbekannt, nicht identifiziert

uniform U1/2	[ˈjuːnɪfɔːm]	Uniform
unit U7/7	[ˈjuːnɪt]	Gerät; Einheit
universe U9/1	[ˈjuːnɪvɜːs]	Universum
university U12/9	[juːnɪˈvɜːsəti]	Universität
unpack U16/7	[ʌnˈpæk]	auspacken
until MORE 1	[ənˈtɪl]	bis
unusual MORE 1	[ʌnˈjuːʒʊəl]	ungewöhnlich
upload EU/1	[ʌpˈləʊd]	hochladen
upset U3/1	[ʌpˈset]	gestört, verärgert, böse
upstairs U3/2	[ʌpˈsteəz]	oben
up to U5/14	[ˈʌp ˌtu]	bis zu
use MORE 1	[juːz]	benutzen, verwenden
useful MORE 1	[ˈjusfəl]	nützlich
usually MORE 1	[ˈjuːʒʊəli]	gewöhnlich, normalerweise

V

valley U7/1	[ˈvæli]	Tal
valuable U15/10	[ˈvæljʊbl]	wertvoll
vampire U4/1	[ˈvæmpaɪə]	Vampir
van C/p.141	[væn]	Kleinbus
vegetable MORE 1	[ˈvedʒtəbl]	Gemüse
vet U18/1	[vet]	Tierarzt, Tierärztin
video game U2/5	[ˈvɪdiəʊ ˌgeɪm]	Videospiel
Vietnam U12/3	[ˌvjetˈnæm]	Vietnam
village MORE 1	[ˈvɪlɪdʒ]	Dorf
visit MORE 1	[ˈvɪzɪt]	besuchen
visit U7/7	[ˈvɪzɪt]	Besuch
voice MORE 1	[vɔɪs]	Stimme
volcanic eruption C/p.139	[vɒlˈkænɪk ɪˌrʌpʃən]	Vulkanausbruch
volcano C/p.139	[vɒlˈkeɪnəʊ]	Vulkan
volume U16/7	[ˈvɒljuːm]	Lautstärke
vote U15/1	[vəʊt]	wählen

W

waiter, waitress U10/5	[ˈweɪtə, ˈweɪtrəs]	Bedienung, Kellner/in
wake somebody up U2/2	[weɪk ˌsʌmbədi ˈʌp]	jemanden aufwecken
walk a pet U18/1	[wɔːk ə ˈpet]	Gassi gehen
walk up U4/3	[wɔk ˈʌp]	hinaufgehen
wall U4/9	[wɔːl]	Wand, Mauer
wallet U2/1	[ˈwɒlɪt]	Brieftasche
war U9/10	[wɔːr]	Krieg
wardrobe U14/3	[ˈwɔːdrəʊb]	Kleiderschrank
warn U7/S3	[wɔːn]	warnen
wash up U7/10	[wɒʃ ˈʌp]	abspülen, abwaschen
washing machine MORE 1	[ˈwɒʃɪŋ məˌʃiːn]	Waschmaschine
do the washing-up U2/2	[ˈduː ðə ˌwɒʃɪŋ ˈʌp]	abspülen
waste of time U17/8	[weɪst əv taɪm]	Zeitverschwendung
watch MORE 1	[wɒtʃ]	beobachten; zuschauen; Uhr
watch TV MORE 1	[wɒtʃ tiːˈviː]	fernsehen
waterfall U7/3	[ˈwɔːtəfɔːl]	Wasserfall
give way U16/1	[gɪv ˈweɪ]	Platz machen
wear MORE 1	[weə]	tragen
weather MORE 1	[ˈweðə]	Wetter
weather forecast U16/3	[ˈweðər ˌfɔːkɑːst]	Wettervorhersage
weather report U16/4	[ˈweðər rɪˌpɔːt]	Wetterbericht
weatherman U16/7	[ˈweðəmæn]	Wettermann
weaver U11/3	[ˈwiːvə]	Weber/in
web U3/6	[web]	Netz, Internet
webpage U1/9	[ˈwebpeɪdʒ]	Internetseite
weigh U5/10	[weɪ]	wiegen
Welcome! MORE 1	[ˈwelkəm]	Wilkommen!
well U6/6	[wel]	gesund, wohlauf
western U16/10	[ˈwestən]	westlich
wet U4/4	[wet]	nass
whale U5/10	[weɪl]	Wal
whale shark U5/13	[ˈweɪl ʃɑːrk]	Walhai
What about? MORE 1	[wɒtˌəˈbaʊt]	Worum geht's?
What a shame! U9/DSC3	[wɒt ə ˈʃeɪm]	Wie schade!
What else? MORE 1	[wɒt ˈels]	Was noch?
What for? U18/NYC4	[wɒt ˈfɔː]	Warum?, Wofür?
What's going on? U2/2	[wɒts gəʊɪŋ ˈɒn]	Was ist los
what sort of U3/6	[wɒt sɔːt ɒv]	welche Art
What's the matter? MORE 1	[wɒts ðə ˈmætə]	Was ist los?
wherever U16/7	[weəˈrevə]	wo(hin) auch immer
which MORE 1	[wɪtʃ]	welche/r/s
while U3/DSC1	[waɪl]	Weile
while U15/14	[waɪl]	während
whisper MORE 1	[ˈwɪspər]	flüstern
who U4/13	[huː]	der, die, das
Who cares? U15/NYC3	[hʊ ˈkeəs]	Wen kümmert es?
whole MORE 1	[həʊl]	ganz; voll
whom U14	[huːm]	wem, wen
whose U5/11	[huːz]	wessen
wide MORE 1	[waɪd]	breit; weit
wife (pl wives) MORE 1	[waɪf, waɪvz]	Ehefrau

wild MORE 1	[waɪld]	wild	
wildlife U15/10	[ˈwaɪldlaɪf]	Tierwelt	
will MORE 1	[wɪl]	werden (Zukunft)	
win MORE 1	[wɪn]	gewinnen	
wind MORE 1	[wɪnd]	Wind	
windsurfing U17/1	[ˈwɪndsɜːfɪŋ]	Windsurfen	
windy U16/2	[ˈwɪndi]	windig	
winner U9/DSC3	[ˈwɪnə]	Gewinner/in	
wish MORE 1	[wɪʃ]	Wunsch	
witch U4/1	[wɪtʃ]	Hexe	
without U12/5	[wɪðˈaʊt]	ohne	
witness U2/7	[ˈwɪtnəs]	Zeuge, Zeugin	
wizard U4/2	[ˈwɪzəd]	Zauberer	
wolf (pl wolves) MORE 1	[wʊlf, wʊlvz]	Wolf	
woman (pl women) MORE 1	[ˈwʊmən, ˈwɪmɪn]	Frau	
(no) wonder U7/7	[ˈwʌndə]	(kein) Wunder	
wonderful MORE 1	[ˈwʌndəfəl]	wunderbar	
wood MORE 1	[wʊd]	Wald; Holz	
wooden MORE 1	[ˈwʊdn]	Holz-, hölzern	
wool U11/3	[ˈwʊl]	Wolle	
work U2/2	[wɜːk]	hier: funktionieren	
work out U12/G	[ˈwɜːk aʊt]	trainieren	
worker U11/3	[ˈwɜːkə]	Arbeiter/in	
workman (pl workmen) U11/8	[ˈwɜːkmən]	Handwerker	
worldwide U5/10	[ˈwɜːldˌwaɪd]	weltweit	
be worried U3/1	[bi ˈwʌrɪd]	besorgt sein	
worry about U16/7	[wʌri əˈbaʊt]	sich Sorgen machen	
worrier U8/10	[ˈwʌrɪə]	Schwarzmaler/in	
be worth U3/2	[biː ˈwɜːθ]	wert sein	
wound U11/8	[wuːnd]	Wunde	
write down U3/DSC1	[raɪt daʊn]	niederschreiben	
writer U15/14	[ˈraɪtə]	Verfasser/in	

Y

yacht U17/10	[jɒt]	Jacht
yachtswoman U17/10	[ˈjɒtswʊmən]	Seglerin
year MORE 1	[jɪə]	Jahr; Jahrgangsstufe
not … yet U13/S6	[nɒt ˈjet]	noch nicht
yours U2/2	[jɔːz]	deine/r/s; Ihre/r/s; eure/r/s
yourself MORE 1	[jɔːˈself]	du/Sie/ihr selbst
youth U7/10	[juːθ]	Jugend
youth camp U7/10	[juːθ kæmp]	Jugendlager
yurt U14/1	[jʊət]	Jurte

Z

zombie U4/2	[ˈzɒmbi]	Zombie

Acknowledgements

The publishers would like to thank the following for their kind permission to reproduce the following photographs and other copyright material:

p70 (CD: Food Icons), p88 Granger Historical Picture Archive, p124 Aurora Photos (Tommy Caldwell) / Alamy Stock Photo; p40 Leslie Banks (kitchen), p44 Margie Hurwich (girl), p46 Warnerbroers (boy on the phone), p65 Elen (UFOs), p85 Auremar (father, mother, uncle) / Darren Baker (aunt) / Ruslan Huzau (grandmother) / Flair Images (grandfather) / Godfer (cousin) /Narimbur (Ben), p90 Lexx72 (pepperoni), p99 Kondratova (trailer), p116 Tracy Whiteside (girl), p120 Russ Ensley (skateboarding), p122 Tracy Whiteside, p128 Kalcutta (girl drying cat) / Wavebreakmedia Ltd (boy stroking dog), p129 Mimagephotography (boy), p133 Tamara Bauer, p136 Vlue, p137 Dmytro Surkov, p139 Mary Katherine Wynn (American football) / Americanspirit (baseball) / Photographerlondon (basketball), p140 Lane Erickson (Yellowstone) / Photographerlondon (grizzly bear) | Dreamstime.com; James Lozeau p99 (treehouse: Finca Bellavista, Costa Rica); p9 J and J Productions (Jacob), p58 Juice Images Ltd (children in tree), p65 Bettman/Kontributor (UFO photo), p80 Egyptian (tomb), p81 Hulton Archive, p128 Steve Teague (girl cleaning out cage), p141 Jim Reed (storm chasers) / Getty Images; Helbling p23, p26, p48, p51 (waterfall), p68, p90, p104, p107, p126, p128 (children playing game); ©iStockphoto.com/ p19 Juanmonino, p26 ajphoto (boy with camera), p31 lisathephotographer, p34 aldomurillo (mother and son) / creatives (pig), p35 GlobalP (dog, fish, rabbit, horse) / mikheewnik (turtle) / viki2win (cat) / Laures (mouse) / tunart (hamster), p36 MR1805 (blue whale), p37 IMPALASTOCK (chimpanzee) / EMPPhotography (giraffe) / BrendanHunter (antilope) / JBryson (boy with white shirt, girl), p51 aabejon (picnic), p87 alynst (Les) / mtreasure (Lisa), p99 robas (houses in Vietnam), p102 pkline (math quiz), p114 mguttman (girl), p116 aabejon (boy) / spencerdare (map), p118 Yarinca (Carina), p121designsimply (Danni), p128 Andrew_Howe (girl feeding cat), p138 EHStock (Susannah); Metro p45 (http://metro.co.uk); p123 Roy Riley/EPA / picturedesk.com; pixabay p130 (house, rat); p9 Anton_Ivanov (Abeeku), p10 Max Topchii, p12 YUSRAN ABDUL RAHMAN, p13 Max Topchii, p24 Antartstock (hand holding phone) / Cienpies Design (background) / lineartestpilot (face), p26 CREATISTA (girl phone) / Iakov Filimonov (girl looking for pen) / Celig (boy eating chocolate), p36 Darrenp (taipan snake) / Bullstar (Eustarine crocodile) / corlaffra (mosquito) / Maros Bauer (cheetah) / Wolfilser (cars), p37 Alberto Loyo (anaconda) / Stephanie Periquet (elephant) / Deborah Kolb (lion) / Andrey Burmakin (giraffe) / tratong (rhino) / A_Lesik (dolphin) / Jan-Nor Photography (ostrich) / Kalmatsuy (boy with red T-shirt), p40 Paul Matthew Photography (living room) / David Hughes (hall) / Photographee.eu (bedroom), p44 cristovao (boy), p46 MJTH (girl on the phone), p47 More Images, p48 1000 Words (traffic light) / chrisdorney (fountain) / Bikeworldtravel (statue) / Pete Spiro (clock tower) / Ron Ellis (bus stop) / Tupungato (bridge), p51 Richard Thornton (climber), p54 Olesia Bilkei, p58 Thomas Pajot (text bubbles) / Hilch (notes) / moosa art (invitation), p60 freesoulproduction, p68 Claudio Divizia (closed sign) / Lester Balajadia (ticket sign) / Carsten Reisinger (lift) / Macrovector (festival poster), p76 amstockphoto (bat) / Cheryl Ann Quigley (hit) / sonya etchison (pitch) / Dennis Debono (team), p80 Jaroslav Moravcik (Tutankhamun) / Waj (pyramid), p84 s_bukley (Angelina Jolie), p86 Olesia Bilkei (campfire) / Aleksey Oleynikov (Vicky) / Catalin Petolea (tractor), p87 Anton_Ivanov (Denise) / singh_lens (Amar), p90 Imageman (cheese) / Roxana Bashyrova (pineapple) / Hong Vo (mushrooms, tomatoes) / gosphotodesign (ham), p99 withGod (yurts) / Rafal Cichawa (Uros' houses), p102 Monkey Business Images (family) / Patricia Hofmeester (school bag) / Chimpinski (cap) / KKulikov (trainers) / Aleksander Krsmanovic (ruler) / Luchi_a (book), p104 OZaiachin (watch strap) / Aaron Amat (sunglasses) / Elnur (jacket), p105 Neamov (leather jacket) / koya979 (straw) / Khvost (socks), p106 Mettus, p109 Ammit Jack (Indian) / Fotos593 (Amazon jungle) / Andrzej Kubik (water lilies), p110 More Images, p112 DavidPinoPhotography (library) / rangizzz (prize) / zhu difeng (internet café), p114 RedKoala (weather symbols), p118 Mike Charles (Lake District), p120 l i g h t p o e t (swimming) / Kwanbenz (ice skating) / CandyBox Images (running) / maxpro (mountain biking) / matimix (football) / hektoR (climbing) / muzsy (volleyball) / Lucy Clark (tennis) / Tumar (basketball) / Dima Fadeev (windsurfing) / gorillaimages (skiing) / 2xSamara.com (snowboarding) / Verena Matthew (cycling) / trubavin (surfing) / Luckylmages (roller-skating), p121 Greg Epperson (Ricky), p126 Rosli Othman (cricket) / Maxisport (football, rugby) / bikeriderlondon (tennis, swimming) / Tony Bowler (golf), p128 sonya etchison (boys washing dog) / kurhan (cat vet) / racorn (girl brushing horse) / Catherine Murray (litter tray) / Sergey Novikov (girls walking dog) / trubitsyn (boy playing with dog), p129 Amazingmikael (girl), p130 Bborriss.67 (dogs) / keantian (cats) / Anton Gvozdikov (birds), p131 Phawat (snake), p132 Jan Martin Will (penguin) / deer boy (map), p134 Tupungato (market) / Africa Studio (money) / Maxx-Studio (phone), p138 Hdyma Natallia (flag) / Monkey Business Images (Mark) / Donna Ellen Coleman (prom couple), p139 sianc (girl) / sergios (boy), 140 welcomia (Redwood National Park) / Sarah Fields Photography (Rocky Mountains) / Everett Historical (Apache), p141 Minerva Studio (tornado) / Guido Amrein Switzerland (hurricane) / Shutterstock.com; Toonz Animation p21, p33, p55, p67, p84, p98; Wikimedia Commons p36 Drahkrub (bumblebee bat, Creative Commons License 4.0, https://commons.wikimedia.org/wiki/File:Pipistrellus_female-1.jpg), p118 Wolfgangbeyer at the German language Wikipedia (Death Valley, Creative Commons License 3.0, https://de.wikipedia.org/wiki/Datei:Death_Valley_Zabriskie_Point.jpg), p124 Octagon (Dawn Wall, Creative Commons License 3.0, https://commons.wikimedia.org/wiki/File:El_Capitan_01.JPG), p141 (Hurricane Katrina) (United States Air Force); cover image ©iStockphoto.com/fstop123

Every effort has been made to trace the owners of any copyright material in this book. If notified, the publishers will be pleased to rectify any errors or omissions.